Last activity   never

D0070242

Cultural Leadership:

The Culture of Excellence in Education

William G. Cunningham
Old Dominion University

Donn W. Gresso
East Tennessee State University

Allyn and Bacon
Boston • London • Toronto • Sydney • Tokyo • Singapore

Dedicated to our parents: Margaret M. and Gerard J. Cunningham,
Alma and Elmer Watson Gresso, and
our spouses and children: Sandra L., Michael S., and Kerri B. Cunningham, and
Marsha B., Jon W., Anne R., David C., and Tom B. Gresso.

Series Editor: Ray Short
Editorial Assistant: Christine Shaw
Cover Administrator: Linda Dickinson
Composition Buyer: Linda Cox
Manufacturing Buyer: Megan Cochran
Production Coordinator: Cheryl Ten Eick
Cover Designer: Suzanne Harbison

Library of Congress Cataloging-in-Publication Data

Cunningham William G.
Cultural leadership: the culture of excellence in education/William G. Cunningham,
    Donn W. Gresso.
P. cm.
Includes bibliographical references and index.
ISBN 0-205-14709-7
1. School management and organization—Social aspects—United States. 2.
    Educational leadership—Social aspects—United States. 3. School improvement
    programs—United States. 4. Danforth Foundation (Saint Louis, Mo.) I. Gresso,
    Donn W. II. Title.
LB2805.C855 1993
371.2′07—dc20   93–542
                                                                                                          CIP

Credits appear on page xvi which is an extension of the copyright page.

Printed in the United States of America

10 9 8 7 6 5 4 3   97 96

Contents

Foreword

Shared vision, participatory leadership, management by results, a commitment to innovation and improvement, provision for continuity and institutionalization, flexibility in the use of time, people and other resources, and the provision of training and personal support constitute the essential components of a comprehensive approach to school redesign. Changing the system of rules, roles, and relationships that determine how these components are addressed is the challenge that confronts anyone who intends to create a culture of excellence in our schools.

With *Cultural Leadership: The Culture of Excellence on Education*, Cunningham and Gresso provide clear examples of ways one might go about addressing the difficult issues that must be addressed if school reform is to move from rhetoric to reality. Their correlates of a culture of excellence are developed through careful observations of experiences gained in a large number of school districts all over the country and with a wide array of teachers and the other school leaders. They have produced a work that persuasively argues the need for fundamental reform while holding out hope that those currently involved in the educative enterprise can accomplish this without wholesale replacements, either at the administrative or classroom level.

Many American and foreign businesses have been restructured, as the authors point out, through innovative leadership at all levels of the organization, and through a change in corporate culture. Why, therefore, should critics of education call for the heads of teachers, principals, and superintendents, when the educators themselves are also victims of a structural/behavioral model for schooling that has been imposed on them for a century?

To a sociologist in an earlier career, but one who has never lost a socio-logical perspective, the case for, and description of a culture of excellence in schools seems long overdue. The authors' view that culture, not mandates or structure, is the telling component in educational organizations is quite compelling. Their comparison of educational mandates to microbic inva-sions of the body resonates with anyone who has ever had to deal with requirements like "minutes per week" in mathematics or other subject areas. The organization surrounds the intrusive object with antibodies to prevent harm and ensure eventual elimination. However, ". . . fighting off foreign substances drains energy and the business at hand gets less atten-tion." (p. 35) The result is a distraction from the real job of educating chil-dren in favor of satisfying federal, state, or local enforcement teams. To be satisfied, the customer becomes the associate superintendent in charge of compliance instead of the student. School systems have ample experience fighting off "infections" and reverting to business as usual, not because they are made up of obstructionist members, but because the culture of the school overpowers any change that does not seek to modify the culture itself.

Inherent in the authors' argument is the notion that school reform will not be easy. They go to great lengths to describe the current state of the reform movement in historical, sociological, and political terms. Fundamental cultural change precludes quick fixes or magic bullets. Despite the emergence of the key correlates of a culture of excellence, Cunningham and Gresso avoid the trap of suggesting a formula for change that can be used in any given district. Such a solution would clearly be false, and their reluctance to embrace it is another factor that separates this book from the multitude of new commentary and prescriptions to be found on the newsstands every month. Because the culture in every district is bound to be unique, the struggle to provide a good education for every stu-dent in the district will likewise be unique.

While the authors' distinction between the structural/behavioral model of organizations and the cultural model obviously results in their favoring a sociological world view, they do not abandon the worth of the individual. They contend that "The culture must emphasize the values which make a classroom, a school, and a school district display greatness. The culture of excellence emphasizes the personal qualities of achievement such as self-image, skill, knowledge, respect, confidence, identity, worth, personal development, enthusiasm, pride, wisdom, and commitment." (p. 260)

While the heart of this book is the development and description of the cultural model of organization, the flesh and bones are the descriptions of the correlates of a culture of excellence. By consulting the tables of contents, the reader can discover these correlates in the titles of chapters three through eleven. Any idea, however, that these correlates represent just

another list of "key points" to be memorized by graduate students is·
quickly dispelled when one begins to fathom the detail of analysis and the
incredible body of research to which the authors had access. After
Cunningham and Gresso discuss the importance of vision and collegiality,
just to name two, the proponents of the strictly behavioral approach to
change will find themselves seriously outgunned. Again, despite the per-
suasiveness of their evidence, it must be noted that the authors refuse to
turn prescriptive, preferring the perhaps unpopular view that a great deal
of hard work remains before anything like a nationwide sea of change will
be seen.

And the authors make clear that nothing less than just such a sea of
change is what is required. They have made a notable contribution to the
continued existence of public education in America, but those who favor
the status quo will find no solace here.

Phillip C. Schlechty
Louisville, Kentucky

Preface

An excellent organization is not about power, it is about empowerment.

These words capture the essence of excellence in America today. The function of leadership is to find new ways to harness the "collective genius" within a school and focus it on improving American education. Such genius is supported through a culture that reinforces the development of individual ability, effort, and performance. Peter M. Senge (1990) stated,

> The old days when a Henry Ford, Alfred Sloan or Tom Watson learned for the organization are gone. In an increasingly dynamic, interdependent and unpredictable world, it is simply no longer possible for anyone to figure it all out at the top. The old model, the top thinks and the local acts, must now give way to integrating thinking and acting at all levels. While the challenge is great so is the potential payoff.

Experience suggests that programs designed to achieve excellence are not directly transferable. Dr. Carl D. Glickman (1990) stated,

> People need to understand that these programs work not because they are so meticulously crafted and engineered but because the faculty in these schools will not let them fail . . . when an empowered school succeeds, it establishes curricular and instructional programs that are unique to its own staff, students, and history. The process of how a school came to such decisions is more transferable than the program. I shudder when I think a superintendent or principal is trying to implement in a top-down manner a program developed through grassroots

participation. To do so merely repeats the mistakes made with "teacher-proof" curricula. It is only the general notions of informed, representational decision making that can be easily transported. Even the specific decision making model of a particular school should not be seen as prescriptive.

Cultures relying on power often create autocratic leaders and horizontal relationships that result in isolation. Each layer of this type of organization lacks the ability to influence other layers, and they tend to resist one another. This culture of power, autocracy, and isolation must change if we are to improve America's schools. School culture must release its talent and energy so the organization can realize its full potential. Dr. John Goodlad (1987) stated,

> One-way directives are replaced by multiple interactions; leadership by authority is replaced by leadership by knowledge; following rules and regulations is replaced by providing more room for decision making; mandated behavior is replaced by inquiring behavior; accountability is replaced by high expectations, responsibility, and a level of trust that includes freedom to make mistakes; and much more.

America can no longer avoid reform and restructuring in its schools. This became clear in 1983, when the National Commission of Excellence in Education compiled a report entitled *A Nation At Risk*. Over 1,000 reports, books, and documents have been published since then, calling for various forms of restructuring and reform. State legislatures and departments of education have developed mandates for how this reform might occur. There is also a growing demand for school-linked programs to provide comprehensive services to all children.

There is no single "silver bullet" to restructure our schools. Restructuring will depend on the hard work of every American. Thomas Jefferson suggested that the states provide "civic laboratories" to deal with the multi-faceted problems that society faces. The great challenge of leadership is to develop a culture that addresses the challenge of creating such "laboratories" that result in continuous improvement. As a result of this need for change, both education and business are moving toward a new paradigm of organizational leadership.

The new paradigms of excellence recognize, develop, support, and encourage all individuals to use their knowledge, skills, and experiences to improve their organization. Administrators should not be threatened by the wisdom and knowledge of their employees. They must develop a culture that supports and encourages participation in the improvement of our schools. The final determinant of success in this endeavor will be measured through the quality of education that our children receive.

This book grew out of a large number of individual efforts to improve American education. It provides an analysis of success in over 42 school districts across America. The book evolved from the work of the Danforth Foundation's School Administrators Fellowship Program, as well as the American Association of School Administrators and Institute for the Development of Educational Activities, Inc.'s District Learning Leadership Team program.

The Danforth Foundation program made an important transition which greatly improved its results. The original strategy of the Danforth Foundation program was to develop a professional growth program by bringing together a university professor as facilitator and secondary school principals. They were encouraged to share ideas, visit schools, and exchange effective educational practices. The principals were invited to observe each other's schools to compare and contrast them with their own. For many, it was the first time they visited other schools, interacted with key educational leaders, shared concerns and needs, and talked about their schools' strengths. The idea was for principals to see other schools and to emulate successes in their own schools.

The participants learned that successful programs cannot be transferred between schools. The development of effective school practices would require an altogether new approach in the redesigned School Administrators Fellowship Program. This revised program addressed the true complexity of the process needed to improve American schools. It was based on the belief that all parties involved in education have important ideas and need to participate in improving schools. People must take individual responsibility for their development, for working with others in the school system, and for moving toward a shared vision of improved education. This is how excellence in organizations works. The Danforth Foundation School Administrators Fellowship program greatly influenced this book, and was used by the AASA in the development of their "District Learning Leadership Team" program.

The first two chapters of this book discuss the context of American education and the culture of school systems that were successful in implementing excellence. The next nine chapters analyze the cultural attributes that encourage and support continuous improvement. The threads that run throughout each of these chapters are the correlates of an effective culture. The final chapter discusses the implications of a culture's supporting participative forms of organizational improvement. The book ends with a discussion of the qualities needed for a truly successful, culturally supported, site-based, participative program for American education.

Acknowledgments

"There is nothing more difficult, more perilous, or more uncertain of success, than to take the lead in introducing a new order of things."

Machiavelli

This book is the outgrowth of a major program called the School Administrators Fellowship Program, sponsored by the Danforth Foundation since 1973. Dr. Donn W. Gresso, former vice president of the Danforth Foundation and current associate professor of Educational Administration at East Tennessee State University, and Dr. William G. Cunningham, professor of Educational Leadership and Counseling at Old Dominion University and a Danforth Foundation Program participant since 1988, had a strong desire to analyze and document the underlying reasons for the success of this very popular and effective program. The authors owe an enormous debt of gratitude to the Danforth Foundation for this program and to the large network of educational administrators who are familiar with its outcomes and activities.

Particular appreciation goes to Dr. Gene L. Schwilck, former president of the Danforth Foundation and to Dr. Bruce J. Anderson, current president, for their continued support of efforts like these. Dr. Schwilck provided inspirational support and Dr. Anderson is a colleague and friend of both authors. Danforth Foundation participants have provided a partial research base for the fundamental principles of successful organizational effectiveness. They also provided anecdotes and examples that clarify and support the many principles of effectiveness that the authors presented. The Danforth Foundation must be given a great deal of credit for creating an environment that supports healthy discourse and encourages papers, articles, books, and practices that have improved the quality of American education. Mr. and Mrs. William H. Danforth and family have proven that one organization can make a significant difference in the professional development of practitioners across America.

As often as possible, the names of educational practitioners and advocates whose ideas were central to this book's development appear in the pages. Their job titles are those that they held at the time of their participation in the Danforth Foundation program. The participating superintendents were:

San Diego, California	Tom Payzant
Seattle, Washington	Robert L. Nelson
Austin, Texas	John Ellis
Colorado Springs, Colorado	Kenneth S. Burnley
Denver, Colorado	James P. Scamman
El Paso, Texas	Ronald K. McLeod
Fort Worth, Texas	Don R. Roberts
Las Vegas, Nevada	Robert E. Wentz
Oklahoma City, Oklahoma	Arthur W. Steller
Tucson, Arizona	Paul D. Houston
Waco, Texas	Jim B. Hensley
Wichita, Kansas	Stuart Berger
Charlotte, North Carolina	Peter D. Relic
Charlottesville, Virginia	Vincent C. Cibbarelli
Jackson, Mississippi	Robert N. Fortenberry
Jacksonville, Florida	Herb Sang
Miami, Florida	Joseph A. Fernandez
Montgomery, Alabama	Thomas Bobo
Norfolk, Virginia	Gene R. Carter
Richmond, Virginia	Lois Harrison-Jones
Prince George County, Maryland	John A. Murphy
Alton, Illinois	David B. VanWinkle
Amarillo, Texas	John Wilson
Atlanta, Georgia	Jerome Harris
Beaumont, Texas	Joseph Austin
Washington, D.C.	Andrew D. Jenkins III
Lexington, Kentucky	Ronald E. Walton
Springfield, Illinois	Donald Miedema
Grand Rapids, Michigan	Robert J. Ferrera
Flint, Michigan	Joseph F. Pollack
Milwaukee, Wisconsin	Lee R. McMurrin
St. Louis, Missouri	Gary Wright

Dayton, Ohio	Franklin L. Smith
Chattanooga, Tennessee	James D. McCullough
Cedar Rapids, Iowa	Newell C. Lash
Springfield, Missouri	Paul J. Hagerty
Youngstown, Ohio	E. N. Catsoules
Kirkwood, Missouri	Tom Keating
Richardson, Texas	Arzell L. Ball
Spring Branch, Texas	Harold D. Guthrie
Victoria, Texas	Larry R. Vaughn
Wichita Falls, Texas	Leslie Carnine

Special appreciation goes to Terrence Deal and Joseph Murphy, Vanderbilt University; Dan Duke, University of Virginia; Paul Hersey, National Association of Secondary School Principals; Jon Paden, John Bohner and Jim Laplant, Institute for the Development of Educational Activities; Carl Ashbaugh, University of North Carolina at Charlotte; Charles Burkett, Floyd Edwards, and Hal Knight, East Tennessee State University; Maurice Berube, Ulysses Van Spiva and Don Myers, Old Dominion University; John Goodlad, University of Washington; and Gene Carter, Association for Supervision and Curriculum Development; for their key insights at various stages during the development of this text. It is difficult to give credit to all of the individuals who influenced this work, but they include some of the best school board members, superintendents, central office administrators, teachers, college professors, and researchers that can be found in this country today. In addition, much thanks goes to Ray Short of Allyn & Bacon for his wisdom in recognizing the importance of this book and for his encouragement along the way. Cheryl Ten Eick of Allyn & Bacon deserves credit for her rare technical and editorial ability.

Although the ideas presented in this book are derived from the successful experience and work of many individuals, organizations, and school districts, the content is the sole responsibility of the authors and does not necessarily reflect the point of view of those who are quoted or discussed.

Special thanks goes to Sandra Evans, a graduate student at Old Dominion University, who did extensive background research on four of these chapters. She was also instrumental in creating the tables of characteristics that appear in this book. The manuscript was proofread and typed by Dawn Hall and Marsha Gresso, who helped to make this book a reality. We also acknowledge Pamela Hopkins, Stephanie Gregg, Sharon Barnett, Penny Smith, and Charles Burkett, all from East Tennessee State University, for their technical assistance. Most of all, we thank our families—Sandi, Mike, Kerri, Marsha, Jon, Anne, David and Tom—for the support, encouragement, and perspectives that they always provide. A special thanks goes to Gail Penn, an exemplary educator and person.

We hope you find this book worthy of the greatness of the people who have had such profound influences upon us. Part of each is in this work.

W.G.C.

D.W.G.

Credits

Credits (cont.)

1

Promoting Excellence in American Schools

There is an intricate tapestry in education today, with each thread providing color, design, and reinforcement to the others. Economics, politics, values, culture, heritage, and environment comprise some of the threads that provide texture to the tapestry. The more the tapestry texture is understood, the greater the chances of transforming American education as it enters the post-industrial era. An understanding of the fabric of American education generates a deep appreciation of its culture and those who work within its confines.

The context of American education provides the historic foundation for the challenges of creating world-class schools. The developments, particularly in the most recent years, have allowed practitioners and theorists alike to get a better handle on excellence. The knowledge of how we arrived at where we are is quite important to the understanding of where we are, and, more importantly, where we want to be to preserve our national well-being. Most would probably prefer to ignore such a nostalgic review of history and move on to the next chapter—what makes organizations excellent. However, that runs counter to one of the primary components of excellence, which is taking time to respect and appreciate the diverse perspectives that make up our culture. These perspectives give color, texture, and vibrancy to a tapestry made by generations of Americans who believe in equal educational opportunity for all of its children. While the threads have become more complex over time and have composed a "mosaic" society that recognizes ethnic, cultural, and racial uniqueness, citizens are experiencing the reverse of the "melting pot" theory of the past decades.

William J. Cook (1990) says amalgamation is being superseded by consolidation. In effective cultures, people take the time to get to know one another, and to value how they think and why they think that way before they begin any tasks. They allow group members to reduce their defense mechanisms and to be able to better listen to and be candid with one another. By understanding the context of education, we can better understand and trust one another and make a commitment to our shared dreams for our school systems. This can occur by sharing personal backgrounds and histories. Excellence is built on a shared understanding of one another.

The Call for Educational Reform

The call for school reform has continued to grow in America. Every major national study of education that has appeared recently has called for major "reform and restructuring" of American education. Perhaps the most compelling of these studies began in 1981, when Secretary of Education Terrel H. Bell created the National Commission of Excellence in Education to examine the quality of education in the United States. School reform was born in 1983 when the commission released their report, *A Nation at Risk: The Imperative for School Reform*. The report was both an indictment of the past and a hopeful solution for the future.

A Nation at Risk was purposefully alarmist in tone. It began,

> Our nation is at risk. Our once unchallenged preeminence in commerce, industry, science and technological innovation is being over taken by competitors throughout the world . . . the educational foundations of our society are presently being eroded by a rising tide of mediocrity that threatens our very future as a nation and a people. . . . If an unfriendly foreign power had attempted to impose on America the mediocre educational performance that exists today, we might well have viewed it as an act of war.

This language was later to be criticized by educational writers and historians as "full of apocalyptic rhetoric and military analogies," however, the report made a significant impact on the educational community and the nation it serves.

The major points were that American students compared unfavorably to foreign students, were weaker in inferential skills, science achievement had declined, and there existed a national problem of illiteracy. The recommendations were to launch a core curriculum, raise academic standards, lengthen the school day and year, improve teacher quality, and attract capable teachers. The report concluded with a challenge,

It is by our willingness to take up the challenge, and our resolve to see it through that America's place in the world will be either secured or forfeited. America has succeeded before and we shall again.

The report went beyond its charge of examining the quality of education in order to issue mandates to educators on what needed to be done to improve American education.

There were a number of other reports during this period of time from respected scholars such as John Goodlad, Ernest Boyer, Mortimer Adler, Theodore Sizer, Chester Finn, Jr., and others, that drew quite similar conclusions. These findings resulted in a concurrent search in America for effective schools. It was hoped that the effective schools research might result in a cure-all for schools in general. There were a number of individuals and groups who took up this challenge and completed major research on school effectiveness. They included such researchers as Ron Edmonds, Lawrence Lezotte, Michael Rutter, Wilbur Brookover, James Comer, Henry Levin, and many others.

The effectiveness research tended to come up with sets of specific formulas by which the United States could improve its schools. The premise was that by adopting these formulas, the schools could be substantially improved. For example, the Research for Better Schools (RBS) pulled together the common features of more than 200 recognized exemplary public elementary schools and found some common factors. These factors were:

- Provide students with maximum opportunity
- The curriculum teaches important content and skills
- Principal provides vision and energy
- Teachers influence and share the values, goals, and standards of their school
- Standards and expectations are high
- Teachers have adequate resources
- The schools accept no excuses
- Schools have specific educational goals

School district programs based on effective schools research multiplied dramatically. This research touched almost every school district in America, including the largest like Chicago, New York, Detroit, Washington, D.C., San Diego, and Memphis. Lawrence Lezotte (1988), drawing on the work of Ron Edmonds, came up with a set of premises about the practices of effective schools which perhaps are the most widely applied. Dr. Lezotte suggests that when these assumptions are transformed into reality, they will improve the performance of the school. These practices of effective schools include:

- Schools will focus on teaching for learning
- Schools will be held accountable for measurable results
- Educational equity will be emphasized as the proportion of poor and minority student increase
- Decision making will be decentralized as the school becomes the strategic unit for planned change
- Collaboration and staff empowerment must increase
- Emphasize the utilization of research and descriptions of effective practices
- Technology is used to accelerate the rate of feedback of instructional monitoring to teachers and administrators
- School administrators will be efficient managers and effective visionary leaders
- Emphasize student outcomes

These premises have been accepted by a large number of schools across America and have been used in developing "school improvement programs" and as core principles for educational reform.

One of the major findings regarding the improvement of American education came from James P. Comer (1980). He concluded,

> . . . focusing on the environment external to the school is short-sighted and may lead to faulty assumptions and conclusions and that the major educational catalyst, the school staff, is a critical variable that has been ignored.
>
> Our findings show that school staff desperately want to be successful. However, because administrators and teachers are not trained to manage in systems and address the social and psychological development of children adequately, staff are often frustrated, knowing what needs to be done but not able to do it. Educators are as much victim of the educational system as students. We found that when given the know-how administrators and teachers eagerly shared their skills, and in the process gained human systems management, child development and relationship skills.

The schools can be improved through participation, cooperation, and trust. Dr. Comer suggested that educators must work together to make schools more productive and happier places to be.

Dr. William J. Bennett replaced Terrel Bell as Secretary of Education in 1985 and kept the educational reform movement alive. Dr. Maurice Berube (1991), in his book *American Presidents and Education,* stated,

Perhaps the key document of Bennett's tenure was his assessment of the excellence reform movement. Entitled *American Education: Making It Work*, Bennett's appraisal was self-congratulatory. He intoned, "The precipitous downward slide of previous decades has been arrested, and we have begun the long climb back to reasonable standards—Our students have made modest gains in achievement . . . we are doing better than we were in 1983 . . . But we are certainly not doing well enough. We are still a nation at risk."

Bennett repackaged the recommendations of *A Nation at Risk* and added concepts like differentiated pay for teachers and CHOICE in attending schools. The tone of the report was that knowing what makes for effective schools, we now must develop the will to build those schools. Much of this belief came from the school effectiveness research and reforms like the first report produced by Chester E. Finn, Assistant Secretary for Research and Improvement, entitled *What Works: Research About Teaching and Learning*.

The National Assessment of Educational Progress (NAEP), Scholastic Aptitude Testing (SAT), American College Testing (ACT), and various state tests of minimum standards are being used to chart the nation's progress regarding student performance. The NAEP is now more commonly known as "the Nation's report card." In 1988, the Hawkins-Stafford Amendments created a governing board for the NAEP with responsibility to select subject areas to be assessed, identify achievement goals, develop assessment objectives, develop test specifications, design assessment methodology, develop standards for data analysis and reporting, develop procedures for interstate, regional and national comparisons, and ensure that selected items are free from racial, cultural, gender, or regional bias. These amendments also added a new dimension in providing for voluntary assessment of eighth-grade mathematics at the state level. A test of this procedure was tried using a stratified random sample of public school eighth-grade students in 37 states. The results of the state by state analysis were released, showing that there had been improvements in achievement; however, the tone of the report was highly critical of education.

After a long period of decline, scores have flattened out or slightly increased at what is described as a "disappointingly slow pace." There is some debate occurring as one set of scores may suggest continued decline where others suggest stabilization or slight improvement. The whole concept of national testing is quite controversial. Dr. Ulysses Van Spiva, president of the Council of Urban Boards of Education, suggests, "Testing kids does not make them smarter any more than weighing pigs makes them heavier." Local educators say that they will have no trouble getting kids to perform well on a standard test, but that does not mean they are well educated or well prepared to meet the demands of American society.

There is also strong debate among experts and the National Assessment Governing Board regarding procedures and use of NAEP data. In an August 1, 1991 report by Daniel L. Stufflebeam, Richard M. Jaeger, and Michael Scriven, it was suggested that the results of the NAEP study should not have been used to infer the quality of 1990 mathematics achievement of grade four, eight, and twelve students in the United States. They believed that the reports had reached premature and flawed closure in response to intense political pressures. The authors of this report stated,

> We have already noted that the achievement levels are not needed to send a message to America that its students are performing grossly inadequately in mathematics; that message has already been sent and received, and without the need for or benefit of achievement levels. . . . The political desire to establish achievement levels in time to report results in conjunction with the June 1991 release of national and trial state Assessment NAEP results drove the timing of NAGB's initial levels-setting project and resulted in a series of unfortunate shortcuts in project design, implementation and evaluation of the project results.

Others express fears about the whole national testing process in that this is the first step in the direction toward a national curriculum—something that has been steadfastly feared from the drafters of the constitution to our citizens of today.

The National Assessment Governing Board was in such strong disagreement with the Stufflebeam, Jaeger, and Scriven report that it terminated the subcontract with these three consultants. In its response to the Draft Summative Evaluation Report, the NAGB stated,

> This draft report cannot be viewed as a competent, objective evaluation of the achievement levels project and, accordingly, the subcontract under which it was prepared has been terminated. A thorough and careful analysis of its contents and recommendations indicate that the draft report represents a political statement by the authors rather than the technical evaluation for which the Board contracted. It amounts to a polemic and is characterized by a pervasive lack of objectivity.

The debate and disagreement regarding testing and many other areas in education suggest wide differences and hotly conflicting beliefs.

During this same period, the Danforth Foundation, acting on reports suggesting that educators had felt largely bypassed in the process of reform and isolated in regard to planning needed educational improvements, modified their long running School Administrators Fellowship program. The redesign included a larger number of participants, including representation at various levels within the school district. The focus was on professional growth, collegiality, school improvement, and transition. Over 42 urban and suburban school districts worked in this redesigned program to improve both the culture of the school district and the effectiveness of the schools. Participants were given an opportunity to attend a national conference with their counterparts to discuss the goals of the Danforth Foundation and the call for national reform.

The American Association of School Administrators (AASA) has had a long history of concern and involvement in school improvement through knowledge and skill development, governmental relations, conventions, and minority affairs. Dr. Lewis Rhodes, associate executive director of the AASA, worked with Dr. John Bahner, president, and Dr. Jon Paden, vice-president of the Institute for Development of Educational Activities, Inc., (/I/D/E/A/) in designing a new program to address reform and restructuring in American schools. This program was modeled after the Danforth School Administrators Fellowship program and was called the District Learning Leadership Team program. /I/D/E/A/ had been heavily involved in the training activities of the Danforth Foundation program and an ideologically related School Improvement Program (SIP) and was a logical choice to work with AASA. The District Learning Leadership Team program was designed to help school systems throughout the country implement a strategy that had potential to engage the capacity of local school districts in continually improving their educational process.

At the same time, Dr. Scott Thompson, executive director, and Paul Hersey, director of professional assistance at the National Association of Secondary School Principals (NASSP), began a long series of work which studied the characteristics of effective school administrators and progressed to a program of selection and development for educational administrators across the United States. Their programs included the Assessment Center; Leadership 1, 2, 3; Springfield Skill Development; Mentor Training; From the Desk of . . . (communications training); and others. They were intricately tied to the reform and restructuring movement by improving the selection and practices of those serving in the principalship. They also received funding from the Danforth Foundation to work with Brigham Young, Virginia Tech, East Tennessee State and Florida State Universities, along with a number of other universities participating in the Danforth Program for the Preparation of Principals. They will design, implement, pilot, and evaluate collaborative models for school administrator preparation and the pedagogy of professors in school administration. The NASSP, the National Association of Elementary School Principals (NAESP), and the Association for Middle School Principals have been quite active in reform efforts through skills training, academies, centers, conferences, and national lobbying efforts.

The National School Board Association (NSBA), which represents some 97,000 local school board members, supports a local school focus and local education effort on reform and restructuring. In a report entitled, *National Imperative: Educating for the 21st Century,* the NSBA "recognizes that special assistance and general aid are appropriate federal activities but it urges that local schools not be subject to federal regulation" so that they have the freedom to be able to experiment and try new ideas.

The National Education Association (NEA) approached the reform and restructuring of American education with considerable cautiousness. The call for reform sounded very much like the relentless criticism that hardworking teachers had been exposed to over the past ten years. The NEA had made a commitment to meeting minimum standards that the nation had mandated as important, including reducing drug use, providing access to all children, and educating the disadvantaged. They were not prepared for a new shift of national focus. In contrast, the American Federation of Teachers (AFT) seemed more prepared to embrace the reform and restructuring movement, even though they were concerned that players from outside the confines of the educational establishment were going to tell teachers how to do their jobs. Many businessmen, doctors, lawyers, politicians, and others would have similar reactions if educators began telling them how to do their work. By this point in time, the teachers' unions were reacting to public pressure and were in danger of losing control of their profession.

Our National Goals

In 1989, school reform was developing from the most ideologically conservative political process of our times. In this setting, President George Bush and the nation's governors came together at the historical educational summit in Charlottesville, Virginia. All agreed that "the time has come, for the first time in the United States history, to establish clear national performance goals, goals that will make us internationally competitive." There was a call among all in attendance for a "renaissance in education," but there was disagreement about just what role Americans would play in seeing that this "renaissance" became a reality by the year 2000. The goals were

- All children will start school ready to learn.
- The high school graduation rate will increase to at least 90 percent.

- United States students will be first in the world in science and mathematics achievement.
- American students will leave grades four, eight and twelve having demonstrated competence in challenging subject matter including English, mathematics, science, history and geography; and every school in America will insure that all students learn to use their minds well, so they may be prepared for responsible citizenship, further learning, and productive employment in our modern economy.
- Every adult American will be literate and will possess the knowledge and skills necessary to compete in a global economy and exercise the rights and responsibilities of citizenship.
- Every school in America will be free of drugs and violence and will offer a disciplined environment conducive to learning.

There was general agreement that public education needed to be fundamentally reformed and restructured in order to ensure that all students meet higher standards. Schools needed powerful incentives for performance and real consequences for persistent failure.

On February 9, 1990, the *Wall Street Journal* contained a special supplement focused on education and the need for reform. The supplement began,

Jobs are becoming more demanding, more complex. But our schools don't seem up to the task. They are producing students who lack the skills that business so desperately needs to compete in today's global economy. And in doing so, they are condemning students to a life devoid of meaningful employment. Better corporate retraining may serve as a stopgap. But ultimately the burden of change rests with our schools. While debate rages about how change should come, almost everyone agrees that something has to be done. And quickly.

Less than one year later, President Bush's administration introduced *America 2000: An Education Strategy* as a far-reaching educational plan to achieve the national goals. Unlike previous federal programs, the Bush proposal was a comprehensive strategy. In announcing the program, President Bush told business leaders, governors, lawmakers, and educators, "For the sake of the future of our children and our nation, we must transform America's schools. The days of the status quo are over." He added, "To those who want to see real improvement in American education, I say, 'there will be no renaissance without revolution.'"

The *America 2000* report was a nine-year plan to move education forward through change in public and private schools, change in every American community, change in every American home, and change in our attitude about learning. The following initiatives made up the crux of the *America 2000* plan:

- *Better and more accountable schools*
  - World class standards
  - American achievement tests (encourage test use by colleges, universities and employers)
  - Presidential citations for educational excellence
  - Presidential achievement scholarships
  - Report cards on schools, districts and states
  - New choice incentives and choice applied to chapter I
  - The school as the site for reform
  - Merit schools' programs to reward schools that move toward national goals
  - Governor's academies for school leaders
  - Governor's academies for teachers
  - Differential pay for teachers
  - Alternative teacher and principal certification
  - Honor outstanding teachers in the five core course subjects

- *A New Generation of American Schools*
  - Research and development through the School Development Corporation to be established by business leaders
  - New American schools to reach world class standards (first 535+ with limited federal and corporation support)
  - Breaking the mold planning
  - Bring American schools on-line with information, research, instructional materials and educational expertise

- *A Nation of Students*
  - Job-related private-sector skills standards
  - Skill clinics
  - Federal leadership on skills upgrading
  - Recommitment to literacy
  - National Conference on Education for adult Americans

- *Communities Where Learning Can Happen*
  - America 2000 communities
  - The Domestic Policy Council to streamline programs and services
  - Individual responsibility for children, family and community

Educators across the nation hailed the comprehensiveness and boldness of the proposal, as well as the visibility and high profile that was placed on improving education. Although the broad concern for education in the report was well received, the specifics of the plan were hotly criticized and debated among educators. There was a concern that national testing and other aspects of the proposal ran against the strongly supported tradition of local control and the management approaches that had been successful in the business community. The spending of large sums of money on new, experimental models when school districts across the nation had just gotten innovative models in place was also a concern. It was also questioned whether it was wise to place so much authority and emphasis on those outside education serving as the innovative force—a further removal of the front line practitioners from the reform process. Such removal has been the cause of failure in American business and education in the past.

There was strong concern that exemplary models in less than one percent of the schools in America would have little impact if they failed to influence the majority of American schools. Past prototype innovations had failed to change the landscape of the schools, and it was determined that there was little to no multiplier effect. There was concern about the validity of measures of performance that would be used in any "merit pay" plan, American Achievement Test, or National Report Card. Possibly the most controversial aspect of the plan was parental choice of schools. There was a real concern that this component would further divide the nation's wealthy from the middle class and poor, and leave public education in complete disarray. The plan may result in a chaotic shift from public to private education with no improvement in the education of American children.

The two major themes of overall concern were that the plan seemed to further remove the experts—the teachers—from the process, while ignoring the real problems that exist in the community with which teachers are having such difficulty. John Goodlad (1992) expressed serious concern about the America 2000 initiatives, and talked about the importance of a more serious reform effort. He stated,

At the outset, America 2000 was declared to be "a nine-year crusade." A crusade involves a mission. But there cannot be a successful mission without the moral imperative of putting in place the conditions necessary to its advancement. Given the fact that high standards and their companion system of assessment can be sustained only if widely regarded as rational and fair, and given our present understanding of the maldistribution of obstacles to fair competition, the nation is called upon to conduct a massive obstacle-clearing campaign far outreaching Desert Storm in complexity, difficulty, and cost.

The nation's moral imperatives seemed to focus on occupational, international competitiveness, and economic conditions as the major driving force for educational reform. However, even these came into question. The economic focus caused schools to be measured on the basis of how well they prepare youth to enter the workforce, and, ultimately, how well that workforce performs. Education was not faring well under this accountability system as a new international economic order was emerging. The general belief in the early 1990s was that poor education had led to poor job skills, which led to unemployment, which led to low wages for all but the richest 30 to 40 percent of the population, which created poverty, which led to welfare, family dissolution, crime and a declining national economy. The total quality management advocates and a few others believed that this was not caused by education but by weak business management. With this new focus on what James Coleman called "economic capital," the policy and mission of the schools must be tied to getting American youth better jobs and higher incomes if they are to receive strong political support.

Many argue that schools must not be adjuncts of corporations. Henry A. Giroux (1992) stated, "The vision of American education should not be limited to making the United States number one in the international marketplace or to more grandiose dreams of presiding over a new world order."

John Goodlad was drawn into the debate regarding the evolving focus of education on the economic capital of the nation in 1986. He was invited to participate in a national network discussion with Governors Thomas Kean of New Jersey and Bill Clinton of Arkansas, on the recently released report of the National Governors' Association, *Time for Results*. Dr. Goodlad expressed concern about the report's narrow focus on expanding economic capital and its need for a broader view of education to provide direction, meaning, and correction. In describing the discourse which followed, Dr. Goodlad stated that Bill Clinton had responded,

> We were not about the business of philosophical discourse . . . We had no time for a course in the philosophy of education. We simply wanted to put out there some practical things we governors might do to improve American education.

Goodlad retorted, "But you did state a value position of sorts. Early on, the report states 'better schools means better jobs.' There can be no backing away from the statement of what our schools are for." The debate regarding a definition and role for education continues, with some narrowing the focus to marketplace definitions and others broadening its boundaries to include developing all aspects of the whole child.

Education was Bill Clinton's first priority as governor of Arkansas since he saw it as the biggest stumbling block to economic growth. He and his wife barnstormed the state, essentially preaching educational excellence and what needed to be done. The Arkansas Education Association and its parent body, The National Education Association, enthusiastically endorsed Bill Clinton for president in 1992, as did the American Federation of Teachers. President Clinton's view that education plays an important role in increasing the productivity, equality, and vocational skills of the nation seems to have gained support. His stress on school safety and only public school choice was also widely supported. The recent themes suggest that the high technology job markets require dramatic educational upgrading to produce a better educated workforce. However, the limitations of the job market outlook in guiding educational reform is still being debated.

$100 Sneakers

The 1990s show a growing number of youth set adrift with minimal chances of success and for whom growing up seems to be a risky business. We often describe this growing body of students as "at-risk." For these students, the family structures have changed drastically, as have the extended support systems. The violence that has been afflicting society in general is creeping into the schools. Other issues that are entering the schools are poor parental and medical care, substance abuse, "crack children," physical and sexual abuse, homicide, poverty, emotional handicaps, neglect, malnourishment, AIDS, latchkey children, mental handicaps, unemployment, lack of direction, lack of motivation, hopelessness, violence, divorce, neglect, suicide, and failure. These and other growing demands have made the work of educators much more complex as they move education beyond its traditional boundaries.

The general fabric of a child's life is eroding. The children of both the rich and poor alike are experiencing a significant array of handicapping conditions which impede their social, psychological, and cognitive development. Although this is more a problem of the urban lower socio-economic, it is growing rapidly among middle-class and wealthy youngsters as well. For example, 50 percent of our students are from divorced families, and some 60 percent are latchkey children.

There are countless other statistics, studies, and analyses that suggest that today's children face far more difficult lives than their counterparts before them. Some of these statistics are:

- One in five children live in poverty.
- Homicide is the second leading cause of death among ages 15-24, preceded by auto accidents and followed by suicide.

- 8.4 million children have no health insurance.
- Drug addicted mothers give birth to approximately 500,000 children a year.
- 2,478 teenagers drop out of school each day of the school year.
- There are 2.4 million reported cases of child abuse.
- There are 37 births for every 1,000 teenage girls between the age of 15 to 19.
- In Chicago, 26 percent of the children have seen someone shot and 29 percent have seen a stabbing.
- Every day nearly 135,000 students carry guns to their classrooms.
- Every 13 seconds a teenager contracts a sexually transmitted disease.
- Boys with antisocial conduct in the fifth grade are likely to engage in serious criminal behavior when they grow older.
- Nearly one in five children experience one or more developmental, learning, or emotional disorder.
- Twelve percent of children suffer damage that prevents them from learning.

What is most shocking about these statistics is that each finding seems to suggest that conditions are a little worse than the findings in previous years. Children are being murdered for jackets and $100 tennis shoes. Eight-year-old girls wear high heels, perfume, and lipstick. Some have described the trends of children's living conditions to be disgraceful.

Our nation was characterized as being made up of "back seat" children as the focus of the 90s became economic. In *Beyond Rhetoric* (1991), the 32 distinguished members of the National Commission on Children described the state of American children:

> . . . among all races and income groups, and in communities nation-wide, many children are in jeopardy. They grow up in families whose lives are in turmoil. Their parents are too stressed and too drained to provide the nurturing, structure and security that protect children and prepare them for adulthood. Some of these children are unloved and ill tended. Others are unsafe at home and in their neighborhoods. Many are poor, and some are homeless and hungry . . . The harshening of these children's lives and their tenuous hold on tomorrow cannot be countenanced by a wealthy nation, a caring people, or a prudent society. America's future depends on these children too.

The problems of single parent homes, high-pressure careers, noncustodial parents and the poverty and violence of the poor are adding stress to the difficult task of raising children.

In recognition of the increasing number of problems plaguing our children, a number of school districts have taken on an increasing role in the coordination and delivery of community services to children and their families. In this way, the school provides leverage on behalf of the students to get them the help that they need. The National Governors Association stated,

> States should encourage providers to integrate their services and create a comprehensive client-focused network...State regulations that impede collaboration at the state and local level should be eliminated and program providers should be held accountable for how well students are being served.

The Kentucky Education Reform Act of 1990 addressed the problem of coordinating services to children experiencing developmental problems. The act called for closer cooperation between schools and social agencies in an effort to ameliorate social conditions that retarded learning. Exemplary programs that exist in Los Angeles, Fresno County, San Francisco, and Ventura County were instigated by a coordinated care system passed by the California State Legislation in 1984. In December of 1988, Connecticut passed legislation to establish three demonstration family resource centers to provide comprehensive child care and family support services to the students and families living within the catchment areas of three school districts. California created a cabinet-level position, secretary of child development and education, in 1991. By 1992, there were a number of such programs nationwide wide that suggested a shift from federal involvement in delivery of services to control at the state and local levels and by the clients themselves.

School-linked services have not been easy to create, however, and they have yet to truly establish themselves. They impose new roles and responsibilities which have not gained wide acceptance. They require educational personnel to work with other agencies and expand the boundaries of their efforts on behalf of students. Establishing collaborative relationships among education, health, social service, police protection, and other human service providers has proved to be quite difficult to balance with the economic focus on a better educated workforce.

The Current Context

There are few in America today who have not concluded that American education is in need of major reform and restructuring. Superintendents across the nation have recognized this need and have worked successfully toward beginning school improvement efforts. Local studies of needed improvement in education abound, such as *Our Children, Our Future: Revitalizing the District of Columbia Public Schools* by the Washington, D.C. Committee on Public Education, *Educational Imperatives: A Community on the Threshold* by the Charlotte Task Force on Education and Employment or the report and recommendations of *The Cincinnati Business Committee Task Force on Public Schools.* The American Association of Colleges for Teacher Education, the University Council for Educational Administration, the National Council of Professors of Educational Administration, and the National Policy Board for Educational Administration have all been involved in "challenging conventional assumptions" and in determining ways to improve American education through reform and restructuring.

State departments of education across the nation have also established new guidelines for certification and accreditation. Most importantly, funding agencies and foundations across America have provided resources needed to complete research on new models to improve American education. Terrel Bell, former United States secretary of education, summed up the mood of the day. He stated,

> We launched the Marshall plan to rebuild the devastated European economy because we knew it was in the best interest of peace and prosperity not only for America, but for the free world. The same self-interest and world interest should govern the need to reform and renew education in America.

Educators, parents, and communities must work together to fashion an education that serves the needs of the community, state, nation, and world in a way that prepares students for their future. We have all perceived a need for the reform and restructuring of education; we must now figure out ways to allow educators to make innovation and improvement routine in American schools. Teachers must be encouraged to experiment and try new ideas in a controlled setting. We must have a grass roots effort to improve American education—one school at a time. This will happen through a better understanding of the "culture of excellence" in American schools.

Bibliography

Alexander, Lamar. *America 2000: An Education Strategy.* Washington, D.C.: U.S. Department of Education, 1991.

Bennett, William J. *American Education: Making It Work.* Washington, D.C.: U.S. Government Printing Office, 1988.

Bennett, William J. *What Works: Research About Teaching and Learning.* Washington, D.C.: U.S. Office of Education Information Office, 1986.

Berube, Maurice R. *American Presidents and Education.* Westport, CT: Greenwood Press, 1991.

Berube, Maurice R. *Teacher Politics: The Influence of Unions.* Westport, CT: Greenwood Press, 1978.

Center for the Future of Children. *The Future of Children.* Los Altos, CA: The David and Lucile Packard Foundation, 1992.

Charlotte Task Force on Education and Employment. *Educational Imperatives: A Community at the Threshold.* Charlotte, NC: Charlotte-Mecklenburg Chamber of Commerce, 1989.

Cincinnati Business Committee Task Force. *The Cincinnati Business Committee Task Force on Public Schools.* Cincinnati, Ohio: Cincinnati Public Schools, September 5, 1991.

Comer, James P. *School Power.* New York: The Free Press, 1980.

Cook, William J. *Strategic Planning for American Schools.* Arlington, VA: American Association of School Administrators, 1990.

Giroux, Henry A. "Educational Leadership and the Crisis of Democratic Government." *Educational Researcher* (May, 1992).

Glickman, Carl D. "Pushing School Reform to a New Edge: The Seven Ironies of School Empowerment." *Phi Delta Kappan* (September, 1990).

Goodlad, John I. (ed.). *The Ecology of School Renewal.* Chicago, Illinois: The University of Chicago Press, 1987.

Goodlad, John I. "On Taking School Reform Seriously." *Phi Delta Kappan* (November 1992).

Lezotte, Lawrence W., and Bancroft, Beverly A. "Growing Use of the Effective Schools Model for School Improvement." *Educational Leadership* (March, 1985).

Lezotte, Lawrence. "Strategic Assumptions of the Effective Schools Process." In *Monographs of Effective Schools.* New York: New York State Council of Educational Associations. Research and Development Committee, 1988.

National Commission on Excellence in Education. *A Nation at Risk: The Imperative for School Reform.* Washington, D.C.: U.S. Office of Education, 1983.

National Assessment Governing Board. *Response to the Draft Summative Evaluation Report on the National Assessments Governing Board's Inaugural Effort to Set Achievement Levels on the National Assessment of Educational Progress.* Washington, D.C.: National Assessment Governing Board, August 14, 1991.

National Commission on Children. *Beyond Rhetoric: A New American Agenda for Children and Families.* Washington, D.C.: U.S. Government Printing Office, 1991.

National School Board Association. *National Imperative: Educating for the 21st Century.* Washington, D.C.: National School Board Association, 1989.

Senge, Peter M. "The Leader's New Work: Building Learning Organizations." *Sloan Management Review* (Fall, 1990). Reprinted by permission of the publisher. Copyright © 1990 by Sloan Management Review Association. All Rights reserved.

Stedman, Lawrence C. "It's Time We Changed the Effective Schools Formula." *Phi Delta Kappan* (November, 1987).

Stufflebeam, Daniel L., Jaeger, Richard M., and Scriven, Michael. *Summative Evaluation of the National Assessments Governing Board's Inaugural Effort to Set Achievement Levels on the National Assessment of Educational Progress.* Kalamazoo, MI: Western Michigan University, August, 1991.

Task Force on Teaching as a Profession. *A Nation Prepared: Teachers for the 21st Century.* Washington, D.C.: Carnegie Forum on Education, 1986.

Washington, D.C. Committee on Public Education. *Our Children, Our Future: Revitalizing the District of Columbia Public Schools."* Washington, D.C.: Washington D.C. City Schools, 1989.

2

Culture, Not Structure

Successful educators spend considerable time developing an effective school culture, since nothing can be accomplished if the culture works against needed reform. Time and effort are spent building and supporting a strong and functional educational culture focused on improving educational performance and effectiveness. Educators have learned that structure and process are important to maintaining the organization, but it is the culture that yields the dividends.

This is not to suggest that formal organization and control are ineffective or unproductive. There must be some level of definition in order to have direction and understand purpose and relationships among employees. Formal structures allow educational employees to apply specialized training and abilities in particular fields, place accountability on performance, and create a hierarchy of authority and responsibility for making arrangements and improving performance. However, when the central focus of the administrator is on formal organization and the control of people, the catalyst for productivity—the culture—becomes muted and blunted. In this case, the primary interest is keeping the organization alive and the structure intact. There is a tendency for such goals of organizational structure to displace the original goals of education.

People are made of flesh and soul and not of steel or wire. They have not been preprogrammed biologically or psychologically for a specific work performance. Each group must work out its own solutions, depending upon the resources at hand, the talents, the needs of the organization's clients or customers, and the state of knowledge available at the time. This is the setting in which employees create a work culture and ensure that new members are appropriately socialized into that culture.

Culture in its most basic form is an informal understanding of the "way we do things around here." Culture is a powerful yet ill-defined conceptual thinking within the organization that expresses organizational values, ideals, attitudes and beliefs. Culture is a strategic body of learned behaviors that gives both meaning and reality to its participants. Edgar H. Schein (1991) suggests three postulates to describe the nature of culture:

1. *a body of solutions to external and internal problems that has worked consistently for a group and that is therefore taught to new members as the correct way to perceive, think about, and feel in relation to those problems;*
2. *which eventually come to be assumptions about the nature of reality, truth, time, space, human nature, human activity, and human relationships;*
3. *so that these assumptions come, over time, to be taken for granted and finally drop out of awareness.*

The vestiges of the culture built on these assumptions are expressed through shared values and beliefs, heroes and heroines, rites and rituals, priests and priestesses, stories and myths, symbols and dress, clans and tribes, norms and practices, legacy and saga, customs and traditions, and common meanings. Members of an organization are enculturated into the work group through these expressions of its work culture. In this way, the process of group socialization goes beyond direct learning and includes a perceived and extraceptive learning that includes unobtrusive systems of symbolic meaning. It is through symbols that man consciously and unconsciously lives, works, and has his meaning.

Lee G. Bolman and Terrence E. Deal (1991) believed that

Culture is both product and process. As product, it embodies the accumulated wisdom of those who were members before we came. As process, it is continually renewed and re-created and new members are taught the old ways and eventually become teachers themselves.

. . . Our view is that every organization develops distinctive beliefs and patterns over time. Many of these patterns and assumptions are unconscious or taken for granted. They are reflected in myths, fairy tales, stories, rituals, ceremonies and other symbolic forms. Managers who understand the power of symbols have a better chance of influencing organizations than do those who focus only on other frames.

Our culture is important because it shapes the different ways we recognize and react to events in our work lives. It shapes how people experience the world of work and how they express meaning in their own work. Structure provides the organization for professional life, but culture produces the reaction. How we approach a situation is shaped by our work structure, but our choice of responses is affected by work culture. The response of the employee shapes organizational success or failure.

Drs. Beth B. Hess, Elizabeth W. Markson, and Peter J. Stein (1990) suggest that

> . . . culture is often defined as the blueprint for living of a group whose members share a given territory and language, feel responsible for one another and call themselves by the same name. . . . People become functioning members of the group as they learn and participate in the culture.

Dr. Wendel H. Oswalt, (1985) an anthropologist, defines culture as

> the learned and shared behavior patterns characteristic of a group of people. . . . Cultural behavior is learned from others in a group and consequently is a sharing of ideas about what is important to that group. Most of what you think and do is based on learning and sharing a behavioral tradition.

Culture causes people to see their work similarly. In this way, they are assimilated into a group and become part of a complementary and productive work team.

Culture is transmitted through observation, shared beliefs, symbolic gestures, mores, folkways, customs, rituals, games, play, art, myths, memories, clothing, methods of physical and emotional relations, and eating. Each helps one to grasp and appreciate the full meaning of the work group. Culture is formed as we observe, listen, talk, and interact with others in our organization.

Washington Middle School

Ralph, a school principal at Washington Middle School, has worked for twenty-two years in the same school district. He was a junior high school science teacher and coach, an elementary school principal, a middle school assistant principal, and is now a middle school principal. He has a diverse and rich staff of people that are bright, young, and very enthusiastic. Although the parents and community are pleased with Ralph and the school, there have been a number of complaints from his staff to Robert, the Associate Superintendent to whom Ralph reports.

The staff is concerned that Ralph is always looking over their shoulders and checking up on them, particularly since the school division has moved toward teacher empowerment and site-based management. Although Ralph is always checking on them, the teachers find that he is unwilling to back them up in experimenting with new ideas or even in handling behavioral, learning or discipline problems. The teachers feel unsupported by the administrative staff. They say, "Ralph checks everything we do, from arriving in the morning to leaving at the end of the day and seems endlessly cynical and critical of our abilities and performance. He acts more like a 'watchdog' than a manager."

There is little or no opportunity to discuss problems or concerns or to be involved in professional development. Staff members are very competitive when trying to get Ralph's support, and there is constant disagreement over how the simplest matter might be handled. The teachers have many ideas that they would like to try in the school but are afraid to voice their feelings, ideas and opinions. They wonder if there are any capable administrators in the school division and if they have chosen the wrong profession and should make a change.

Robert is concerned and has asked Ralph about this, without identifying the teachers involved. Ralph explains that the education of the community's children is very important and that the professional behavior of the teachers is simply too important to take chances with. He says,

> The teachers on my staff tend to be primadonnas, particularly the younger ones, and they are not as smart as they think they are. It takes a lot of time to develop good teaching skills, and these teachers are constantly looking for short cuts and wanting to change things.

Robert can tell that Ralph is very angry about the fact that this problem has left the walls of his school and fears that Ralph may even tighten his administrative style to ensure that it does not happen again.

The situation at Washington Middle School is not shocking to anyone who has been involved with public education over the last fifteen years. It is well documented in studies like *The Nation at Risk, A Nation Prepared, Time for Results, Leaders for American Schools* and hundreds of other reports that document existing conditions. *America 2000: An Educational Strategy* sourcebook documents President Bush's and the Governor's historical educational conference results and calls for massive educational reform.

Dr. John Goodlad (1984) suggests that the culture of education has changed very little over the past two decades. He states,

> Teachers talk at pupils; students work on written assignments or answer specific narrow questions; there is little feedback or guidance from the teacher; students work with textbooks and complete written

homework assignments; and students are judged by how well they perform on paper and pencil tests.

The only way education will improve is if we invite ideas from the people who work in the school. The people who work in the culture are the ones who know which reforms are acceptable, and which ones can be implemented successfully. These are the only improvements that will influence the school positively. When asked the secret of his success as the baseball manager of the world series champion Cincinnati Reds, Sparky Anderson said, "If your team wants to win, let them." In other words, make sure you have a winning culture, then let the educators do their magic.

There are many structural adjustments and controls that might be considered in order to improve the situation at Washington. Ralph needs to be retrained on how to be an effective administrator, or replaced. The new teachers need to be trained in the "Washington ways." Washington Middle School needs to be reorganized so that the trouble-makers are defused or neutralized. The induction process needs to be improved so the new middle school teachers realize that they must follow established practice. The school needs a better evaluation system and merit pay so it can discourage Ralph and the new teachers from displaying inappropriate behavior. Parents should consider their choice to send their children to Washington, and whether to allow such problems to be corrected by competitive market economics. It's time to shift Ralph to a new school and get an open-minded administrator at Washington Middle School. Washington's pre-service and in-service programs need to be restructured. Business and community leaders can assist with ideas to help Washington Middle School.

Structural aspects that might be used to improve this situation include training, performance appraisal systems, salary and wage plans, recruitment and selection techniques, principal and teacher preparation programs, organizational patterns and structure, staffing patterns, student tracking, planning and control mechanisms, accounting procedures, testing and accountability systems, policies and procedures, new curricula, and centralizing or decentralizing authority. The leadership notion being practiced is that conditions will improve if we tinker with the structures.

Structure, Behavior, Culture, and Performance

Obviously, structure has an impact on employees within an organization. If you modify the structure, you modify the employee's behavior. People will be moved into new grooves or ruts as the new structures change their directional patterns. The change of structures will change expectations and methods, and this is expected to change the behavior patterns. The trick is to modify the structure to get the correct behavior. Change a structure to change the situation.

What we have learned from a long history of structural change is that it does not work! This indirect process is too slow, too random, and too imprecise to be successful in today's fast-paced, multi-talented organizations. The behavior of people has too great a staying power to be modified by external restructuring and reform. Structure will never change attitudes, abilities, interests or human spirit. More importantly, it will rarely change the culture or result in improved school effectiveness.

Structure should not be used to change organizational performance and effectiveness. It should be vice versa—focus on the culture of excellence and the structures will evolve to support that culture. It is through the school culture that we have the greatest chance of improving what our students learn. Alexis DeTocqueville recognized the wisdom of this almost 200 years ago when he stated,

> It would seem as if rulers of our time sought only to use men in order to make things great; I wish that they would try a little more to make great men; that they would set less value on the work and more upon the workman; that they would never forget that a nation cannot be strong when everyone belonging to it is individually weak.

Using the Washington Middle School example, Robert needs to encourage the development of a joint vision within the school. This will require the development of collegial relations; trust, understanding and support; broad involvement; life-long development; knowledge and skill; continuous improvement; and empowered employees. This is no easy task, but it is the responsibility of educational leaders who are interested in improving school effectiveness and student learning.

Structure and behavior are two forces that have governed the leadership literature in the past and are dominant in almost all current forms of administrative training. These forces do not allow us to fully engage the immense ability or to adequately use the humanity that exists within the profession. The problems that cause ineffective schooling are typically related to the culture and its malice toward the initiatives of effectiveness and those who serve as a driving force for those initiatives. There is a lack of excitement in the symbols, traditions, stories and sagas of the institutions. The culture serves as a self-perpetuating counterforce to effectiveness. For example, at Washington Middle School the culture suggests that the school administrators are old, out of touch, and impotent. The administrators see the staff as young, inexperienced, and requiring close supervision. All of the traditions, symbols, and stories perpetuate these beliefs, regardless of the structural or behavioral changes that are made.

Culture-building requires that school leaders give attention to the informal, subtle and symbolic aspects of school life which shape the beliefs and actions of each employee within the system. The task of leadership is to create and support the culture necessary to foster an attitude of effectiveness in everything that is done within the school. Once this attitude is achieved and supported by the culture, all other aspects of the organization will fall in line. This is why culture-building is the key to organizational success.

The first thing that needs to be addressed at Washington Middle School is the work culture itself. Unless the work culture is changed, none of the traditional structural or behavioral changes, whether suggested by educational leaders, politicians, business persons, or other service professionals, will have any long-term impact. We have used too few of our educators to solve the immense problems that confront education today.

There is a need for American education to shift the focus from mundane structures and practices to the energy and spirit that generate excellence in education. Greatness does not grow out of a focus on structure and process, but is found in the culture of the organization and the spirit and purposefulness of the lives of people who belong to that organization. Students, parents, the community, and employees take pride in results that grow out of common efforts to achieve excellence. Leadership must focus on these simple human values in the public school systems in order to make them great.

This human spirit of "can do" was exemplified by Della Burrus, a teacher in Lexington, Kentucky who was a member of the 1986-87 Danforth Foundation Fayette County Public School District vertical team. She had met often with the members of her vertical team and had been enculturated into the spirit of expecting great things from herself and others. She believed in both her own greatness and that of her fellow colleagues. The vertical team and its culture had given her the confidence to use her abilities in ways she would never have imagined before.

A series of very impressive examples were provided by Ms. Burrus, the most impressive being her involvement in a district-wide meeting involving several hundred teachers from the school district. She shared how she and vertical team members had been working with Dr. Van Meter, the vertical team facilitator, to develop their skills of leadership through personal and professional growth. She explained,

The other day while attending a district-wide meeting with several hundred other teachers from many different schools, it was announced as we sat patiently in the room that the speaker hadn't arrived. All of a sudden something intrinsic took over and I came out of my chair, and without administrative approval, went to the front of the room and said, "Get yourselves organized into small groups; time is valuable and I have some activities that will help all of us get to know each other better and support unity in this district." I have never been the same since. Associating on a regular basis with people from all levels within the school district in a rich culture of trust and support has allowed me to think differently. In addition, the evaluations at the end of the district-wide meeting indicated the audience liked my activity better than the tardy speaker.

Leadership must emphasize the personal values that make a teacher and classroom, a principal and school, and sometimes even an entire school district, display real greatness. The emphasis should be on cultural and personal qualities of achievement, such as self-image, respect, confidence, identity, worth, enthusiasm, pride, wisdom, and commitment. The central themes of an effective work culture are vertical integration; vision and optimism; collegiality; values and interests; diverse perspective; personal/professional development; long-term focus; information, cooperation and communication; trust, support, care, and bold action; continuous and sustained improvement; and vulnerability and risk.

Those who like the safety of working in their office, exerting "paper control" over people, operating and making decisions on the basis of plans, reports and memorandums, as well as implementing structural changes and evaluating processes, will feel a bit uncomfortable. If the techniques of excellent school systems are not being practiced, making the shift will take some nerve. The leaders will have to listen, have convictions, communicate with and support people, grow, cooperate, develop vision, support action, take risks, and be responsible for results. The administrators will be closely observed by the employees of the school district. The personal values of respect, confidence, trust, self-esteem, and commitment come in as the leader realizes that she or he may not always be appreciated and that others may have ideas that will be equally as effective or possibly even more effective. However, when school leaders practice the principles of excellence, they will discover the essence of great achievement through the commitment, zest, energy, care, fun, friendship, enthusiasm, extraordinary individual efforts, and celebration which can pervade public education.

The methods of developing effective work cultures have been consistently supported as having greatly improved a school division's ability to achieve excellence. Washington Middle School's future success will depend upon the development of a culture that values excellence and prominently projects that value in all aspects of the educational program. Ralph cannot mandate, impose, or coerce an effective work culture. He can only create one by allowing the school staff an opportunity to get to know and understand one another; by supporting their personal and professional development; by focusing their talent, energy, and passion on excellence in their schools; by giving them enough power and time to really make a difference; by building trust, support and a desire for continuous improvement; by encouraging experimentation and tolerating risks; and, finally, by measuring and feeding back results. This is what Ralph must do if he truly cares about the education of children in Washington Middle School.

Culture Imbedded in Administrative Theory

Elton Mayo (Bendix & Fisher, 1961) was one of the first to challenge the domination of the scientific, rational, and structural approach to administrative practice. His colleague at Harvard, Chester Barnard (1968), concurred, asserting that the leader's role was one of harnessing the human potential within the organization. Barnard stated,

> The essential functions (of administration) are first to provide the system of communication; second to promote the securing of essential efforts; and third to formulate and define purpose.

Both men focused on human properties and how to provide the synergistic force to bring the energy and abilities of employees together in such a way that they create a positive force within the organization.

In discussing the art of leadership and institution-building, Philip Selznick (1957) wrote,

> To institutionalize is to infuse with values beyond the technical requirements of the task at hand. The institutional leader, then, is primarily an expert in the promotion and protection of values.

He went on to suggest that such values are enhanced and promulgated by the work culture.

Charles Lindbloom (1980) suggested that individual values, beliefs, and behavior were not individualistic and distinct from one another but were intertwined among the people shaping an organizational culture. Warren Bennis (1989), the author of a number of articles and books on leadership, suggests that "American organizations have been overmanaged and underled." The total quality management (TQM) scholars go a step further and suggest that all problems in American education and business are the result of poor management. Leadership is effective when it unleashes the energy of those within the organization and facilitates this ability to achieve the objectives and goals that they can believe in and support.

Thomas J. Peters wrote three very successful books. The first, with Robert H. Waterman (1982), was entitled *In Search of Excellence*. Following that was a book written with Nancy Austin (1985) entitled *A Passion for Excellence*, and then a book (1988) entitled *Thriving on Chaos*. Peters suggests that the consistent high performance of excellent companies is due in large part to their focus on people, not structure. Such a work force accomplishes great things because it is motivated by "compelling, simple—even beautiful—values." What is important to the success of organizations is the individual and group initiatives for innovation and creative energy—not the facilities and organizational structures within which they work. In fact, these authors suggest that the most effective organizations have lots of informal communication and a "can do" attitude. They don't constrain themselves with attention to structure, plans, evaluation, or memorandum when the people within the organization are most important. One of their basic beliefs is that if you find an organization staffed with people who want it to live and prosper, they will find a way to make it succeed and a structure in which to do so.

Peters and Waterman (1982) talk about a college-educated first-line department chair who manages ten engineers in a structure that does not allow him to buy an item that costs only $8.95. Although such employees may not be experts on the need for such rules, they are surely experts on the meaning of "trust." And, according to these authors, trust is what organizations are all about. They suggest that

> People are why managers are there and they know it and like it . . . There was hardly a more pervasive theme in the excellent companies than respect for the individual. These managers encourage exuberance and collegiality within the organization. Management just plain talk to their employees on a regular basis and in such a way that direct communication takes place between the highest and lowest levels within the organization. Organizations must support people and their development. The basic philosophy, spirit and drive of an organization have far more to do with its achievement than do technological or economic resources, organizational structures, innovation and timing.

Thomas Sergiovanni (1991) pointed out the importance of culture to the roles and responsibilities of educational administration. He stated,

> Excellent schools have central zones composed of values and beliefs that take on sacred or cultural characteristics. Indeed, it might be useful to think of them as having an official 'religion' which gives meaning and guides appropriate actions. As repositories of values, these central zones become sources of identity for teachers and students, giving

meaning to their school lives. The focus of leadership, then, is on developing and nurturing these central zone patterns so that they provide a normative basis for action within the school.

Karl E. Weich (1982) also recognized the importance of the intangiable aspects of culture to the effective operation of the organization. In his words,

> People need to be part of sensible projects. Their action becomes richer, more confident, and more satisfying when it is linked with important underlying themes, values and movements . . . administration must be attentive to the "glue" that holds loosely coupled systems together because such forms are just barely systems.

Although Terrence Deal and Allan Kennedy's (1982) book focused on corporate culture, they spent considerable time studying culture and school performance. They concluded,

> The importance of culture is an old fashioned idea that great business leaders have known for years. Many school principals also spend considerable time building cohesive school cultures. They might not label it as such, but it's precisely what they're doing. The wisdom of their efforts is supported by educational researchers who have documented the power of culture. Sarason demonstrated how school cultures can undermine innovation. When culture works against you, it's nearly impossible to get anything done...The problem is to make something powerful and ill-defined work for us and to show that building strong culture is intimately tied to improving educational performance.

The Functional Paradigm of Administration

Most models of the administrative process are composed of the same fundamental components. These organizational components are typically categorized under structure, behavior, culture, and performance. The *structure* is how the organization is set up to accomplish its goals and objectives. Thomas Sergiavonni (1991) suggests,

> By emphasizing such concepts as planning and time management technologies, contingency leadership theories, and organizational structures, the leader provides planning, organizing, coordinating and scheduling to the life of the school.

A "management engineer" is skilled at manipulating strategies and situations to ensure optimum effectiveness.

Behavior denotes the way that various roles and responsibilities within the organization are approached, and forms the work process of the organization. Sergiovanni (1991) stated,

> By emphasizing such concepts as human relations, interpersonal competence, and instrumental motivation techniques, she or he provides support, encouragement and growth opportunities to the school's human organization.

The skilled "human engineer" is adept at building and maintaining morale and using such processes as participatory decision making.

The *culture* defines the way individuals respond to one another, and the expectations of the work that is to be done. It is the system of informal rules and regulations that spell out how people within the organization conduct their work life. The cultural leader assumes the role of "high priest," seeking to define, strengthen, and articulate those enduring values, beliefs, and cultural strands that give a school its unique identity. Sergiovanni (1991) stated that,

> Leader activities associated with the cultural force include articulating school purposes and mission; socializing new members to the culture, telling stories and maintaining and reinforcing myths, traditions, and beliefs; explaining the way things operate around here; developing and displaying a system of symbols over time; and rewarding those who reflect this culture.

Performance is the outcome created from the combination of organizational structure, behavior, and culture. It is often referred to as the bottom-line reason why work organizations exist. Problems with performance signal need to take corrective action, and good performance means the objectives and goals of the organization are being met efficiently, effectively, and excellently.

The Structural Model

Some administrative scholars suggest that structure, behavior, culture and performance reinforce one another, and that culture, and performance flow from structure and behavior. Thus, appropriately shaping the structure and behavior will produce an efficient and effective work culture, resulting in appropriate work performance. In this arrangement it is believed that organizational behavior and structure shape the culture. The central focus of administrative theory and practice based on these beliefs are presented in Figure 2–1. In this paradigm, corrective actions are based on the premise

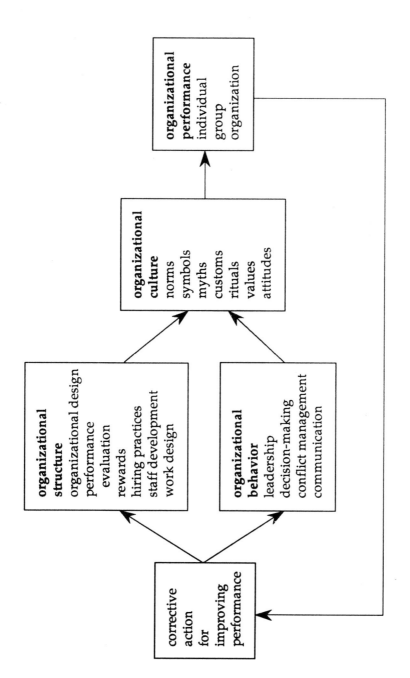

FIGURE 2–1 The Structural, Behavioral, Control Approach to Leadership

organizational
structure
organizational design
performance
evaluation
rewards
hiring practices
staff development
work design

organizational
behavior
leadership
decision-making
conflict management
communication

organizational
culture
norms
symbols
myths
customs
rituals
values
attitudes

organizational
performance
individual
group
organization

corrective
action
for
improving
performance

that changes to culture and performance are best made by an indirect approach of modifying structural and behavioral components such as job descriptions or leadership styles. Research suggests that this indirect approach has established a relatively long track record of poor success. Sergiovanni (1984) suggested that "the structural and behavioral components are essential to competent schooling, and their absence contributes to ineffectiveness." However, he believed that they were "not sufficient to bring about excellence in schooling . . . The greater the presence of a cultural or symbolic leadership force the less important beyond some unknown minimum presence are others below." (Those below are structural and behavioral components of administrative practice.)

Culture has a very strong staying power, even in cases where no one seems to benefit from it. Dr. Scott Thompson (1988) suggests that "the culture is the thoughts, words, deeds and hearts of everyone in the school and it is not easily modified by national reports, state mandates, or the latest change in practice." Intense inservice training efforts bring about changes in teacher behavior for a period of time, but research suggests that reversion to the traditional behavior will occur if the culture is not changed. When a strong administrator uses a new style of leadership with teachers, the teachers may behave accordingly, but their actions do not necessarily imply that they have changed their ideas, values, or beliefs from the predominant ones that exist in the culture. The culture will have existed long before the latest structural package or behavioral practice was tried and will exist long after both have evaporated.

The cultural tapestry has a unique color and texture of its own which must be addressed directly if we hope to achieve any long term results. Culture defines the manner of operation that is acceptable to members of individual work groups and is the basis by which most of us live. Culture pervades people's minds and forms their models for perceiving, relating, and interpreting their management, their work, and their selves. The professional lives within a school culture derive importance, meaning, identity and belongingness from this culture.

The Cultural Model

Although the notion of organizational culture is gaining credibility in literature, little has been done to focus on it as the key to administrative practice and organizational improvement. Yet, this is exactly what must be done to improve the quality of education that American youth receive in our schools. Dr. John Goodlad (1984) states, in *A Place Called School,*

The ambience of each school differs. These differences appear to have more to do with the quality of life and, indeed, the quality of education in schools than do the explicit curriculum and the method of teaching.

It is this ambience, this culture, that must be the central focus of practicing administrators. Mary Anne Raywid, Charles A. Tesconi and Donald P. Warren (1984) in *Pride and Promise: Schools of Excellence for all the People* state that what is most frightening is that the general strategy taught in most educational administration classes, adopted by most education reports, and implemented in a growing number of states, may be distinctly opposed to the development of a culture of excellence.

Recent research on school effectiveness has identified many characteristics common to an effective school culture. The work of the Danforth Foundation in their School Administrators Fellowship program, particularly their work with 42 different school districts over a six-year period, has drawn on this research and greatly added to the knowledge base. Other research such as the school effectiveness studies and the work of the Institute for Development of Educational Activities, Inc. (I/D/E/A/), American Association of School Administrators (AASA), National School Board Association (NSBA), National Association of Secondary School Principals (NASSP), National Association of Elementary School Principals (NAESP), and University Council for Educational Administration (UCEA) has also contributed much to our understanding of effective school culture and the responsibility of the leader in relation to that culture. The overall conclusion of these studies is that it is the shared culture provides the cohesion needed to sustain individual excellence in the teaching profession.

Culture must be at the center of all administrative efforts if we hope to continuously improve organizational effectiveness. The organizational behavior, structure, and performance all flow from the culture, as shown in Figure 2–2. The culture produces the performance and shapes the structure and behavior of the organization. The mechanism for improving performance is the organizational culture. The behavior and structure will naturally evolve and support the appropriate culture. The reverse, changing behavior and structure directly, has at best haphazard, temporary, or random effects on performance, and is seldom long-lasting unless a corresponding supporting change occurs in the culture.

Dr. Harrison Owen (1987), a management consultant from Washington, D.C., uses the term "organizational transformation" to describe the cultural approach. The culture shapes the energy of the work force and focuses it on the work needed to accomplish organizational goals and objectives. The energy and spirit of the organization, as well as its performance, is born out

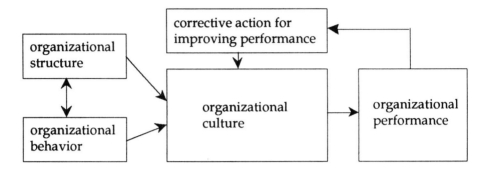

FIGURE 2–2   The Cultural Approach to Leadership

of the culture. However, most administrative researchers and practitioners practice what Harrison calls a "flatlander's view of the organization," focusing their attention on organizational structure, purpose, technology and behavior. Harrison found that there is something very important underneath all that, which he calls the "depths," or the culture, of the organization. The depths give the organization its form, color, style, approach to work, and ultimately influence performance. Today's administrators must first "chart the depths" and then influence and change the culture to support effectiveness and efficiency.

The cultural forces for change are situational and contextual, deriving their unique qualities from specific matters of education and schooling as well as the school district and school. These qualities differentiate the leadership of one type of organization—for instance, education—from the leadership of another—say, business. The culture flows through the entire organization in the form of myths, rituals, customs, symbols, beliefs, heroes, and even what Harrison calls "liturgy," and holds the organization together.

New people are initiated, inducted, and assimilated into the organization, not by a structured induction processes, but by the culture in which they find themselves working. The culture, not the behavior or structure, of the organization gives support in troubled times. It is not the leadership, rules and regulations, or memoranda that carry the spirit of the organization, but the culture. And, most importantly, it is not administrative practice or organizational structure that results in organizational effectiveness, but the work culture, which grows out of those who dedicate their life's toil to the organization.

The culture must be understood, cared for, and transformed if we ever hope to sustain improved productivity and effectiveness. As the culture takes on new wrinkles, we must be careful not to kill it, but allow it to move with the flow of the organization, providing new energy and nutrients for those working in the organization. Let the culture create the new stories, and when they are disruptive to the organization's purpose, help those in the work culture to find the stories that will produce effective results. The stories will unite people, and the culture generates those stories.

One cannot install a "packaged" approach that has worked well in one school division and expect it to work well in another. Its results will be random, at best, since both the culture and the response will be different. Certainly, much can be learned from what has worked well in other cultures, but each organization must solve its own problems through its own culture. Unfortunately, those with the best intentions often misunderstand this basic premise of organizational function as they mandate solutions to problems. These mandates become the central focus of the culture and rob it of precious time needed to solve its real problems.

Mandates are handled by the culture much as germs, viruses, and bacteria are handled by the human body. Antibodies collect around the germ for the purpose of carrying it through the human body in a way that it will do the least harm, and ultimately eliminate it from the system. Of course, fighting off foreign substances drains energy, and the business at hand gets less attention. The more understood, accepted, and cohesive the culture of a school, the better able it is to move in concert toward ideals.

A Structural and Cultural Example

The difference between the structural and cultural approaches to administration can be clearly represented through the experiences of two different school districts—the Virginia Beach Public School System in Virginia and the Amarillo Independent School District in Texas. There were an amazing number of similarities in the intentions of the school divisions and their new superintendents. Both superintendents, Dr. E. Carlton Bowyer and Dr. John Wilson, wanted to reduce failure rates, raise test scores, address the needs of at-risk students, and reduce dropout rates; both saw whole language curriculum, cooperative learning, writing across the curriculum, and improving thinking skills as directions that the divisions should take to accomplish their goals; and both had high ideals, hopes, and a vision of excellence for their school divisions.

The two superintendents were, however, quite different in their approaches to making these changes. Dr. Bowyer was asked to implement a major curriculum change in a one year period. He had some concern regarding this expectation and stated, "We are attempting to do in one year what would normally take five years." Superintendent Bowyer used a structural and behavioral administrative style to achieve the agreed upon goals. He was hired because of his aggressive leadership style, his "can do" attitude, and a number of successful initiatives he had implemented in previous jobs. He created curriculum and instructional development committees to revise and rewrite the curriculum, first for the elementary schools and then for the middle and high schools. The teams were to use the whole language approach by combining vocabulary comprehension, literature, information resources, speaking, listening, phonics, handwriting, structural analysis, writing, and grammar through the language arts program. Some of the outcomes of the curriculum committee's work were 1.) to eliminate reading groups and go to flex-group approaches, 2.) to use more hands-on object learning and fewer dittos, and 3.) to incorporate thinking skills and learning styles into all lessons. Stress was also placed on cooperative learning and the development of leadership, communications, trust-building and cooperation skills among students. A number of teacher's manuals and resources were developed by these committees, supervisors, and instructional leaders, and made available to every teacher within the school system.

In order to implement these changes in the curriculum, a number of staff development and training (inservice) activities were established within the school district. First, all grade-level leaders and department chairs were asked to attend training in the new programs and to act as resource people within their schools. Next, almost all of the teachers within the school division were provided workshops on the new curriculum and instructional approaches. The training emphasized teachers' building upon existing strengths needed to implement the curriculum. Teacher training and evaluation was based on "correlated strategy related to the new curriculum." The manuals were comprehensive, explaining how the curriculum was to be taught and even providing a number of hands-on activities from which the teachers could select to accomplish various objectives within the curriculum. This was a comprehensive, systematic, and structural approach to teacher development.

Superintendent Bowyer did not underestimate the difficulty in getting close to 4,000 teachers to change their approach and felt that some administrative pressure would be needed as well. He said,

> You don't get 4,000 teachers to move without pushing some to get them to moving. Please don't misunderstand. We have an excellent teaching corps. I would put our teachers against any in the state and any in the nation. But change comes hard.

He expected himself and his principals to have hands-on control of their teachers and to see that this program was implemented correctly.

He had a number of administration meetings with principals and leaned on them to see that the curriculum changes were implemented within their schools. He knew that administrative support was essential to the plan's success and wanted to establish a strong sense of loyalty to the plan among all principals. He made these wishes known to administrators quite emphatically. An evaluation system was devised based on the curriculum to ensure that teachers and principals were being evaluated on the basis of what was now being expected of them. Other structural approaches regarding newsletters, hotlines, resources, and support services were provided to the teachers.

A year after having implemented a comprehensive, well thought-out structural approach to this plan, the superintendent was given a vote of "no confidence" by the teachers within the school division. Most serious analysts would suggest that it was the style of implementation, above all else, including the content of the curriculum, that resulted in the vote. In fact, a survey by the Virginia Beach Education Association showed that almost 50 percent of the teachers supported the new curriculum but did not support the superintendent who was responsible for implementing it. There are currently a number of signs that show that support for the curriculum is actually growing.

The chief complaint from more than 70 percent of the over 3,000 teachers who completed the VBEA survey was that pressure from the administration to implement the plan was having a negative effect on their schools and that the central administration was trying to accomplish too much, too fast. Teachers portrayed the administrative style as heavy-handed and unsupportive, using threats to motivate teachers. Eighty-four percent of the teachers said that there seemed to be a breakdown in the communication channels in the school division.

Soon after the VBEA survey, the school board, which had supported Dr. Bowyer and the school division's new directives, also lost confidence in Dr. Bowyer. The board wanted the curriculum changes to continue but not under the leadership of Superintendent Bowyer. The superintendent was fired by an eight to two vote with the motion citing "lack of effective communication with personnel" as a primary reason. In trying to reduce the negative effects of the situation, all school administrators were asked to put aside politics and begin a new era, free from "acrimony." Virginia Beach employees were told,

> We've been through a time of acrimony. We want to put that behind us . . . we've been focusing too much on ourselves. What we really need to focus on are these 70,000 kids.

The true culprit in all of this was not the superintendent, but the traditional structural/behavioral approach that was chosen in implementing what many observed as needed and beneficial changes.

On the other hand, Dr. John Wilson, superintendent of Amarillo Independent School District, was highly successful using a cultural approach. Dr. Wilson was faced with the same challenges that existed in Virginia Beach—reduce failure rates, raise test scores, and reduce drop outs. He, too, was looking at whole language curriculum, cooperative learning, writing across the curriculum, and thinking skills to accomplish these goals. However, this is where the similarities end, since Dr. Wilson chose to use a cultural approach to improve school effectiveness. Although the goals were roughly the same, the methods of design and implementation were quite different.

Dr. Wilson chose to use the vertical and horizontal team concept as a method to achieve the goals of the school division and to enhance decision-making and communication within the district. The purpose of the teams was to help develop the culture needed within the district to achieve the agreed upon results. Dr. Wilson wanted the culture to value and support enhanced communication, collegiality, trust, teacher empowerment, and a sense of team spirit. He also hoped to establish a district-wide vision that would embrace the goals of the school district. He would then give that culture the freedom to alter the structures and behaviors to support the desired performance.

These objectives were greatly facilitated by the fact that the Amarillo Public School District was part of the Danforth Foundation School Administrator Fellowship Program during this same year. First, the school district set up a vertical team composed of a school board member, the superintendent, a central office administrator, four principals, and three teachers. In addition, cluster groups were formed, comprised of administrators and teachers from each of the high school attendance zones within the school district. Dr. Wilson stated, "I met as often as possible with the clusters from each of the attendance areas to insure that we shared a common vision and were moving in directions that would support that vision."

The initial purpose of these groups was to develop a work culture that would promote collegiality, trust, support, and involvement of different levels of the staff. Dr. Wilson said,

> I have some deep concerns about the segmented nature of the staff and its ability to work together to achieve the goals we have established for this district. We need to improve understanding and communication within the division, that is, among elementary and secondary levels and among administrative echelons both at the central office and within the schools. We need to build a culture that can design, implement and support the type of changes needed within this school division.

Any significant change within the district needed to grow out of the culture and its group process.

Principals were encouraged to provide opportunities for their staff to participate in school-based management. A "can do" culture was expected from the staff. A belief formed within the division that along with the freedom to exercise their best professional judgment came the responsibility to work towards and accomplish the common vision and goals of the school district. The key theme promoted throughout the staff was "ownership" of the future of the school division. Groups were then formed within the schools, including vertical team and cluster group members, to develop opportunities and programs that would address district-wide initiatives. These school committees were asked to develop implementation policies and procedures for a "zeros are not permitted" program, whole-language instruction, cooperative learning, and tutorial programs.

Rebecca Harrison, principal at Caprock High School in Amarillo, stated,

> The Strategic Plan Committee at Caprock worked to analyze division directions, look at school data, discuss national movements, etc., and to present their findings to the staff and lead the staff in developing, enhancing and implementing programs to achieve three goals for Caprock. The goals relate to improving the retention rate of students staying in school, improving the number of students passing the TEAMS, and improving the number of students recognized as National Merit Scholars. Through involving the staff in the decision-making process, an atmosphere of ownership has been established. The team process, integration of employees, collegiality, trust and respect in our school improvement efforts have resulted in our teachers accepting and supporting new school programs.

Vertical teams and cluster groups were used to identify priorities for district training that were directly related to the district's strategic plan. A strong emphasis was placed on the "teachers training teachers" concept at the campus level. Team members often made outstanding trainers, since they had been part of the discussion across a number of levels within the school division. These "in-services" included several "sharing times" for teacher ideas in the academic needs area, forum-type in-services addressing concerns and suggestions, and planning sessions to discuss implementation of the school's new strategic plan. Dr. Wilson stated, "A culture is developing in the sessions to be risk takers in attempting new methods which might achieve school division goals."

Sandra Blacksten, a teacher at Emerson Elementary School, said that as a result of the committee and inservice process, as well as the attitudes of colleagues and administrators, she felt she was ready to begin implementing some of the ideas she had learned about whole language instruction and cooperative learning. In discussing the results of her efforts, she said,

> By February, I was amazed by the growth my students had made in both reading and writing skills. I was so impressed with the results of the whole language and cooperative learning strategies that I decided to work up a presentation for other teachers. At the present time I have done this inservice presentation for six elementary schools in my district. I am presently helping plan a whole language conference that will be held in Amarillo in August.

Obviously, the division plan has not been implemented evenly in all schools. Some took a little longer to get started or to come aboard. In some cases, other problems got in the way that needed to be addressed first. However, there is now a strong base, and probably an unstoppable momentum, that has been built into the culture of the school division. At this point, Dr. Wilson is a resource, there to help his teachers succeed in their individual efforts to improve student learning within the division's goals and objectives. He is there to see that the structures and behaviors within the district support the teachers in their efforts.

According to Superintendent Wilson,

> the initial reports are very favorable. Reports and verbal feedback from the participants have indicated that this is a very viable arrangement to achieve results within the school district.

Even though the program is only in the early stages of its implementation, failure rates at Caprock High School have lowered an average of two percent. Staff perception of the school's focus, along with the sharing of power and the improvement of communication, have increased, as measured on an Organizational Health Instrument used within the school district.

There is general agreement that the staff has made progress in working together and working to improve the learning environment. Principal Harrison states,

> My attempts to involve teachers in the decision-making process have been extremely rewarding. I have watched teachers become very involved and excited to watch improvements falling in place because of their hard work. I have worked with teachers to develop cooperative learning skills, writing across the curriculum activity, code of ethical behavior and the faculty advisory committee. The school division

seems to have a higher level of trust and respect for each other and for all levels within the school division.

One teacher said, "Understanding the 'why' behind previous decisions helped a great deal along with many good suggestions from staff members." In general, the program is seen as successful and is growing in leaps and bounds.

Recently, Dr. Wilson reported,

I thought that you might like to know that we have continued after three years to use the fundamental vertical team method we learned through the Danforth Foundation Program. We have slightly changed the makeup of our team in order to accommodate more of the administrators in our district, but it is essentially the same. Since the initial experience, we have funded our team locally and call it the Superintendent's Leadership Team. I have expanded the concept in the district to create vertical teams within the different high school clusters,. We have four high schools, thus four clusters. The benefits we have incurred through team building, building trust relationships, working together to solve problems, collectively becoming a "think tank", and the basic modeling of the vertical team concept have been invaluable in moving our district forward.

Correlates of the Effective Culture

The question now becomes, how does one work with the culture to keep it healthy while transforming it to improve the performance of the organization? The early answers are found in a number of correlates of the culture of excellence. Terms used to describe these correlates of cultural excellence are "the vertical slice," "vision not deficiencies," "collegial relationship," "trust and support," "values and interests, not power and position," "broad participation," "lifelong growth," "present life but long-term perspective," "access to quality information," "continuous and sustained improvement" and "individual empowerment."

These correlates, when taken together, allow the organization to develop the most effective and efficient work culture. They become the basic tenents that guide the work of administrators, regardless of the level at which they work. They are the very simple forms and tools with which the administration must work in taking corrective action to improve performance.

Cultures can be changed, but managers must know how to create situations in which such change can occur. The following are the cultural conditions that have been found to be effective. These correlates have promoted effective cultural changes in schools and school district administrative offices across America. Many of these same correlates are a major part of the Danforth Foundation "School Administrators Fellowship Program," and the American Association of School Administration's program entitled, "District Learning Leadership Team," and are also a major part of the Institute for Development of Educational Activities, Inc.'s, "School Improvement Program." They are also the basis for a number of programs that have been developed by the NASSP. These are the cultural supports that are needed in order for participative decision-making, site-based management, Total Quality Management, and learning organization-type programs to work.

The Vertical Slice

It is essential that influential individuals across all levels of an organization are given an opportunity to come together on a regular basis to discuss their values and visions. Employees at all levels must have an opportunity to periodically communicate on a face-to-face basis. Those working in the organization will not support the directives of others, regardless of their power, until they gain a clear understanding of each individual's values, beliefs, and traditions, and are given an opportunity to renegotiate areas that they believe need to be addressed. This requires the establishment of a vertical culture that crosses over all of the horizontal cultures within the organization.

In the Danforth Foundation program, a vertical or diagonal team is chosen and meets for a full day on at least a monthly basis. When members on the same level meet, the culture is horizontal, and when members on various levels within the organization meet, the culture becomes vertical. In school divisions, a vertical slice might include a school board member, the superintendent, an assistant superintendent or division director, principals, and teachers. Another type of team might also be called an implementation team, a school improvement team, or a restructuring team. This team might include central office administrators, principal, assistant principal, teachers, secretaries, clerical worker (janitor), parent, and student. A major function of the team, after it has been formed, is to transform its vertical nature to one of horizontal team relationships in which all feel free and open to communicate. Each vertical team operates with a well-trained facilitator. Regardless of method, an effective work culture provides employees at all levels of the organization an opportunity to come together to get to know and trust one another.

The power of a team is that each member has an opportunity to hear and learn the diverse perspectives of fellow team members, creating a culture within the organization. In a vertical team, team members gain understanding of the entire organization and respect for each person up and down the line. They become a vertical, cultural catalyst for their work group.

When interested participants throughout the organization have a legitimate opportunity to discuss their views and hear the views of others, they will be better able to understand organizational direction and become a part of a broader culture that will support that direction. This is absolutely essential in modern organizations where implementation efforts have reached a level of complexity that requires cultural support well beyond a group of individuals at any one level within the organization.

Vision, Not Deficiencies

According to this correlate, the school should work together to develop a collective vision of what school should be like. Once the long-range vision can be described, it can be achieved. This is an especially important point if group dynamics and synergistic effects are to support the effectiveness of the school.

Effective group dynamics cannot develop if the central focus of the team is on work problems or "fixing" deficiencies. This is as true working in the classroom with students as it is being a member of the vertical team. The team must not use what Dr. Jon Paden at the Institute for the Development of Educational Activities, Inc. calls a "deficit model." The "deficit model" is probably more commonly known as the problem-solving approach, in which one collects information about the problems within the organization, focusing on correcting deficits or solving problems. The deficit model is particularly problematic when organizational personnel from various levels of a work organization are on the same team.

The visionary model is necessary for appropriate team dynamics to develop, and to minimize the unproductive characteristics of defensiveness and fear. It focuses on a collective view of the ideal, and everyone's efforts are focused on creating that ideal. The visionary model allows team members to feel comfortable discussing where effort is required in order to achieve the vision. The focus is on specific areas that need to be addressed if the vision is to be realized, rather than on tearing down or berating what has already been done. The visionary model inspires the team to work toward achieving an ideal.

Collegial Relationships

Participants enter a group with many highly developed perspectives and talents. Through collegiality, the team learns how to respect, appreciate, and foster the individual identities of group members. Building a collegial group composed of diverse talents and perspectives requires a special sensitivity to make each person feel like a valued and appreciated contributor. The group must develop a sense of mutual, shared responsibility. Team members cannot work toward a desired outcome until they have formed a sense of community or team spirit and learned to trust and support one another.

Collaboration allows individuals to develop a common understanding and language out of which a common culture can emerge. It stimulates dialogue and the sharing of values, knowledge, expertise, thoughts, aspirations, visions, and difficulties in a supportive and positive environment. People cannot work together effectively unless they get to know one another—what they value, how they think, and why they think that way. This creates understanding, and ultimately respect, for one another. The words "collegial" and "collaborative" are often used synonomously since they both refer to working together in a positive manner of support and interest. Before a work group or vertical team can be effective they must institutionalize collegial relationships.

Effective collegial relations develop within the organization only when all levels within an organization have opportunities to come together at the beginning of the project. Collegial relationships stress the common interest and good above all else, and especially stress individual self-interest. Kenneth Sirotnik and John Goodlad (1988) in *School-University Partnerships in Action* suggest the typical approach among organizations is, "I'll help you with your concerns and you'll help me with mine." In collegial relationships, concerns are mutually owned; they are *our* problems. As long as problems are defined in the context of any one group, it is exceedingly difficult, if not impossible, for all partners to own them and feel a part of them. Visions within the organization cannot be created by any one party at the expense of another, or collaboration and collegiality will not exist. No party can be given a monopoly if a collegial relation is to develop.

Trust and Support

An effective work group must engage in purposeful activities that establish and continually build upon a climate of mutual understanding, trust, and commitment to one another and the organization. Trust and support tend to reduce individuals' fears regarding potential repercussions and embarrassment resulting from being a member of the group. The dream must belong to the group if it is ever to materialize, and that will only happen when the group has learned to trust and support one another. Members of the group must value one another's strengths while at the same time treat each other as trusted colleagues. As collaboration and collegiality grow, so do support and trust. Trust is essential to working together and it comes through understanding and knowing one another.

Mistrust disempowers the work group and reduces the quality of work performed. A team cannot come together and work effectively until they have had a chance to develop an understanding and trust of one another. The practices, symbols, and stories of the group must freely express a trust for every member. Without trust and support, the work team will not be able to develop the group dynamics and synergistic relationships necessary for the organization to move toward a new vision of effectiveness. The culture will resist individual and group efforts unless trust and support have been developed.

Values and Interest, Not Power and Position

Groups need to work through, discuss, and resolve their own interpersonal and intra-group problems. Problems occur when individuals take different positions on a particular issue. In almost every case, shared, or at least compatible, interests lie behind opposing positions. Therefore, the focus of the group should always be on reconciliation of interests, not positions. Roger Fisher and William Ury (1981) in *Getting to Yes* state,

> When bargaining over positions, they tend to lock themselves into those positions. The more you clarify your position and defend it against attack, the more committed you become to it. The more you try to convince the other side of the impossibility of changing your opening position, the more difficult it becomes to do so. Your ego becomes identified with your position. You now have a new interest in 'saving face'—in reconciling future action with past positions—making it less and less likely that any agreement will wisely reconcile the parties' original interests.

Interests serve to motivate and give people direction. Your position is something you have decided upon; your interests are what caused you to decide. The role of the leader is to reconcile interests rather than develop compromises among positions.

It is imperative that decisions are based on reconciled interest and not a battle of wills. In a positional battle, it is almost certain that the highest ranking official of the team will use power to see that he or she saves face and that his or her position is accepted. As James McCullough, superintendent of the Chattanooga Public Schools found,

> The team members put aside rank, position, and responsibilities, and reminded us again that individuals can communicate on the authority

of their own competence and worth regardless of their titles and responsibility.

This is why the focus of the work team must always be on member values and interests. Otherwise, narrow, and just plain wrong, decisions can be made on the basis of one person's source of power.

Access to Quality Information

A major source of power in any organization is the free and open access to needed information. Unless those who are employed within the organization have easy access to important information, they will not be able to use their abilities effectively. Information stimulates thought and feeds future innovation. Information holds the work group together and allows it to develop a common culture. The quality of a group's knowledge and decision can only be as good as the quality of information available. Therefore, it is essential that as much information as possible be made available to all members of the group in a concise and easily comprehended format. We are living in the "age of information" and organizations must master that information if they are to have any hope of achieving excellence. Information fuels development.

Everyone within the organization must be given accurate performance information. Employees naturally want to be effective and will automatically make adjustments to continuously improve their work if they know where they stand in relation to where they ought to be. No one tries to do a mediocre or poor job. The absence of accurate and timely feedback regarding employees' work allows poor performance to continue. Data is not used to mass-produce results but to help each employee to constantly improve his or her performance.

Teachers must know on a weekly basis if their students are attaining high levels of achievement. Lesson outcomes, not lesson plans, are important. Teachers' support for a vision and a program greatly increases after its effectiveness has been verified within their own classrooms There is nothing more rewarding than knowing your ideas are making improvements in the way a job is performed, and in the way students are learning. However, improvements are usually gradual, incremental, and long-term, and systems of measurement must be able to pick up this gradual improvement.

Broad Participation

A group appreciates and fosters the diversity and commonality of experiences, interests, talents, skills, and knowledge among its members. The strength of a group is found in its diverse perspectives among various levels within the organization. Excellence in performance develops by sharing perspectives and searching for threads that hold the levels together, allowing each member to trust and support one another.

Each person in a group can provide a unique experience based on his or her particular knowledge and work experience. A superintendent, for instance, can see the need for a system-wide student/school/community interface to address students' needs, while a teacher deals with what to do with a student in class tomorrow. Both gain a better understanding of what needs to be done at their own level by exchanging knowledge and experience regarding shared concerns. In this way, decisions are not "half-baked." Those involved in the organization become aware of the opportunity for improvement with all of its ramifications, related concerns, and possibilities fully developed.

The old adage that "two heads are better than one," or more practically, "several heads are better than one," is well founded. The group encompasses more knowledge, experience, and information than any single member. The talents of these individuals can be amassed in a work group in such a way as to achieve far more than would ever be possible if the individuals worked independently of one another—the synergistic effect. As individuals gain greater understanding of other organizational members' values, beliefs, interests, visions, and commitments, they find it easier to design and understand the overall plan.

Lifelong Growth

Organizational excellence promotes personal and professional growth. The group provides positive reinforcement to the individual while finding ways to help the individual reach for new and higher developmental goals. Fellow group members are used for resources and support as each person develops an annual plan for personal/professional development, carries out that plan, and verifies that effective growth has taken place. Employees constantly redefine themselves and what they are capable of doing. Dr. William G. Cunningham suggests that it is "immoral not to grow throughout your life." Without growth, an individual will constantly apply old strategies to new problems with a very low probability of success.

Dr. Malcolm Knowles (1984), often given credit for popularizing the term "lifelong learning," states its underlying premise as "in a world of accelerating change, learning must be a lifelong process." Therefore, a major function of an organization is to provide the resources, support, and encouragement for self-directed inquiry and growth. Almost all developmental theorists suggest that personal development is a lifelong process and that individuals will stagnate, atrophy, and degenerate unless they are continually growing, learning and developing.

Today, the time span for useful information is considerably shorter than that of human life, and, therefore, individuals must constantly prepare to stay informed. Half of all the information available at any point in time will become obsolete within ten years. Thus, the nature of today's organizational life requires an individual to maintain a continuing process of inquiry and self-development.

Individual Empowerment

Each individual has a unique potential and a unique historical context, with special opportunities and obligations reserved just for him or her. This means that each person has potential power to release within the organization. This is not always easy for someone whose maturation process was always controlled and guided by external sources. The individual begins to look externally for direction and may mistrust his or her own abilities and skills.

The paradox here is that one is empowered by becoming more confident in one's own ability and knowledge, and yet, one's process of maturation requires one to learn under the direction of external influences. The problem is that we learn to follow the directions of those around us instead of developing skills to direct our own lives. We cannot bring our full potential to our work. Such individuals operate below their potential, and the sum total of such loss determines the difference between effective and ineffective organizations. In Tom Peters's Public Broadcasting Service special, "The Leadership Alliance," Pat Karington suggests that most employees are trained to "leave their brains at the door before they come in." Governance can be shared with such employees, but if they have not developed confidence and knowledge, they cannot participate. This is why concepts like shared governance, site-based management, and participative decision-making are not the same as employee empowerment. Employees must first be empowered if they are able to take advantage of the various forms of shared governance.

The organizational culture must support individual uniqueness for the natural individual within the employee to unfold and flow. In this way, employees are free and empowered to take risks, to be different, and to make a difference. One grows by being more of what he or she is, not by becoming something that others desire. Empowerment is the ability to feel one's own feelings, think one's own thoughts, and support one's own behaviors. As e. e. cummings suggests,

The hardest battle is to be nobody but yourself in
a world, which is doing its best, night and day,
to make you like everybody else.

Continuous and Sustained Innovation

The research on effective schools suggests that significant improvement in
educational practice takes three to seven years. Planning is the foundation
upon which all activity is based, and if that activity is to be successful, it
must be based on a long-term perspective. "Quick fix," and "solution of the
year" approaches have proven to be very ineffective. Quick fixes have not
demonstrated any form of staying power or long-run impact. Ideas that
have proven successful in other school systems need to be considered and
given attention, but the primary focus of the work group should be on the
achievement of a collective vision. This requires a long-term, concerted
effort, including evaluation and follow-up. Therefore, the effective work
group looks to long-term accomplishments and not to quick cosmetic
changes or the administrator's or politician's "pet project" for the year.

We use a vision of the future to create direction and goals, not to
become obsessed with the achievement and accomplishment of a specific
future state. We use visions of the future to set priorities, to think through
actions, and to gain perspective on how we wish to live our present lives.
The long term vision is there to help us make present decisions and
commitments. By looking to and anticipating the future with all its
possibilities, we can be better prepared for the changes that present
conditions bring. We do not postpone present focus, work, or enjoyment in
the hopes of a better future, but we do make decisions with a vision of the
future in mind. We look to the future to be better prepared to live in the
present.

Effective cultures invite and support continuous improvement from
within rather than externally developed reform and restructuring efforts.
Continuous improvement creates a long-term systematic, cumulative
improvement of education practice, as opposed to a sequence of unrelated
programs. It is often the difference between a reasoned, tested, continuous,
proactive response by the practitioner and the reactionary, externally
engineered, packaged, "quick fixes" by those who are not in the trenches.
School improvement is a cultural, ongoing, cumulative process, not one of
implementing the latest approach. Problems often cause abandonment of a
reform, weakening with assault, but providing information and related
critical analysis for improvement. The culture of improvement provides
stable building blocks, breeding a sense of success and confidence in
cumulative innovation. The idea of continuous improvement must be

planned as a long-term process. Improvements are made milestone by milestone.

Ralph's Challenge

Sergiovanni (1991) suggests that

All schools have cultures: strong or weak, functional or dysfunctional. Successful schools seem to have strong and functional culture aligned with a vision of excellence in schooling.

Strong, functional cultures must be nourished, nurtured, and supported through the correlates of cultural development. The correlates of excellence are highly interrelated. They must all be addressed if the culture is to ever support the desired vision and performance.

At Washington Middle School, Ralph must develop a culture of excellence if he is to have any hope of improving the existing conditions. Teachers, administrators, and support staff have formed subcultures around their attitudes toward one another and their parochial interests that pull the school in opposite directions. Motivation, effort, consistency, and other ingredients essential to good education are being damaged by the existing culture. The subcultures are angrily resisting one another. Ultimately, it is Washington students and their city, state, and country that are feeling the pain. The culture must be changed to one of internal cohesion that supports maximum school effectiveness. Ralph certainly has his work cut out for him as he learns from the new culture that will emerge.

Ralph will first need to be in touch with the values, heroes and heroines, stories and myths, rites and rituals, common meanings and shared assumptions, and informal networks that exist and are a central part of the school. He will then have to determine how that culture encourages or undermines school effectiveness. Lastly, he will have to implement the correlates of an effective culture.

Structural changes may have to be made, although most will grow out of an improved culture. Ralph's whole style of leadership may change, or he may change the way that employees are evaluated or trained or even hired. The decision-making process, as well as how the school is structured and what is included as curriculum or instruction might change. The important point is that Ralph will not change any of these directly. He will simply allow the evolving culture with its shared vision to make these changes that he will sustain and support. He will learn not to be threatened by and be resistant to culture, but to be supportive of an effective culture. He will examine results and evaluate performance using both hard and soft measures. He will help to achieve a shared vision of excellence for Washington Middle School. He will help to develop his staff by creating a learning organization. This is what Ralph and all school administrators must do if they want to improve the conditions that now exist in our schools and achieve the American vision for our educational system.

Bibliography

Barnard, Chester I. *The Function of the Executive*. Cambridge, Mass: Harvard University Press, 1968.

Bendix, Reinhard and Fisher, Lloyd H. "The Perspectives of Elton Mayo." Amatai Etzioni (Ed.). *Complex Organizations: A Sociological Reader*. New York: Holt, Rinehart, Winston, 1961.

Bennis, Warren G. *On Becoming a Leader*. Reading, Ma: Addison-Wesley, 1989.

Bolman, Lee G. and Deal, Terrence E. *Reframing Organizations*. San Francisco, CA.: Jossey-Bass Inc., 1991.

Chandler, Alfred. *Strategy and Structure*. Cambridge, Mass: MIT Press, 1962.

Deal, Terrence E. and Kennedy, Allan A. *Corporate Cultures: The Rites and Rituals of Corporate Life*. Reading, Mass: Addison-Wesley Publishing Company, Inc., 1982. Copyright by Addison-Wesley Publishing Company, Inc. Reprinted with permission of the publisher.

Deal, Terrence E. and Kennedy, Allan A. "Culture and School Performance." *Educational Leadership* (February, 1983).

Fisher, Roger and Ury, William. *Getting to Yes*. Boston: Houghton Mifflin Company, 1981. Copyright by Roger Fisher and William Ury. Reprinted by permission of Houghton Mifflin Company. All rights reserved.

Fullan, Michael. *The Meaning of Educational Change*. New York: Teachers College Press, 1982.

Goodlad, John I. *A Place Called School*. New York: McGraw-Hill Book Company, 1984.

Hess, Beth B. and Markson, Elizabeth W., (Eds.) *Growing Old In America*. New Brunswick, N.J.: Transaction Publishers, 1990.

Knowles, Malcolm. *Androgyny in Action*. San Francisco: Jossey-Bass, 1984.

Lindblom, Charles E. *The Policy Making Process*. Englewood Cliffs, N.J.: Prentice Hall Inc., 1980.

Litskey, Dennis and Fried, Robby. "The Challenge to Make Good Schools Great." *Today's Education* (January, 1988).

Miles, Matthew B. and Louis, Karen Seashore. "Mustering the Will and Skill for Change." *Educational Leadership* (May, 1990).

Owen, Harrison. *Spirit, Transformation and Development in Organization*. Potomac, MD.: Abbott Publishing, 1987.

Owen, Harrison. *Leadership*. Potomac, MD.: Abbott Publishing, 1990.

Oswalt, Wendel H. *Life Cycles and Lifeways: An Introduction to Cultural Anthropology*. Palo Alto, CA: Mayfield Publishing, 1985.

Peters, Thomas J. and Waterman, Robert H. *In Search of Excellence.* New York: Harper & Row Publishers, 1982.

Peters, Tom and Austin, Nancy. *A Passion for Excellence.* New York: Random House, 1985.

Peters, Tom. *Thriving on Chaos.* New York: Alfred A. Knopf, 1988.

Quinby, Nelson. "Improving the Place Called School: A Conversation with John Goodlad." *Educational Leadership* (March, 1985).

Raywid, Mary Anne, Tesconi, Charles A. and Warren, Donald P. *Pride and Promise: Schools of Excellence for all the People.* Washington, D.C.: American Education Studies Association, 1984.

Sarason, Seymor. *The Culture of Schools and the Problem of Change.* Boston: Allyn and Bacon, 1971.

Schein, Edgar H. *Organizational Culture and Leadership.* San Francisco: Jossey-Bass, 1991.

Selznick, Philip. *Leadership in Administration.* New York: Harper & Row, 1957.

Sergiovanni, Thomas. "Leadership and Excellence in Schooling." *Educational Leadership* (February, 1984).

Sergiovanni, Thomas. *The Principalship: A Reflective Practice Perspective.* Boston: Allyn and Bacon, 1991.

Sirotnik, Kenneth A. and Goodlad, John I. (Ed.). *School-University Partnerships in Action: Concepts, Cases and Concerns.* New York: Teachers College Press, © 1988 by Teachers College, Columbia University. All rights reserved. Selected quotes from sections by Sirotnik/Goodlad and Schlechty/Whitford. Reprinted by permission of the publisher.

Thompson, Scott D. "The Principalship: Ingredients of Programs to Prepare Effective Leaders." *The NASSP Bulletin* (May, 1988).

Weich, Karl E. "Administering Education in Loosely Coupled Schools." *Phi Delta Kappan* (June, 1982).

3

The Vertical Team
Approach

All organizations have their own culture, since each one is an inter-related system of people who share a common direction and way of doing things. Some of the cultural properties of the organization are the clarity of goals and objectives, the commitment of individuals to achieve them, and the norms and standards of conduct that each expects of all the others. Other cultural aspects include the ways by which joint efforts are coordinated, the manner in which disagreements and conflicts are resolved, the way decisions are made, and the degree of candor with which people express their convictions.

Education can be greatly improved by simply strengthening the connections among people who work at all levels within the organization. In this way, a shared belief system, a common set of assumptions and norms, an understood set of decisions and directions, and, most importantly, an organizational commitment can be achieved throughout the organization. The RAND Corporation (1989), in a report entitled *Steady Work: Policy, Practice and the Reform of American Education,* stated that

> . . . the mistakes of the past can be remedied by strengthening the connection between the decision-making process of policymakers, administrators, and practitioners . . . so that new knowledge is translated into the experience of principals, teachers and district administrators.

The report stresses that the decision-making process is interdependent. Decisions at each level set the conditions and limits for the next level's decisions, but can't predetermine how those decisions will be made. Policymakers, administrators, and teachers must draw upon each other for needed information if the common goal of helping children learn is to be realized. Unfortunately, management processes that would connect and support group interaction are not part of common practice.

The vertical team concept was developed to meet this need for interrelatedness, interdependence, and interaction among various levels within the organization. The purpose of the vertical team is to allow for the important exchange of information among individuals who share a common purpose but operate on different levels and who thus have very different organizational perspectives. It is through vertical integration that the organization begins to develop a shared culture that supports implementation efforts and creates long-term school effectiveness. Without a supportive organizational culture, school effectiveness programs are either never implemented or disappear after implementation.

In their School Administrators Fellowship Program, the Danforth Foundation experimented with a vertical team program for 5 years in 42 different urban and suburban school districts in the United States. In 1985, the Foundation redesigned the program to embrace the vertical team concept. The new format placed greater emphasis on a team of educators at various levels within the school district working together to focus on the objectives of collegiality, personal/professional development, school effectiveness and transition.

The program dealt with effective change, stressing that it must involve all groups within a school system, including all those affected by the change. In addition, it must be focused upon commitment to specific goals and principles, lead to continuous personal/professional growth of educators, and be based on the knowledge and experience of educators. The vertical team concept develops a work culture in which participants at various levels within the organization express a clear commitment to work together and support school improvement. The major premise of the program was that effective change was more likely to occur in a school where interested parties had an opportunity to communicate about, as well as make and monitor, decisions regarding effective school program design and implementation.

The overall results reported by the participants in the Danforth Foundation Vertical Team Program were that the approach was quite effective and that the basic beliefs upon which the program was based were well-founded. The program was especially effective in creating collegiality, personal/professional development, and school improvement. The vertical team concept was a powerful tool for developing a productive, supportive, and integrated work culture within the school system. Team members believed that the interaction of people at various levels within the organization was important to the improvement of both the quality of and the commitment to decisions within the school district.

These results were further substantiated in a dissertation completed by Mary Lewis Hensley (1989) at Baylor University. In a comprehensive study of ten school divisions that participated in the Danforth Vertical Team program, Dr. Hensley (1989) concluded that it was important to both individual and organizational effectiveness that team members have close communication with key leaders at various levels within the school district. She stated,

> each of the ten vertical teams commented on the effectiveness of the vertical team as a method of staff development for personal and professional growth. . . . The vertical team approach opened doors of communication and opportunity that had previously been closed; not purposefully, but for one reason or another, no one had thought to open them.

The American Association of School Administrators, in cooperation with the Institute for Development of Education Activities, Inc. (/I/D/E/A/), is currently involved in implementing a vertical team activity called the "District Learning Leadership Team." In announcing this program, the AASA stated,

> As the educational enterprise, as a whole, has become complex, the fragmentation of communication and subsequent actions make it appear that the system is in a state of disarray. Everyone wants to help, but the many suggestions for improvement, legislated mandates, and reform initiatives, although well intentioned, generally fail to bring about widespread substantive change. Meanwhile, dedicated teachers, administrators and board members remain in relative isolation from each other as they apply their expertise and experience to the needs of children whose lives they touch.
>
> The American Association of School Administrators (AASA) in cooperation with the Institute for Development of Educational Activities, Inc. (/I/D/E/A/), a non-profit educational foundation, is helping school systems throughout the country implement a strategy that has potential to affect in a very real way the local meaning of, and capacity to engage in, continuing educational improvement. The AASA District Learning Leadership Team program provides training and support for a collaborative, vertical team that transcends hierarchical barriers in a district and community.

Both /I/D/E/A/ and the AASA believe that many schools are implementing team structures, in such forms as school improvement teams, faculty and planning councils, site-based teams, colleague coaching, and support teams, allowing for valuable exchange of information among colleagues. Unfortunately, these team structures are made up of people with the same limited information and who share the same horizontal bond. These structures tend to focus on building relationships and knowledge through horizontal peer networking. This can create cohesive groups or subcultures within the school or department, but there tends to be a lack of knowledge regarding a district-wide perspective—a school district culture. There are few opportunities for individuals at various levels within the school district, or outside the school building, to communicate and share information.

Both /I/D/E/A/ and the AASA have found that vertical team strategies have remedied these weaknesses in school districts that have implemented them. They state,

> These strategies connect a "vertical" slice of a district's decision making levels to help those whose decisions influence the quality of classroom instruction and learning to better understand competing or conflicting priorities, share perspectives, unfreeze assumptions, and develop support that permits greater risk-taking.

Horizontal teams that have not been vertically integrated tend to resist, demean, and fight each other, reducing organizational effectiveness.

Vertical team strategies have been included as part of an effort by Motorola Corporation to assist in improving American education. Motorola executives found the District Learning Leadership Team program to be an effective component in helping schools bring about systematic change. The program was also quite effective in creating "learning organizations." As a result, Motorola Corporation has been actively involved in the implementation of this program in Illinois and Massachusetts.

Edward W. Bales, director at Motorola University, said

> Motorola Incorporated, as a customer of the education system, saw that the output of education was no longer meeting the needs of the new work force which had shifted from an industrial base to an information base model. Therefore, Motorola Incorporated saw their role as customer to help define the educational requirements of students to ensure successful employment, but not to tell educators how to do their jobs. The role of education is to transform the system to meet those newly developed needs. Our experience in transforming our corporation into a global leader indicated that the most powerful way to

implement change is to have all of the constituencies involved in the process. The "district leadership team" concept was identical to our experience in that it includes all of the parties who have a legitimate investment in education.

Motorola Incorporated is presently a partner with /I/D/E/A/ and the Illinois Math and Science Academy, with 32 school districts in Illinois, and has begun the process with two districts in Massachusetts. Motorola plans to expand its partnerships into the states of Texas, Arizona, and Florida, where they presently have facilities.

The vertical team helps to eliminate the cultural isolation that results from conflicting and unintegrated subcultures. The vertical team helps to develop connections among subgroups, increases organizational cohesiveness, and ultimately provides an opportunity for members to develop a sense of shared vertical culture. The AASA-/I/D/E/A/ program focuses on communication between levels of decision-makers, and requires participants to talk openly in order to gain new perspectives, insights, commitments, and cooperative efforts. The program broadens the information, knowledge, and decision-making base in order to support and develop caring and committed practitioners as part of a school division culture.

Bonding and Cohesiveness

Formal and informal teams typically develop in any situation where people are together over a period of time. As the teams form, their behavior develops a cultural mode of operation. The longer the group is together, the stronger is the sense of team and culture, resulting in a strong sense of bonding and cohesiveness. Bonding is a predisposition for individuals to join with others in the group. Cohesiveness allows the group to accomplish far more than the sum total of the individual efforts, producing a synergistic effect.

A very important aspect of the cultural approach to leadership is the development of work teams that believe in the importance of school effectiveness. Once an effective work culture has been developed, operations flow more smoothly, implementation efforts are supported, and appropriate corrective actions are taken. The culture allows participants to work together toward commonly understood and shared goals. Employees that have bonded develop commitment, enthusiasm, and loyalty to the other members of the organizational team. They are revered as they become part of an ideological system dedicated to an almost sacred mission. It is through team formation, the bonding process, and acculturation that employees develop a sense of personal importance and significance.

This desire to bond is an instinctive, natural process in all humans that cannot be denied. Through bonding, work takes on a new meaning, characterized by richer satisfaction, an expanded sense of identity, and a feeling of belonging to something important. After examining cultural bonding within organizations, Karl E. Weich (1982) concluded,

> . . . their action becomes richer, more confident, and more satisfying when it is linked with important underlying themes, values and movements . . . administrators must be attentive to the 'glue' that holds a loosely coupled system together because such forms are just barely systems.

People are willing to make significant commitments of time, knowledge, skill, and energy toward a work team with whom they feel a cultural bond. Shaping and encouraging this bond is often an overlooked role of organizational leadership.

As leaders are better able to understand and incorporate bonding and other cultural forces, they will discover a very powerful influence over improved school effectiveness. Thomas G. Sergiovanni (1991) states,

> Symbolic and cultural forces are very powerful influences of human thought and behavior. People respond to these factors by bonding together into a highly normative-cohesive group, and this group in turn bonds itself to the school culture in an almost irrational way. The "cult" metaphor communicates well the nature and effect of extremely strong bonding.

Cultural bonding helps a team achieve a satisfactory level of cohesion and trust. Cohesion is a sense of togetherness, or community, within a group. A cohesive group is one in which there are incentives for remaining in the group and a feeling of belongingness and relatedness among the members. According to Marianne and Gerald Corey (1987),

> Our conviction is that cohesion is largely the result of the group's choice to work actively at developing unifying bonds. Members do this mainly by choosing to make themselves known to others, by allowing caring to develop, by initiating meaningful work, and by giving honest feedback to others.

Research suggests that cohesive teams are much more capable of implementing planned changes and responding favorably to unplanned changes. In fact, I. D. Yalon (1985) maintains that research shows that cohesion and bonding are strong determinants of positive team outcomes. The inability of a group to bond and develop cohesion may have long-term, harmful effects on all phases of the team's working together.

Cultural bonding is measured by the strength of the relationships that link the members of a work team to one another and to the team itself. Kurt Lewin (1953) suggests that linkages develop from each member's attraction to other team members, whether the attraction is based on liking, respect, trust, or understanding. The strength and potential of the team develops once people join together to form a single, united, and cohesive culture. Purposefulness, pride, confidence, enthusiasm, empowerment, commitment, loyalty, and satisfaction are much more pronounced in teams that share a common culture. These qualities are much less pronounced, though, when an organizational culture has not formed. In this case, there is little or no bonding, and a lack of cohesiveness.

In a work culture in which bonding has taken place, the team members are more supportive, participate more fully, communicate more frequently, and, are generally more responsible for themselves and the work of the team. According to Dr. Cartwright (1968), cohesive teams experience heightened self-worth and motivation and lowered anxiety and professional burnout. Cohesive teams have fewer absences and an increased capacity to retain their members. After examining research on group culture, cohesiveness, and performance, Donelson R. Forsyth (1990) concluded that "so long as group norms encourage high productivity, cohesiveness and productivity are positively related: the more cohesive the group, the greater its productivity."

When cohesive groups establish a call for increased productivity as part of their performance norms, productivity increases occur. This same phenomenon is not true for noncohesive groups. Furthermore, when cohesive groups call for a decrease in productivity standards, the decrease in productivity brought about by these messages is greater than the increase brought about by the positive messages. This implies that organizational culture and team bonding are important, but if the culture is not well-integrated within the organization and supportive of the organization and its leadership, the horizontal culture that naturally develops can work quite powerfully against the organization. Well-integrated, cohesive vertical cultures will increase productivity, but poorly integrated horizontal cultures can cause serious reductions in productivity. This is a very important, but often misunderstood, point. Group cohesiveness is a necessary prerequisite to activity that requires teamwork, but is does not insure success. The team members must share a desire to achieve the desired outcomes, and all members understand the vision.

This underscores the importance of integrating work teams into a shared culture for the entire organization. Work teams that bond and form cohesive units on a horizontal level within the organization become sub-cultures of the organization. These cohesive subcultures are powerful tools for increasing productivity when they are integrated into a vertical organizational culture. However, they are even more powerful forces for decreasing productivity, restricting innovation, and bringing down leadership when they are not well-integrated into the entire organizational culture.

According to Abraham Zaleznic and David Moment (1964),

> Not only must groups build their own cohesion and continually resolve their own internal problems, they must also maintain a positive identification with other groups and with a larger organization. The fact that small groups satisfy important human needs assures their survival as a form of organization. But this does not assure the development of effective groups and consequently effective organizations in the larger institutions of society.

The need for cultural integration in large organizations is becoming as important as the need for cultural integration in the global world. We need to maintain our unique cultures, but in order to survive and prosper, we must be part of a larger culture.

Just as athletes on a team must learn how to integrate their skills, abilities, and energies into a cohesive group, work groups must learn to coordinate their efforts with other groups in the organization to form a cohesive, unified organization. Group goals must be set, work patterns structured, and a sense of group identity developed, but always in relation to a broader vertical organizational vision. Members must learn to coordinate their abilities and actions within both the subculture and the vertical organizational culture. Both must complement and support one another.

Effective Cultural Development

During the early stages of cultural development, members need to get to know one another through self-disclosure. Self-disclosure helps to promote a sense of shared community, beginning the cultural bonding process. However, genuine cohesion typically comes about after the group works through disagreements over such things as vision and work methods, and differences in values. Once members have taken some level of risk with one another and have worked through tensions, they will develop a sense of acceptance, belonging, and security.

Some positive characteristics of team culture are 1.) a willingness to show up at meetings on time, 2.) an effort to make the team a safe place,

3.) the existence of support and caring, 4.) a willingness to listen to others and accept them for who they are, and 5.) a willingness to trust and express honest (but considerate) reactions to one another. In an effective culture, members can openly express their ideas and concerns, share their own re-actions, have a clearly stated purpose for their meetings, become active participants, experience a sense of shared leadership and member-to-member interaction, accept conflict and honestly work through differences, listen non-defensively and respectfully, support team decisions, and express appreciation for the group.

Effective cultures develop best when there is a facilitator who models the attitudes and behaviors necessary for excellent membership. The success of cultural development depends on how well the facilitator prepares the members as the culture is developed and enriched. The facilitator should inform members of their rights and responsibilities, teach and model effective group process, prepare members for what will occur, and try to ensure that members have successful, positive experiences. The facilitator's behavior in meetings is the key to the success of developing an organizational culture.

Why Culture?

Culture provides members of organizations with a sense of identity and a meaningful direction. The culture defines what the group is committed to and what members think of each other. It provides an informal structure by which membership is defined and the process by which members become acculturated. It creates a core group of "priests and priestesses" that can go out and communicate the commitments of the culture to other members within the organization. The strength of the culture is in the members' actively supporting and committing to its teachings and communicating that support and commitment to other members within the organization.

Without active cultural articulation of support and commitment, even the best plans break down during implementation. Each level or subculture within the organization must have all available information, points of view that were expressed, approaches considered and priorities established, strategies developed and selected, and resources and time lines that were finalized.

The more people who are part of decision teams, the greater the probability that they will be able to build understanding and shape the culture and commitment of non-decision makers. In this way, the culture and commitment are transferred from decision makers to other members of the organization. As Michael Fullan (1990) argued,

... implementation or change in practice is not a thing, a set of materials, an announcement or a delivery date; rather it is a process of learning and resocialization over a period of time involving people and relations among people in order to alter practice.

The culture must take on an "enabling" function in which it helps to create a work force that supports activity leading to improved school effectiveness.

Why Vertical Culture?

One problem that occurs in organizations is that supportive and enabling cultures naturally form on a horizontal level. These subcultures become a very important part of the members' professional lives, and their allegiance, enthusiasm, loyalty, and commitment are directed toward the horizontal subculture instead of the organization. If horizontal subcultures support the overall direction and plan for the entire organization, this does not cause any great organizational problems. However, there is often no mechanism set up to ensure that the horizontal subcultures are integrated into and supportive of a single organizational culture. When individuals feel a sense of importance and significance from a horizontal culture, the subculture becomes cohesive and is able to work at odds with higher level administrators who are not part of that culture.

When cultures are formed on a completely horizontal level, all of the bonding forces occur there. This means that all of the connecting links and binding mechanisms within the organization are horizontal. Most of the symbolic and cultural forces for influence are formed on the horizontal level. Thus, work groups at the various levels within the organization are very cohesive but there is little reason to expect these subgroups to bond to an overall vertical organizational culture. They know and care for one another, they will share with and support one another, and they will provide honest feedback to one another on a horizontal plane, but that culture does not necessarily support other subcultures forming up and down the organizational channel.

In Tom Peters' 1992 PBS special on management, Mike Walsh, Chairman of Union Pacific Railroad, said

I couldn't cause it to happen. I personally think that is what is wrong with American business today. You have by and large a set of frustrated CEO's because they can't make the organization respond to what they want because of the layers.

This statement is true for school system administrators as well. The vertical team provides a mechanism to resolve this problem by running through the layers, to develop clear communication, and to develop openness, trust, and a direct link to the action.

Rensis Likert (1967), in *The Human Organization*, was the first to describe the "overlapping group" form of structure. In this form, groups were linked to those above or below them by an individual called a "linking pin," who was a member of groups on two different hierarchical levels. In this way, the individual was a member of the group above, as well as the leader of the group below. Dr. Likert believed that the "linking pin" would be a catalyst for coordination, cohesion, interaction, integration, involvement, and commitment. He believed the cross-linked groups and their "linking pins" would create a vertical organizational culture out of the various horizontal cultures that had developed at each hierarchical level. This is called a "multiple overlapping organizational structure."

The "linking pin" concept has not proven effective in achieving this vertical integration of horizontal cultures. Dr. Likert himself recognized that problems could develop with the theory when he stated,

> . . . if the existing linkage channels cross many work groups and hence are long and cumbersome, the persons or groups involved should take the initiative in establishing face-to-face groups to provide direct linkages for handling the problems.

Effective organizations have found that a form of "face-to-face" interaction is required to create a vertical culture. Face-to-face interaction of people at various levels within the organization has proven to be an absolute requirement if a vertical culture is to be developed.

Vertical Communication

An effective vertical culture develops high levels of support and assistance running from top to bottom. The vertical culture has a much greater commitment to innovation and a sense of competence among its employees. The vertical culture greatly enhances the flow of accurate information and helps to reduce the number and impact of detrimental rumors and stories.

Vertical culture tends to have a long-term survival focus. It looks at potential and organizational flexibility, whereas horizontal culture is concerned with existing positions and facts. Vertical culture is visionary, looking to effectiveness and future challenges, while horizontal culture focuses on experience and proven standard procedures. Vertical culture is more willing to take risks than horizontal culture. Vertical culture tends to develop a more dynamic strategic direction, whereas horizontal culture develops a more static, operational outlook.

There are other concepts that support the wisdom of a vertical team structure. Information circulated among employees is naturally distorted based on the number of people through whom the information is passed. Anyone who has played the game "telephone" is aware of how information becomes garbled as it is passed from one person to another. After the information is passed through many people, it changes into something unrecognizable from the original message.

Upper-level administrators who spend time at more strategic levels within the organization quickly lose touch with the work, staff, and clients. This is a very unhealthy position for those who are involved in planning the strategic direction of an organization. Employees within the organization need to have tangible, visceral, contact among the various organizational levels to feel important, heard, respected, appreciated, and, most importantly, informed. Managers in Peters' and Waterman's (1982) study confirm that "visible management" or "management by walking around" (MBWA) is a very important approach to organizational effectiveness. The vertical team concept insures that this "visible management" is an organizational reality.

Research suggests that the vertical team structure is not prevalent and that school district improvement efforts are not often formulated by simultaneous interaction and discussion among individuals at various levels within the organization. In the last twenty years, educators have become fragmented into separate groups of professionals, each pursuing separate interests and concerns in their own way. Fred Wood and Donn Gresso (1990) found that fragmentation of effort often results when individuals at various levels are not well-integrated in the planning and implementation process. They state,

> The more central office administrators, school board members, and teachers pursue their own interests, the less they have tended to pursue common goals and to expose their ideas to educators in other roles.

Problems will develop, regardless of how good the ideas are, because little communication among various levels within the organizations has addressed what Wood and Gresso see as, "how each job in the district might be affected by district improvement goals and what potential problems might be associated with implementation of such goals." Wood and Gresso (1990) concluded,

> The current fragmentation and lack of cooperative effort among the key stakeholders . . . has resulted in a lack of understanding of various roles

and problems each role group faces in carrying out their responsibilities.

They believe that this has resulted in a "lack of trust and increasing confrontation among teachers and administrators" that are "ineffective and inappropriate for our changing world."

The Impact of Vertical Teams

One of the most common benefits expressed by those who participated in vertical teams was the increased insight that occurred from being exposed to a broad diversity of perspectives. Members saw themselves as part of an organization in which individual horizontal groups were able to achieve far less than what was possible by working together as an entire organization. They began to recognize, value, and actively seek members at all levels within the organization who might help them achieve improved organizational effectiveness. Most participants on vertical teams concurred that exposure to the expertise and viewpoints of others enabled them to function more effectively in their jobs.

For example, members of the El Paso Independent School's vertical team liked the exhilaration of working together, and found that the vertical team provided a forum for the enrichment of points of view. The teams believed that "It is not often that one has the opportunity to communicate at some length with leadership at various levels within the organization." Other vertical teams shared this same belief. Betty Riddle, a high school principal in Charlotte, North Carolina, expressed the beliefs of many team members when she said,

> Our vertical team meetings have constituted one of the few opportunities that I have had to spend entire mornings discussing and thinking about issues in education, both locally and nationwide. Perhaps this should not be true, but those of us in the field have very little time to sit and think and brainstorm with colleagues at various levels within the organization. The vertical team format has contributed to this opportunity in that it has broadened the perspective for all of us involved.

Many vertical team participants explain that a major benefit of the program is the discovery that the school is both a separate part within the system and an integral part of the entire system. The individuals could identify their unique horizontal nature and still see how they were integrated into the entire system. Thomas Bobo, superintendent of the Montgomery, Alabama public schools captured this sentiment in his statement,

Our vertical team experience had led us to look at schools as schools. Our vertical team experience has led us to look at schools as separate institutions apart from the system as a whole, and I think that is good in many ways. I feel that it has led people to buy more into ownership of what is going on in their schools. The team members also realize through the vertical team that they are part of the system as a whole.

The opportunity to hear fellow professionals discuss common issues from different perspectives and different levels was an enlightening experience for all team members. For example, central office administrators wondered how programs could be devised to help school personnel deal with specific types of student problems. A teacher wanted to learn new techniques for a student's need, realizing that tomorrow morning she would again face that student in the classroom. One begins to recognize that each member wrestles with problems of significant complexity, that each shares a sincere concern for the problems, that there is typically no easy or quick solution, and that decisions at each level influence what occurs at other levels. However, in order for the program to be effective, this has to be discovered by people in each of the horizontal layers.

Eddie Roberson, Jr., a school board member on the Chattanooga, Tennessee public school's vertical team, described the development of cohesiveness among team members when he said,

. . . as the degree of confidence and trust was strengthened you could sense the sharing of problems and ideas. This, without a doubt, made me feel the vertical team experience was working. There were times in the beginning that it seemed hard for some members of the team to understand and accept responses to issues. But as each explained their roles and functions, I could see an understanding of how each member faced team issues. The diversity of the team led to the most interesting discussions regarding all areas of education. But with all the exercises and frank discussions one thing became clear, we all loved children and wanted to improve the Chattanooga Schools.

Participants often reported an increase in communication and trust among employees at different levels. The teams often helped to close the gap of misunderstanding that existed between the boardroom and the classroom. New lines of communication were opened and new perspectives were gained as a result of vertical networking. Roberta Cartwright, a teacher at Chaparral High School in Las Vegas, said, "If everyone on every level could hear the reasoning behind decisions and know we're all working together, school districts would run a lot more smoothly."

Dr. Jorge Descamps, facilitator from the University of Texas at El Paso, believes that staff often fear and feel distant from the superintendent—even if those fears are unfounded. He believed this attitude existed toward Dr. Ronald McLeod, Superintendent of the El Paso Independent School District. Some mistakenly saw the superintendent as "distant from his district." After Superintendent McLeod and his staff participated on the vertical team, perceptions completely changed, and staff at all levels saw McLeod as being "in touch with his constituency."

Superintendent Don R. Roberts from the Forth Worth, Texas public schools saw the vertical team as an opportunity to cut through the organization and get needed information. He said,

> When I first went to Fort Worth, I didn't want to be involved in a vertical team. I thought it wasn't going to be good. I thought that I really needed to be doing other things. But in hindsight, I thought it was a good experience, and something that helped me later on. I would not have known those people to the degree that I did. I would not have learned some of the things that were going on in some of the schools. I did learn from team members. They were free to talk. They were not defensive or protective of what they talked about. I could see the different problems. I could see the specifics.

A sense of trust developed in Fort Worth as team members were given opportunities and support to take risks and try some exciting new approaches to education. Participants were made to feel comfortable, especially when expressing opinions about matters being discussed in the vertical team meetings. Dr. Stuart Berger, superintendent of the Wichita public school's vertical team, believed that the vertical team "allowed me to have individuals at different places in the school district upon whom I can rely." An important outcome was the development of an established network for obtaining information and support that was unavailable prior to their involvement.

Some vertical team members in districts that had strong unionization and difficult professional negotiations believed that the vertical team process had helped to "re-connect" teachers, principals, central office staff, superintendent and board members. The linkages and common interests of all educators had taken precedence over the disagreements and conflicting positions that often hindered communication between the union and school administrators. Increased respect and collegiality developed, which had not existed since unionization and professional negotiation had begun taking hold. James McCullough, superintendent of the Chattanooga public schools, said,

I feel the system is better for its involvement in the vertical team program, and I have a great degree of satisfaction in my reflections upon this year. Through representation of teachers and principals on the team, a feeling of confidence and understanding that existed for a long time, but was damaged when professional negotiations began, has been reestablished. My hope and belief is that this feeling will continue. The team members put aside rank, position, and responsibilities, and reminded us again that individuals can communicate on the authority of their own competence and worth regardless of their titles and responsibilities.

This same sentiment was expressed by Anthony C. Julian, school board president on the Youngstown, Ohio vertical team.

I saw improved communication and the feeling of involvement in a team effort working toward common goals. We all have a better understanding of the problems of each other's professional responsibilities. And we have built up our trust and confidences in each other and we have developed a personal bond for one another.

Many who participated on vertical teams discussed the benefit of relationships that developed among the members. Dr. Kenneth Burnley, superintendent of the Colorado Springs schools, particularly appreciated the relationships he developed with other members of the team that far exceeded what he had experienced in other organizational settings. In describing her experience on a vertical team, Elva Cooper, a principal in Charlotte, North Carolina, stated,

I have been privileged to rub elbows and share ideas with people for whom I have the deepest amount of respect. These people work hard, love children, and are what excellence in education is all about. Because of them, I believe even more in myself and am inspired to maintain, extend and create a better school environment for student learning.

Karen Gaddy, a school board member on the Charlotte, North Carolina vertical team, affirmed Cooper's feeling. She stated, "Perhaps the most overwhelming surprise of this project for me has been the intense pride I have developed in the participating people and schools."

Participants gain courage from vertical teams to try exciting new approaches and to take risks to increase school effectiveness. The vertical team often gave its members courage to be the best that they could be. The vertical team process encouraged participants to try to make needed changes in order to improve school effectiveness. In addition, participants developed an excitement about their efforts. They served as cheerleaders and supporters for new innovations and innovators.

Most importantly, vertical team members provided non-team members with a better understanding, respect, and appreciation for their colleagues' job responsibilities, the school system, and the direction in which the school system was moving. Frank Brusa, principal of Las Vegas High School, responded, "The vertical team was a great concept for everyone involved and a great way to communicate ideas to all levels."

The benefits that participants on vertical teams experienced affected non-team members within the school systems. The general conclusion of team members, particularly principals, was that the culture created in the vertical team was contagious and that it slowly influenced the perceptions of non-team members. As the energy level and professional interests of the participants evolved, they served as role models and they directly and indirectly expressed the system-wide views that had developed during their vertical team meetings. This was also observed by non-team members, and typically resulted in one of two reactions. The first, and most desirable, was a sincere interest in learning from the individual who had participated on the vertical team. However, in some cases there was a feeling of jealously, and non-team members began to isolate the vertical team member. Those not on the vertical team felt excluded from this critical opportunity for direct involvement and concerned that the members of vertical teams were favorites, and had special privileges. Because of this, they cut themselves off from colleagues at their own level.

The most prevalent reaction of non-team members, however, was a sincere interest in what was discussed at vertical team meetings and a desire for sharing of new creative ideas. This was reflected in a joint statement made by all participants on the Youngstown, Ohio, public school's vertical team. They stated,

> The participants believe that the people they work with and for have also benefited from the vertical team program. It is our belief and hope that the benefits derived thus far for students, faculty, staff, administration, and Board of Education will continue to grow as a result of the seeds that were sown by this year's participants on the Youngstown, Ohio, public school's vertical team.

The Youngstown team believed that confidentiality was maintained when necessary, but developments that would improve the schools were generally shared and discussed with colleagues.

In relation to controversial and heated topics, Youngstown team members stated, "These discussions never left the group. This unusual degree of confidentiality enhanced the level of trust, loyalty, and confidence among fellow members." Their motto was, "we have met the remedy and it is us."

Members of the Wichita, Kansas public schools found that the knowledge and understanding that team members developed during team meetings later helped them when they were promoted to higher-level positions. Paul Longhofer, a Wichita high school principal, said, "The opportunities afforded by the vertical team have made adaptation to new job responsibilities easier and in that respect, do contribute to personal and school district improvement."

Members of the vertical team in the El Paso, Texas Independent School District believed that the vertical team concept developed a very positive vertical cohesiveness that does not naturally form in organizations. Dr. Ronald McLeod, superintendent in El Paso, found that,

> Vertical Teams are effective because position differences among the members melt away as the group begins to care about and appreciate each other as persons and fellow professionals.

In a joint statement, the Chattanooga public school's vertical team participants concluded,

> Together we have encountered new and provocative ideas for the improvement of our schools, gained an appreciation of each other and the complexity and importance of each job there is to do in the school system, and enjoyed the collegiality and support that the vertical team made possible as we progressed through our daily responsibilities.

A number of vertical team participants, particularly teachers, referred to the revitalization that occurred as a result of being a team member. Some top-notch teachers were asked to participate on vertical teams at a point when they were very nearly burned-out in the profession. The opportunity to be a member of the vertical team re-sparked their interest in education and their desire to be top level teachers. In describing this phenomenon, Frances J. Logan-Thomas, an elementary school teacher in Dayton, Ohio, stated,

> Prior to my vertical team involvement, I had entertained thoughts of leaving the teaching profession. As a result of my past year involvement on a vertical team my self-esteem has been bolstered. I feel certain that this experience has and will continue to enhance my teaching experience.

Budgeting time for vertical team meetings adds stress to the lives of very busy vertical team members. Linda Ethridge, a school board member in the Waco, Texas Independent School District, said,

School people are busy. Everyone has reams of papers to read, fill out and process. Calendars are full of places to go, meetings to attend and deadlines to meet. The phone is ringing, people are waiting to see you, and you are only on number three on your to-do list of 29 urgent tasks. The need to think, plan, evaluate, and consider new options often gets lost in the hubbub. The vertical team was a valuable time to step back, reflect, and even take the time necessary for creative thought. The give and take which developed in our group fostered creative planning and reinforced the value and necessity of careful, well-considered leadership.

Many who have implemented vertical teams suggest that when members did not have the time to commit to the team or when the membership changed, the teams were usually much less effective. The team's inconsistency of membership and/or unfamiliarity with a new member affected the bonding process and cohesiveness of the team and created apprehension and a lack of trust in the process. Frequent absences by team members were not appreciated and were read as a lack of interest in the vertical team concept. Also, such changes waste time, as new or poor attending members had to be brought up to speed if the process was to be effective.

Richard Penry, a high school principal in the Dayton, Ohio public schools, captured the positive sentiment regarding vertical teams. He states,

Being involved with the Danforth Foundation Vertical Team Program has meant a great deal to me. It has been the most beneficial and worthwhile professional growth venture I have experienced.

Raymond Swann, another principal representative on the Dayton public school's vertical team, concurred,

During my 28 years of professional experience, I have never experienced the quality of professional development that the vertical team involvement provided. . . . to me the true vertical team experience is the "special feeling" you have because you are a part of the team. A team that fostered the positive self concept of all the participants. A team that encouraged the honest, open and candid thoughts of the members; a team that consisted of a board member, superintendent, deputy superintendent, building principal from each level and classroom teachers, yet all were equal and the contributions of all were equally valued.

Dr. Donald Miedema, superintendent of the Springfield, Illinois public schools, said,

> I believe the Danforth vertical team experience has helped me to grow professionally and has helped this district to move forward, particularly in the schools represented on the vertical team.

Dr. Donn Gresso had the unique experience of working with these vertical teams over a five-year period. In summing up the concept, its problems, and its benefits, he stated,

> From the very beginning, the superintendent of schools, assistant superintendents and/or high ranking school officials are key to determining the degree of success which can be realized by the vertical team members. Such high ranking administrators must personally make this experience a part of their professional commitment by attending each vertical team meeting. They must demonstrate a willingness to listen to what professionals in different job roles believe are necessary to create a culture of excellence. They must be willing to support the vision that the vertical team members are creating. And, they must be willing to allow team members to be catalysts for constant improvement within the schools.

Bibliography

Cartwright, D. "The Nature of Group Cohesiveness." In *Group Dynamics: Research and Theory*; edited by D. Cartwright and A. Zander, New York: Harper and Row, 1968.

Corey, Marianne S. and Corey, Gerald. *Group Process and Practice*. Monterey, CA: Brooks/Cole Publishing Company, 1987.

Cunningham, William G. *Systematic Planning for Educational Change*. Palo Alto, CA: Mayfield Publishing Company, 1982.

Eiseman, Jeffrey W., Fleming Douglas S. and Hergert, Leslie F. *The Role of Teams In Implementing School Improvement Plans*. Andover, Mass.: The Regional Laboratory for Educational Improvement of the Northeast and Islands, 1989.

Elmore, R. and McLaughlin, M. *Steady Work: Policy, Practice and the Reform of American Education*, Santa Monica, CA: RAND, A-3574-NIE, 1989.

Forsyth, Donelson R. *Group Dynamics*. Pacific Grove, CA: Brooks/Cole Publishing Company, 1990.

Fullan, Michael. "The Regional Lab." In David Hopkins (Ed.) *School Organization.* Lewes, East Sussex: Falmer Press, 1990.

Hensley, Mary Lewis. *A Vertical Team Approach to Professional Growth, School Improvement and Collegiality in Ten Urban School Districts.* Doctoral Dissertation, Baylor University, 1989.

Lewin, Kurt. "Studies in Group Decision." In D. Cartwright and A. Zander (Eds.) *Group Dynamics: Research and Theory.* Evanston, Ill: Row, Peterson, 1953.

Likert, Rensis. *The Human Organization.* New York: McGraw-Hill Book Company, 1967.

Peters, Tom and Waterman, Robert. *In Search of Excellence.* New York: Harper and Row Publishers, 1982.

Schein, Edgar H. *Organizational Culture and Leadership.* San Francisco: Jossey-Bass, 1991.

Sergiovanni, Thomas J. *The Principalship: A Reflective Practitioner Perspective.* Boston: Allyn & Bacon, 1991.

Weick, Karl E. "Administering Education in Loosely Coupled Schools." *Phi Delta Kappan,* (June, 1982).

Wood, Fred and Gresso, Donn. "For Your Next Change, Think Vertically." *School Administrator* (December, 1990). Copyright by the American Association of School Administrators.

Yalon, I. D. *Theory and Practice of Group Psychotherapy.* New York: Basic, 1985.

Zaleznic, Abraham and Moment, David. *The Dynamics of Interpersonal Behavior.* New York: John Wiley & Sons, Inc., 1964.

4

Vision, Not Criticism,
Supports Excellence

The mentality of a high performing educational organization is one of working toward a shared vision of what an ideal school or district should look like. The shared vision serves as the bonding agent within the culture. The visionary model has long been the centerpiece of the very successful School Improvement Program (SIP) developed by the Institute for the Development of Educational Ideas, Inc. (/I/D/E/A/). In describing this program, the staff at /I/D/E/A/ states,

> Much of what we do in schools today is shaped by visions from our past. If schools are to improve and continue to respond to new demands and new challenges, change efforts must include a commitment to some key elements of effective school improvement that find definition in a vision of excellence related to the future.

According to Jon Paden, executive vice president of /I/D/E/A/, a critical concern facing education is "the need to develop and remain committed to a vision of what our schools should become." The desired result of the first stage of the SIP model is to "develop an awareness of what schooling could be—a vision of 'what we want our school to become in five years.'"

/I/D/E/A/ is credited with developing and articulating the visionary model of planning that many school districts use today. The visionary model focuses stakeholders' thinking and direction on the ideal school they wish to create. This opposes traditional deficit models that focus attention on correcting the problems that exist within the school system. The visionary model focuses on shared visions, while the deficit model focuses on problem solving. Dr. Paden suggests that the Danforth Foundation School Administrators Fellowship Program does not include

> a deficit or problem-solving approach which destroys the major components of an effective work culture. Problem solving tends to promote defensiveness, a breakdown in openness, a lack of trust, a lack of support, disempowerment and a destruction of collegiality. The problem solving or deficit approach typically results in a very ineffective work group."

On the other hand, when everyone focuses on a shared vision and how to accomplish it, the team is able to work more effectively. Problems facing the organization become one piece of information to be used by the team in deciding how to accomplish its vision. Problems are not the center of focus for the work group as they are in the problem-solving approach. In describing the visionary model, Dr. Paden states,

> /I/D/E/A/'s School Improvement Program (SIP) is a long-term vision-driven process. Each year school planning teams create a vision projecting five years hence. This visionary model focuses on the future and the best a school and it's community can become, rather than a deficit model that looks at fixing things that are wrong."

Vision is developed through in-depth study of nine basic principles of education that are the heart and soul of what a good school should try to become. The nine principles of the SIP model are:

1. Education is increasingly used to prepare students for successful life transitions.

2. Schools should make every effort to link students with appropriate community resources that could make a positive contribution to the students' education.

3. Students become increasingly self-directed through planned activities leading to self-educating adulthood.

4. Schools explicitly teach and reward the agreed upon values of the school and community.

5. Parents are expected to be active participants in the education of their children.

6. Each student pursues excellence in an area of his or her own choosing.

7. Everyone affected by a decision is involved directly or representatively in the making of it.

8. Schools strive to integrate the interdependent efforts of home, school and community in order to enhance each student's self-concept and education.

9. Every participant involved in educating youth models the role of learner.

Training for the SIP model gives participants the ability to use these principles in creative ways to broaden the vision of their school.

The stakeholders associated with a school or school system develop a clear ideal of what the school or school district may become, based on the nine principles and any other relevant information. Goals, objectives, programs, and performance are woven together in a tapestry that clearly illustrates the school's vision. In this way, the culture becomes the "keeper of the vision."

One approach to envisioning a school is to use a well-established model like SIP which is provided by a successful consultant. This is what occurred at Lindbergh High School in St. Louis, Missouri. Cynthia Jaskowiak, principal, believed it was imperative to think toward the future and use diverse experience and knowledge. She believed that it was imperative for administrators and leaders to broaden their own perspectives as they developed the vision for their school. As a result, she believed that it was important to involve her staff in a formalized process of "visioning".

Jaskowiak selected the SIP model because of its long track record of significant school improvement. The program suggested that the major stakeholders in the high school—parents, staff members, teachers, administrators, and students—work together to develop a vision for the school. The result would be a school that continually tries to improve the high school experiences of students. The ten stages of SIP are readiness, planning, retreat, design, training, implementation, monitoring, continuous improvement, evaluation and recycle. A triad of facilitators are trained to guide the process. An administrator, a key teacher, and a key parent are part of the team and they serve as facilitators for the team.

SIP is designed to create a process that plans for priorities and implements improvement based on a vision of the best a school can possibly be in five years. The vehicle for achieving this goal is a school-based planning team. Once the school's tentative long-range vision has been described, a design task group is formed to develop a first-year plan by identifying those modifications that will enable future improvement. The plan includes practices that lead to attainment of the long term vision. After acceptance and modification, participants plan needed staff development, and determine the coordinating and governing structures that will be needed to support the improvements. All stages are guided by a continuing commitment to the vision of schooling developed by the planning group.

Dr. Gary Awkerman (1991) calls the visionary model "ends planning," or an exclusive focus on "a future result or expectation." Establishing a clear description of a desired future, vision, or end is an important function of an effective culture. Awkerman defines "visionary planning" as

> any collective effort of stakeholders to focus their planning exclusively on creating a best future for a complete system, that is, the development of a set of vivid, written statements describing a desired future for a system.

With the visionary focus, Awkerman found that organizations do not move to the kind of "quick-fix" mentality that is often found in the problem-solving or deficit models. The greater the clarity of desired ends, the greater the probability that the selected means will accomplish the desired ends.

Visioning

The first step in any organizational effort is developing the vision for the organization. This means that everyone associated with the school needs to gain an understanding of what constitutes this vision, best achieved through a vivid and comprehensive description of a desired future. The vision is typically worded as if it describes part of the present reality. Then, for each recommendation, the work group develops action plans to implement and move toward that ideal future. The present conditions within the school or school district are simply baseline data to help develop action plans to achieve the vision and to serve as estimates from which to measure progress.

Warren Bennis and Burt Nanus (1985) focused on the visionary model as a primary correlate of effective organizations. One of the major themes that evolved from their study of ninety effective corporate leaders was "attention through vision." Attention through vision is created by an organizational focus. Bennis and Nanus (1985) state,

> The visions these various leaders conveyed seemed to bring about a confidence on the part of the employees, a confidence that instilled in them a belief that they were capable of performing the necessary acts. These leaders were challengers, not coddlers. Edwin H. Land, founder of Polaroid, said, "The first thing you naturally do is teach the person to feel that the undertaking is manifestly important and nearly impossible . . . That draws out the kind of drives that make people strong, that put you in pursuit intellectually." Vision animates, inspirits, transforms purpose into action.

Vision translates intentions into reality. Sergiovanni (1991) states,

> The fleshing out of this vision requires the building of a shared consensus about purposes and beliefs that creates a powerful force bonding people together around common themes. This bonding provides them with a sense of what is important and some signal of what is of value. With bonding in place the school is transformed from an organization to a community.

This community becomes a school and a school system that is quality-driven. Roland Barth (1986) points out the importance of teachers' having a vision in which they can believe. He states,

> All of us who entered teaching brought with us a conception of a desirable school. Each of us had a personal vision and was prepared to work, even fight, for it. Over time our personal visions became blurred by the visions, demands, and requirements of others. Many teachers' personal visions are now all but obliterated by external prescriptions.

In a later work, Barth (1990) states,

> Without a vision, I think our behavior becomes reflexive, inconsistent, and shortsighted, as we seek the action that will most quickly put out the fire so we can get on with putting out the next one. In five years, if we're lucky, our school might be fire-free—but it won't have changed much. Anxiety will remain high, humor low, and leadership muddled. Or as one teacher put it in a powerful piece of writing, "Without a clear sense of purpose we get lost and our activities become but empty vessels of our discontent." Seafaring folk put it differently; "For the sailor without a destination, there is no favorable wind."

Thus, it is the vision that outlines a possible future while at the same time lifting and moving people.

Charles Kiefer and Peter Stroh (1983) found that organizations capable of inspired performance appear to have several key elements:

- A deep sense of purpose often expressed as a vision of what the organization stands for or strives to create.
- Alignment of individuals around that vision.
- An emphasis on personal performances and an environment that empowers the individual.
- Effective structures that take the systematic aspects of organization into account.
- A capacity to integrate reason and intuition.

By unifying these elements, the organization can create its destiny and guarantee a successful future.

In defining vision, Bennis and Nanus (1985) concluded,

> The critical point is that a vision articulate a view of a realistic, credible, attractive future for the organization, a condition that is better in some important ways than what now exists.

This improved condition does not presently exist. Vision provides the bridge between useful knowledge and purposeful, coordinated action. Consultants report they are able to feel the energy in businesses with a shared vision, as well as its notable absence in organizations focused on problem-solving. Bennis and Nanus continued, "By focusing attention on a vision, the leader operates on the emotional and spiritual resources of the organization, on its values, commitment and aspirations." In this way, organizations work to create an "empowering vision of the future."

Tom Peters (1988) talked about the importance of visions being "lived convincingly." He stated that effective visions are inspiring, clear and challenging, are about excellence, make sense, stress flexibility and execution, are stable but constantly changing, are beacons and controls, are empowering, are future oriented while honoring the past, and are delivered in detail and not broad strokes. A vision is only successful if it communicates and effectively institutionalizes a set of guiding principles or directions. Thus, creating a vision is not an exercise in power or coercion. Vision must grow out of an effective work culture, and must be acted upon, personified and modeled in the action of every employee. Progress is measured as the "realization of the vision."

Visioning in the Norfolk Public Schools

A basic vision can be partially communicated through a slogan. The slogan in the public schools in Norfolk, Virginia is, "Believe, Achieve and Succeed." In fact, the right slogan transcends verbal communication altogether, and like a poem or song, it resonates with the listener's own emotional needs. This is the case in the Norfolk public schools. The Honorable Gerald L. Baliles, former governor in Virginia, wrote,

> I particularly like the theme on your partnerships brochure: "Believe-Achieve-Succeed!" It is this type of challenge and inspirational message that can make a difference.

Dr. Gene Carter, superintendent of schools in Norfolk, is a believer in the importance of a strong and well-understood set of organizational values, vision, and purpose. He stated,

A clear and focused vision is necessary to any form of school improvement effort. Without a clearly focused vision for our schools, much of the school improvement we need and seek will not be realized. All programs in Norfolk public schools are developed under the umbrella of a shared vision and a set of common mission statements for school improvement.

The administrators and staff in the Norfolk schools are expected to look at their schools as what they could be, not what they are, and work toward those visions.

The use of vision to achieve results is exemplified by Norview High School in Norfolk. There was a "respect" problem at Norview. Not only did students disrespect their parents and teachers, but parents and teachers seemed to disrespect students as well. To turn the tide, the school was envisioned as a supportive place where there was mutual respect among parents, teachers, and students. The school developed the following slogan to reflect this vision: "Respect—the more you give, the more you get." This slogan was placed on wall banners and worn on buttons by teachers, students, and parents. As everyone worked more positively with one another in achieving mutual interests, the vision slowly became a reality.

To inspire visions for the school division and the schools, Dr. Lawrence W. Lezotte, a professor from Michigan State University, was invited to Norfolk to discuss characteristics of an ideal school. Community members, board members, administrators, faculty, and other stakeholders were encouraged to study the effective school's research to learn more about the vision of an ideal school. The school division held two-day institutes each fall, which employees were encouraged to attend and envision their ideal schools. In addition, workshops on instructional skills, school improvement programs, as well as teacher orientations were designed to improve teachers' and administrators' visions of the ideal school. Instructional skills workshops were based on the models for instructional improvement developed by Dr. Madeline Hunter, from the University of California, Los Angeles.

The vision that developed for the district encompassed a number of areas such as essential skills, cooperative learning, school climate, high expectations, remediation and acceleration, monitoring, and parent and community involvement. In describing the basis of the focus on shared visioning, Dr. Carter stated,

Effectiveness is enhanced when teachers, administrators, and classified staff are committed to changes and self-improvement because of intrinsic motivation to become better at what they do. This is greatly enhanced by creating a vision of what their ideal school would look like. The vision becomes a strong guiding set of principles and convictions for all that they do and provides inspiration for exceptional performances.

The Norfolk public school system wants to be the finest in the country. Regarding his visit to Norfolk schools, Dr. Max. Heim, superintendent of Geary County Unified Schools in Kansas, stated,

> . . . Norfolk Public Schools has the premiere effective schools program in the United States. At every juncture we see happy children and enthusiastic teachers, and the best news of all is the fact that Norfolk learning is occurring in an equitable way . . . Never have we visited a district where there is so much positive instructional improvement going on . . .

The major theme for the Norfolk public schools and their vertical team was, "Set your sights high! Make success happen!" This was also the theme for Norfolk's Annual School Effectiveness Institute. The keynote speaker for the Institute, Dr. Lawrence Lezotte, stressed,

> The question being asked becomes, "what are the prospects for school improvement if one goes straight to the individual school district and individual schools' in that district and invites schools improvement from within?" The literature on planned change and effective staff development would suggest that this strategy tends to be the one approach that will bring about enduring change because it builds in commitment and local ownership through the involvement process . . . One needs to find a powerful motive for change. One way to create such a motive is through a powerful vision of new possibilities for the school and district and most significantly, the students it serves.

In Norfolk, the goal is to move from ideas to action, and from action to results. They believe that there are no perfect ideas and there are no ideas totally without merit. As a result, they summarize what they like about ideas, explain their concerns, and encourage everyone to explore ways to develop strengths. There are, however, a number of ground rules regarding the visioning process. Some of these include:

1. Address the plan as a continuous process.
2. Discuss improvement plans often.
3. Make decisions based on what is best for students.
4. Encourage research-based experimentation.
5. Strive for high quality in all you do.
6. Seek central office support and commitment.
7. Sustain the momentum of the process.
8. Evaluate staff on the basis of the vision .
9. Align all components with the vision.
10. Continuously monitor outcomes.
11. Desegregate student data by socioeconomic status.
12. Eliminate ideas that have not brought about positive results.
13. Celebrate success.

In discussing local school efforts in a school district like Norfolk, Lezotte stated,

> Cultural change takes time, tends to occur in a "million little actions" and is clearly incremental. Building on these notions, school improvement can be described as an endless succession of incremental adjustment.

Each adjustment is made in order to try to better achieve the ever improving vision of the ideal school. In Norfolk, system-wide visioning is succinct, direct, and open to a great deal of freedom of interpretation regarding the ideas and visions of each school. The Norfolk mission simply states,

> The mission of Norfolk Public Schools is to provide both "equity" and "quality" in terms of educational opportunities for each of its students, systemwide, through continuous school improvement. We believe that *all* students can learn and that schools improve one at a time.

The Norfolk school system developed a bank of test items to determine whether students had successfully completed main learning objectives within subject areas. Norfolk student test scores on these tests, as well as standardized achievement tests, improved slightly each year since the district began focusing on a shared vision of excellence for their schools. Dr. Carter believes

> The trend of improved test scores of students in Norfolk public schools is a testimonial to the fact that the dedication and commitment to a

vision of excellence is working in Norfolk. The beneficiaries of this dedication and commitment are the students who annually are displaying their sense of purpose through steadily rising test scores.

In updating their vision of an ideal school, a number of different ideas surfaced, including improved placements for special education students; developing a creditable learning-disabled curriculum; improving services to dropout/dropins; providing assistance to students with a high risk of suicide, students in trouble with the law, students preyed upon by wealthy drug dealers, etc.; providing opportunities for more social activities for children; developing greater family support for childrens' education; insuring that success occurs in all children's lives; and, most importantly developing more of a "human touch" when implementing the mechanisms and structures that are in place.

There was a belief that the structures and the delivery systems in Norfolk were sound and well-supported, but the culture of the school was not changing. Norfolk educators believed that there needed to be a vision of the school as a care provider in which teachers took a more active interest in students, seeing that their needs were being met at whatever level they were operating.

In reflecting on her three-year experience with visioning and vertical team programs Norfolk teacher Julia Cameron stated,

> It is not, as we commonly believe, that the past plus the present form our vision of the future; rather the past plus our vision of the future form the present. These words of Phillip Schlechty echo in my mind as I review my Norfolk vertical team experience. The years have been filled with enlightening experiences, proactive discussions and intellectual growth. I have had the opportunity to work with a dedicated group of people to sharpen our vision of what we hope to achieve in both Norfolk City Schools and at Maury High School. My vision of the future—optimistic.

In describing a few of the changes that occurred at Larrymore Elementary school, Principal Peggie Robertson, stated,

> Some of the changes that have improved the work culture at Larrymore are cooperative groups including classified personnel and parents, sharing at bi-monthly grade level meetings, published weekly announcements, monthly news-letters, formation of the schoolteacher assistance teams, monthly faculty breakfasts, secret pals, apple and silver charm awards, seventeen annual school inservices, the vertical team meetings, and the pride in working toward an ideal school.

She described the experience as

> ... a highlight of my professional life. I have changed my approach to the principalship to one of facilitating, supporting and rewarding the talents of my staff. Not only has the staff expressed appreciation for the dynamic and exciting work culture, but, I find that I am more excited about my job and have a stronger sense of respect and pride in what we are achieving in this school even though I have less involvement in the day-to-day operations.

Visioning, Not Problem Solving

The model of change commonly applied in our schools and business organizations is one of problem-solving. In the traditional model, school districts are asked to address deficiencies, which are most often identified through needs assessment. In an article entitled "The Quality School," William Glasser stated,

> In contrast to the coercive core of boss-management, persuasion and problem solving are central to the philosophy of lead-management. . . . A lead manager emphasizes that problems are never solved by coercion; they are solved by having all parties to the problem figure out a better way that is acceptable to all. If the first solution doesn't work, the problem is addressed again. Because coercion is never an option, the lead manager and the workers cannot become adversaries.

Problems, central to the focus of the organization may be societal, political, or educational. The problem-solving approach tends, however, to produce results opposite to those Glasser calls for. Problem-solving creates a group dynamic of defensiveness, protectionism, power struggle, mistrust, and an ultimately adversarial relationship. Applied to the improvement of schooling, the model usually results in feelings of failure, incompetence, and depression, which must be covered-up in some way or another. The individuals feel that they, as well as the organization, are incapable of operating effectively because all efforts are placed on trying to improve one problem area. A sense of inadequacy develops within the culture. Power is often removed from the problem solvers under the assumption that more intelligence exists outside the organization or the problems would not have developed in the first place.

Those involved in the organization develop a sense of impotence and passivity, making them easy targets. When this happens, school effectiveness actually declines, creating more problems to be solved in a spiraling deflation of spirit, energy, and performance. At this point, educators within the organization begin to see themselves as victims and develop self-defense mechanisms to protect themselves from burnout or an urge to leave the profession.

Intense utilization of problem solving accompanied by mandates from politicians, communities, and businesses have not produced the intended effects in our schools. After an abundance of national reports from various commissions decrying the problems in American education and the endless attempts to "fix" the nation's schools, most believe that education is no better off than it was before. Worst of all, school educators are left with problems and little or no power to create an improved vision for their schools.

The Ill-Fated Problem-Solving Model

Administrators have often been taught that a necessary condition for a decision is a problem or organizational deficit. That is, if problems do not exist, there is no need for decisions. Such administrators spend time finding problems to which they can apply their skill. Administrators that pride themselves in their problem-solving skills often subconsciously encourage employees to provide them with problems to be solved. Recognizing that administrators relish the task of fixing problems, employees create problems with which they can gain the administrator's attention. The administrator feels good solving the problem, and the employee is recognized. In this way, problem-solving gets the attention of the organization and ultimately dictates the rewards. This can reach an unhealthy state, as solving organizational problems can become an end in itself rather than a means to a greater end. As problem-solving becomes an isolated act and other factors are excluded, cognitive dissonance begins to build up as stress, bitterness, conflict, and disenfranchisement. Such a situation often creates the need for tighter control and more problem solving, resulting in a very unsuccessful approach to education.

Simply getting rid of problems is qualitatively different from creating solutions. Getting rid of a wrong does not mean achieving a right. The performance is limited to correcting what the person already knows how to do so they are doing it better or at least problem-free. The focus is not on what ideally they might do to achieve excellence.

As soon as a problem shifts and fades, a more important problem surfaces. Thus, a feeling of never succeeding develops within the work culture. Problem-solving approaches shift to and fro in an attempt to resolve the shifting problem base. This turbulence is well understood by practitioners who have been living in the aftermath of such occurrences caused by constantly changing public demands, special interest groups that lose and gain power, and constant political shifts on policy and governing boards.

The Visionary Model

School districts that have taken a visionary approach to their future are surviving and prospering. They have restructured outmoded deficit and problem-solving models and shifted to a visionary approach that is far better suited to the culture of excellence. They have wrestled control from politicians and businesspeople and placed it back with the schools, where it always belonged. Naisbitt and Aburdence (1985) note that,

> Once we accept the challenge of re-inventing education, we are free to stop justifying our failures and move ahead to the creative part which asks, "Where do I go from here?"

Such school districts do not ask where they are but try to determine where they want to be. This shared vision can drive an organization to excellence.

This visionary approach to the functions of organizational leadership allows the development of the synergy needed for effectiveness. Figure 4–1 characterizes the qualities of this synergism.

Visionary Models in Practice

The central theme of an effective work culture is a deep, even noble, sense of vision, purpose, and inspiration to develop the best school or school district possible. Although adjustments usually need to be made to achieve the vision, it is the vision, and not the adjustments, that are the focus for the organization. The organization will naturally and continually make needed adjustments if the vision becomes a part of the work culture. Dealing with problems promptly, actively, and with some depth is a very important determinant of whether the vision will ever be achieved. Passivity, denial, and doing nothing are the main enemies of success in any visionary venture. The organization should not focus on the problems, but on the vision of the ideal school.

Perhaps these concepts are best summarized by Matthew Miles and Karen Seashore Louis (1990). As a result of their study of five high schools in Boston, New York, New Jersey, Cleveland, and Los Angeles, they

Visionary Model	*Problem-solving Model*
• is proactive	• is reactive
• is effective	• is efficient
• is based on perception, creativity, innovation, experimentation, intuition and imagination	• is based on logic, rationality, problem-solving, sequential, linear, deductive, scientific approach
• involves synthesis	• involves analysis
• shares responsibility for success and failure	• points the blame
• works to build/renew	• works to repair/correct/replace
• driven by values, ideals and inspiration	• driven by coping and surviving
• is continuous, farsighted and foresighted	• is immediate, routine and myopic
• is led (empowered/enculturated)	• is managed (commanded/structured)
• lends itself to synergistic efforts of creation	• lends itself to individual efforts of correction
• builds toward the best system to contain the water	• puts "fingers in the dike"
• is planning in the present with an eye on the future vision	• is planning in the present with an eye on anticipating needed adjustment
• is initiating and stimulating	• is scanning and responsive
• encourages reformation and restructuring	• protects the status-quo
• is cultural and conceptual	• is structured and concrete
• has a visualization, experimentation orientation	• has a crisis, firefighting orientation
• impacts upon organizational context	• is impacted upon by organizational context
• is holistic and "ecological"	• is unilateral and focused on parts
• is program/performance-oriented	• is operational/process-oriented
• thrives in a "innovating, learning" environment	• thrives in a "knowing, problem-solving" environment
• removes boundaries set by precedent	• breeds "poverty of possibilities"
• has a growth and development orientation	• has a safety and security orientation
• is based on hope and inspiration	• is based on experience and standards
• is important	• is urgent

FIGURE 4–1   Characteristics of Visionary and Problem-solving Models

identified the key theme for improvement as an active involvement in achieving a vision for the school. In discussing one of their major findings, they concluded,

> Our findings were that broad, ennobling, passionate, shared images of what the school should become do much to guide successful improvement. People in one of our successful schools said, "We are not only a school for kids, but a university for teachers"—a vision that led to a strong internal cadre's running an immense and rich range of staff development. Visions may either emerge from or lead to smaller "change themes," such as "get successful small projects going" or "model improved supervision and teaching." Gaining real ownership of visions by school staff is critical and requires serious time investment, patience, and empowerment for success.

Visioning is a joint process; hope depends on successful and optimistic interaction among people.

Issues of will. Will looms very large in vision building. Many people experience fear and uncertainty about the future, since they feel it cannot be known.

Advice: Asking people to look on the future as if it had already happened is very helpful. An example: "It's October 6, 2000. The governor's office has just cited this school as one of 10 outstanding schools in the state. Write the citation." Furthermore, people often stop themselves from vision building by doubting themselves and their ability to be out front, leading, making a commitment. And they weaken the power of their visions by taking present structures and procedures as given, not as things to be transcended.

Key skills. Here we can point to the skill of "going outside the frame," thinking laterally and creatively. An associated skill is the ability to **design**, invent new structures and procedures.

The basic skills of collaboration are key. Visions can't be shared without direct, joint work on decisions that matter, nor without the ability to support and encourage others in dreaming.

Time is required before a vision will develop these qualities, for everyone to think, talk, and struggle with the vision before they can adopt and live it. If the vision needs to be written in order to be communicated, there is no shared vision. In fact, the least important thing an organization does is to develop documentation for its vision. If an organization needs to begin with a formal declaration, it is probably doomed.

As the mission becomes a part of the work culture, the work group begins to operate in a highly aligned manner. The group knows what needs to be done and can sense when convergence and synergy is being achieved. Employees talk until they can each tell they are seeing things in the same way. There is little need for formal statements of agreement, as agreement is understood. At this point, the work culture has achieved a deep level of understanding that will propagate throughout the organization. Michael G. Fullan (1991) found that effective vision "permeates the organization with values, purpose, and integrity for both the what and how of improvement. It is not an easy concept to work with, largely because its formation, implementation, shaping, and reshaping is a constant process."

Building on Strengths

School visions can build on existing conditions of excellence within the school, as is the case at Lincoln High School in San Diego, California. This is a particularly interesting school in that many fine athletes—Marcus Allen, Lew Barnes, Damon Allen, Steve Taylor, Steve Pierce, and Malcom Glover, to name a few—are graduates. The school athletic program is steeped in tradition and pride, and its athletic teams are often ranked among the top five in the state. However, this attitude has not been as pervasive within the academic program. The faculty and administrators believed that this strong school attitude toward athletics could be used as a foundation for a "new attitude" toward academics at Lincoln. This was a real challenge, since Lincoln had the lowest test scores in the San Diego Unified School District in reading, math, and language, and the second highest dropout rate in the district.

The new vision would be based on achieving high grades in the classroom as well as on the field. Wendell Bass, Lincoln's vice principal and athletic director, explained,

> Lincoln Preparation High School marks the beginning of a period in which academics, the preparation of students for life, will merge with an athletic prowess to make Lincoln Prep the best institution of learning that the San Diego Unified School District has to offer. At Lincoln Prep we have a new attitude about learning, about ourselves and about our school. This is a shared vision among administrators, teachers and students who are all striving to improve the academic image of this grand old school.

There were a number of changes made at Lincoln Prep in order to improve academics. This positive attitude was expressed in the teachers' motto:

> You must believe that anybody can achieve. You have to believe that this kid, this human being, can achieve regardless of what his status in life is. Once you believe that, then you can make it happen!

The mission of the school was to adequately prepare students to graduate with optimum choices for the future. Each student was to graduate as a responsible, self-fulfilled, and productive citizen. The stakeholders believed in each other, and accomplished great things by working together. Randy Hasper, a teacher at Lincoln, told fellow teachers,

> Find more information on that area of your subject that you are weak in. By means of this you will avoid being the teacher in the chair behind the desk. Effective teachers are up and doing, directly involved in offering a palpable serving of what they have discovered . . . students will readily learn from someone who listens to them, someone who welcomes questions, someone who is kind. Care enough to stay after school to talk to Clarence about his sense of isolation. Care enough to call Wendy at the hospital after her surgery. Care enough to ask Charles the second time, when he will complete his late project. Exceptional approachability is a force that weakens resistance to learning.

A newspaper article in the *San Diego Union* described Lincoln as a local success story:

> Lincoln has strengthened its curriculum and faculty, become a full-fledged magnet school, added more than 250 students, developed a strong PTA, and last month held its first ever college night.

The vision for Lincoln became contagious as administrators, teachers, community, parents, and students gave of themselves to make the ideal become the reality.

Abraham Lincoln High School in Denver involved all the school stakeholders in a mission. The stakeholders developed a vision of their high school as one in which students maximized their success, developed strong reading achievement, and learned in an atmosphere of inspiration and high morale. Some of the results that grew out of this mission were improved articulation and communication with feeder schools; improved student placement; more student, parent, and teacher conferences; an increase of staff; motivational speakers at assemblies; improved student monitoring and programming; and an increase in reading strategies in the content areas. Overall school morale was improved through increased oral and written forms of recognition, increased social and extra-curricular activities, and an improved reward system for academic performance.

The school began to market its symbol on hats, jackets, and shirts, and presented the school through slides at community organization meetings. They also advertised events at Lincoln High School in the local newspaper. This new vision of excellence at Abraham Lincoln High School had a significantly positive impact on the school as reflected in both test scores and individual attitudes.

Research-Based Visions

The visions of an effective school can take on different forms based on the values that are most prominently shared by stakeholders within the school. Visions can be refined using research based on what we know about quality schools. Ideas can also come from knowledge of the best available practices. Research and knowledge tell us that some things do tend to work better than others, and represent a place from which to begin the improvement journey.

A combination of research and experience was used by the faculty and staff at Beaumont Junior High School, in Fayette County Public Schools in Lexington, Kentucky, to create a vision for their school. The staff had read a number of national research reports expressing concern about the sense of isolation that teachers felt in the classroom. It was pointed out that teachers in schools shared with colleagues tended to perform much more effectively. As a result, the focus of Beaumont's school improvement efforts was on creating a sense of teacher support and communication within the school.

The school district's mission was to focus on teaching and learning, so Beaumont's vision of sharing, support, and communication was directed at these processes. They envisioned their school as one in which teachers spent time with one another, provided positive feedback and support to one another and provided helpful, personal testimony. A high point of the results of the school improvement effort was reported by Russell Behanan, principal of Beaumont Junior High School. He stated,

> A major focus for the year was dealing with the issue of teacher isolation. As one activity of particular significance during the year, an internal teacher visitation day was conducted, with everyone in the building involved. Each teacher during their planning period made a visitation to another teacher's class to observe. Forms were developed so that teachers could provide feedback to one another. This visitation day was

used as a stimulus to familiarize teachers with the process of constructive visitations as a means of reducing teacher isolation, and subsequent visitations were encouraged and tracked throughout the year. In addition, in-service planning and programs for the year were focused on issues of reducing teacher isolation.

The school also set up systems where teachers were able to substitute for other teachers so they could visit a particular class to share and develop ideas.

Collegiality became a major theme in the development of various in-services within the school. Efforts were underway for one-day and one-week switches of faculty between schools in the district so that teachers could work with colleagues from other schools. The teachers developed a system by which they were able to trade "good classroom ideas." They also tried to arrange more opportunities for all teachers within the subject area to meet to discuss needs and future direction. These activities resulted in a more professional and productive work culture where much professional growth occurred, and new activities were planned for the future.

Another high school within the Fayette County Public School District also created a vision under the district's general mission. The teachers and administrators at Bryan Station High School recognized that teachers needed to have viable input in the decision-making process, and it became an important vision for their school. The research on quality circles suggested that these seemed to be a viable means by which to have greater influence on school practice. Quality Circles are small groups of employees that meet on a regular basis to discuss ways to improve the outcome of organizational efforts, while at the same time reducing costs.

A group of twenty-one teachers volunteered to serve on various advisory groups to evaluate decisions that directly affected the entire school program. In describing this program, Principal Jon Akers stated,

> A major focus for the year was the establishment of quality circle teams of teachers within the school. This program was so successful that a writeup about the program was presented in *Education Week* as an exemplary staff improvement concept.

The vision for Akers' quality circle program was to make Bryan Station High School a more effective high school.

Decisions evolve from an idea of how the shared vision of the employees can be achieved. Problems or failures become one more piece of information used to develop and implement strategy to achieve the desired, shared vision. The administrator becomes a facilitator who provides resources (i.e. financial, human, information, knowledge, etc.) that are used by the organization to obtain its vision. In such an environment, loyalty, commitment, professionalism, maturity and many other such characteristics begin to grow, as does productivity. In this way, professional relationships are fostered and a very positive work culture can develop.

This shifts the role of management from one of control to one of facilitation and support. The employees shift their attitude from forced acceptance to development and commitment. Administrators don't manage people, because people manage themselves. The vision, not the contracts and organizational structures, is the basis of the organization. Of course, this can only work if people have both the capacity and opportunity to shape their vision of the future.

In these times of turbulence and uncertainty, it is even more important that employees are empowered to take instant action from "the trenches" in the schools and classrooms. This front line action-taking requires that everyone have a clear understanding of what the community, school district, and school are trying to achieve. This must be clearly and forcefully articulated on every possible occasion so it becomes an integral part of the culture. Members of the organization become the priests and priestesses, preaching the vision to all who will listen. They are constantly involved in retreats and revivals, and the vision is the word for the organization. No opportunity is inappropriate for reiterating the vision. This means that it is a vision—shared, clear, believed in, even fought for—that draws out and inspires the type of initiative and high-quality performance that excellent schools demand. A compelling vision and committed staff are a surefire combination for success.

Teacher-Developed Visions

The vision that was developed and clearly communicated by the staff at E. J. Brown Intermediate School in Dayton, Ohio, was "promoting more effective classroom instruction and improved student attendance during that instruction." The teachers in the school felt that they needed as much time as possible during the day for instruction, and the interruptions of that instructional time had to be reduced. As a result, a number of procedures were implemented to reduce disruption of classroom teaching. Two examples of changes made were 1.) a daily bulletin of announcements was read and posted in each homeroom, lessening the number of PA announcements, and 2.) an activity period was utilized weekly, where one hour at the beginning of the school day was allotted for assemblies, club, and class meetings. All classes were reduced ten minutes to provide this hour, but the remainder of the school day was devoted to the instructional program only—with no interruptions.

Monthly meetings of teachers in each of the disciplines were held in order to support and encourage the exchange of ideas. A coordinator was appointed to schedule and design the meetings around specific instructional strategies and teaching techniques. The discipline units got together and arranged large group presentations on the mastery learning concept, using teachers who volunteered to be resident consultants and present the inservices. Cheryl Johnson, principal of E. J. Brown Intermediate Magnet School, stated,

> The staff was more receptive to their own colleagues being the presenters than someone from the outside. Four staff members now have an in-service package which they developed and presented at the Ohio teachers of English conference held in Columbus, Ohio. In addition, four language arts teachers refined the writing curriculum to assist our students in creative writing. The district has developed a committee chaired by our language arts chairperson to develop and expand the Written Expression Course of Study.

In addition, "golden apple" awards were given to staff members for outstanding service to students.

In an attempt to obtain a 98 percent attendance rate at E. J. Brown, a number of programs were developed. An "adopt-a-student" program was developed in which 100 poor attendance students were paired with 50 staff members to provide a continuous support system. Bi-weekly drawings of students with perfect attendance were held, and a total of $5,000.00 in cash prizes was awarded in an attendance lottery. Other activities implemented included posting homerooms with perfect daily attendance, providing donut and soda treats for rooms that maintained high attendance rates for the week, and providing a monthly bowling and pizza party to homerooms that maintained a high attendance rate for the month. Students who had great attendance received an "E. J. Brown Great Attender" T-shirt.

All of this had a significant effect on performance. The students improved their gains on the California Achievement tests, showing more than one year's growth for one year's instruction on all three grade levels. In addition, student attendance for the year was up 4 percent, and teacher absence days were only 457, as compared to 771 during the previous school year. The spirit of the school improved and students had more positive attitudes about fellow students, teachers, and their school in general.

Salute to Academics Programs

The Flint Community School District in Flint, Michigan, developed a vision of their schools in which academic achievement was formally promoted and recognized in order to improve school spirit and classroom results. Flint school district developed a "salute to academics" campaign. This was a year-long campaign to promote and recognize the academic achievements of Flint students. It began with a pep rally of inspirational and rousing speeches and the release of several hundred balloons proclaiming Flint's "salute to academics." Superintendent Joseph Pollack stated, "Each Flint school will engage in activities aimed at improving attitudes and personal goals toward academics."

The school system decided to honor academics with a school letter like the kind that had been reserved for athletic performance. In Flint, 250 students from tenth through twelfth grades were honored with letters for earning at least a 3.5 grade point average in the previous semester. The letters were presented as part of an academic pep rally. Deputy superintendent Nathel Burtley told the students, "You not only represent Flint's finest, you are Flint's highest achievers. You have indicated you have the right stuff."

The school system's program of a "salute to academics" served to inspire more students to achieve at the highest level possible in the hope that they, too, might earn a letter. An academic booster's club consisting of parents and others in the community was formed to help promote the campaign and to develop ways to recognize academic excellence.

A number of other schools in the district also developed related programs. For example, Holmes Middle School's theme for the year was, "We produce winners here." One of the teams at Holmes developed a reward system for improvement in behavior, test results, homework, and special assignments. The school developed an attitude of pride in academic work. Students developed an attitude that they wanted to learn and needed the school to help.

Our Noble Purpose

A vision is not a statement of practicality, but a statement of dreams. More precisely, it is the link between dreams and action. Dream your most vivid, lucid, idealistic dreams and they can become your possibilities for the future. Dreams are measured by such terms as inspiration, alignment, empowerment, and noble purpose. Each communicates values, quality, creativity, and purpose.

Visions are essentially intangible. They are descriptions of ideals that may not necessarily be achieved, but are certainly worth aspiring to. A vision of where the organization would like to be in one year, three years or five years guides, cajoles, inspires, directs, and facilitates performance. Visions also provide the basis for a sense of pride in being part of the effort.

Vision is responsible for creating our new future. This occurs when educators are aligned, engaging employee's imagination and dedication in the pursuit of these visions. To do this, we must put aside the status quo past and open our minds to the infinite possibilities that lie ahead. Society is changing from an industrial base to an information base. This and many other conditions require new missions for our schools. Their leadership and culture must be developed in such a way that they can face the challenges and opportunities of our future world.

Synergy requires that people are able to function in an easy, almost unconscious synchronization with each other, translating individual energy into collective results. The vision and the culture orchestrate the synergy between personal and organizational goals, resulting in truly outstanding performances.

It is a deep, noble sense of organizational purpose that brings all these elements together and creates the shared meaning for our professional lives. In this way, the noble mission becomes a sacred value of our profession. The vision embodies the organizations highest values and aspirations. It inspires people to reach for what they can be. This high road to greatness requires stamina and courage, but most of all it requires noble purpose.

Bibliography

Awkerman, Gary. "Strategic Ends Planning: A Commitment to Focus." In *Education Planning: Concepts, Strategies and Practices*, edited by Robert V. Carlson and Gary Awkerman. New York: Longman, 1991.

Barth, Roland S. *Improving Schools From Within*. San Francisco: Jossey-Bass Publishers, Inc., 1990.

Barth, Roland S. "The Principal and the Profession of Teaching." *Elementary School Journal* 4 (1986).

Bennis, Warren and Nanus, Burt. *Leaders: The Strategies of Taking Charge*. New York: Harper & Row, 1985.

Fullan, Michael, G. *The Meaning of Educational Change*. New York: Teachers College Press, 1991.

Glasser, William. "The Quality School." *Phi Delta Kappan* (February, 1990).

Kiefer, Charles and Stroh, Peter. "A New Paradigm for Organizational Development." *Training and Development Journal* (April, 1983).

Leyotte, Lawrence. "Strategic Assumptions of the Effective Schools Process." *Monographs on Effective Schools*, New York State Council of Educational Associations, Research and Development Committee, 1988.

Leyotte, Lawrence and Bancroft, Beverly A. "Growing Use of the Model for School Improvement." *Educational Leadership* (March, 1985).

Reprinted by permission of the publisher from Louis, Karen Seashore and Miles, Matthew B. *Improving the Urban High School: What Works and Why?* New York: Teachers College Press, 1990. © by Karen Seashore Louis and Matthew B. Miles, All rights reserved.

Miles, Matthew B. and Louis, Karen Seashore. "Mustering the Will and Skill for Change." *Educational Leadership* (May 1990).

Naisbitt, John and Aburdence, Patricia. *Re-Inventing the Corporation.* New York: Warner Books, 1985.

Peters, Tom. *Thriving on Chaos.* New York: Alfred A. Knopf, 1988.

Senge, Peter. "New Management Enters the Mainstream: Alignment, Vision." *Management World* (January 1987).

Senge, Peter M. *Fifth Discipline.* New York: Doubleday Currency, 1990.

Sergiovanni, Thomas J. *The Principalship: A Reflective Practice Perspective.* Boston: Allyn & Bacon, 1991.

5

Collegiality is the Catalyst

An effective work culture supports individuals in an atmosphere of collegiality. Collegiality is a closeness that grows out of an understanding and caring for one another, resulting in group members getting to know one another better, wanting to listen to one another, being interested in one another's values, and, perhaps most important, wanting to be together. Collegiality is an emotional feeling of closeness to the group. Collegiality is to bosses, subordinates, and colleagues what a sense of family is to parents, siblings, uncles, aunts, grandparents, and cousins.

An appropriate synonym for collegiality is community. When people have a sense of community, they belong, and have pride in the group. John W. Gardner (1990), in his book *On Leadership,* describes the potential difficulty in developing such relations. He states,

> One of the difficulties in creating a sense of community today is the sheer heterogeneity of almost any population one deals with. Gone forever, except in a few out-of-the-mainstream localities, is the community in which a stable set of shared values rests on the even more stable bedrock of a single religious denomination, a single ethnic identity, and an unchallenged tradition. Today we live with many faiths. We must nurture a framework of shared secular values (justice, respect for the individual, tolerance, and so on) while leaving people free to honor diverse deeper faiths that undergird those values.
>
> Having visited innumerable schools, the author concluded years ago that some were communities in the best sense of the word, while others were simply geographical locations where students gathered to perform specific tasks. Later the same diversity struck us with respect to "congregations, workplaces, and cities."

Collegiality is the means by which cultural, religious, ethnic, and gender differences are free to be expressed and understood. Collegiality results in comfort and trust, allowing each member of a group to feel safe. Members are comfortable sharing both successes and failures, happiness and sadness, problems and opportunities, good things and bad, as well as hopes and fears. Collegiality promotes respect more effectively than power, authority, knowledge, or experience.

Some of the characteristics of a collegial group are honesty, trust, loyalty, commitment, caring, camaraderie, enthusiasm, support, patience, cooperation, and synergy. In such an environment, members are able to express themselves frankly. Collegiality is characterized by the amount of open and honest interaction within the group and a clear and quick understanding of what group members are saying.

School effectiveness research suggests that an effective work culture depends on a shared ethos. Drs. Raywid, Tesconi, and Warren (1984) suggest that,

> Collegiality can produce the coherence good schools require, and a vitality far beyond the reach of formalistic rules. In different words: in any undertaking, such as a school, where success depends on a substantial degree of autonomy, a shared ethos provides the cohesion needed to sustain individual efforts.

Collegiality exists when each member feels free and encouraged to participate, and when members feel that they share equally in influencing the group.

In a collegial group, flexible patterns of communication are used so that all members feel free to participate equally and at will. Minority opinions are encouraged and understood. Individuals know and understand one another, and are sensitive to each other's ideas and reactions. There is a level of trust and mutual respect that results in members dealing candidly with one another without fear of harmful effects. Doubts, resistance, and concerns are discussed and resolved so that each member feels comfortable.

All members feel a sense of responsibility toward the group's success and are committed to the work of the group. The group is an important natural resource to each of its members. Drs. Donn Gresso and Fred Wood (1990) believe that collegiality is the key element to the success of any team effort. Without it, the work of a team will not have an impact on the organization. They found that,

> Collegiality is the most important element in the success of and commitment to school improvement. Collegiality is the key component to the effectiveness of teams. It cannot be achieved by coercion,

persuasion, duplicity or unconditional positive regard. The levels of trust that are established among and across role positions are the catalyst for important and honest interaction among team members.

Perhaps one of the most important aspects of collegiality is that it improves trust and interaction. Dr. Jay Hall (1971) completed a study of over 400 discussion groups and found a high correlation between reported levels of participation in collegial groups and levels of felt commitment to organizational goals. He also found a strong positive relationship between the degree to which one participates in a collegial group and his or her subsequent level of commitment to group results. An ancillary finding was that the degree of collaborative involvement was strongly associated with the amount of satisfaction members derived from their experience in the group. Hall suggests that collegiality and commitment coexist with one another and it is difficult to achieve one without insuring to some degree the existence of the other. In this way, collegiality—creating openings for members to enter deliberation, prodding and supporting, showing interest and caring about what the individual has to say—became imperative to group effectiveness and commitment.

Dr. Hall also found that groups with a history of collegial interaction and relationships handled conflicts differently and responded to them as opportunities for creative visioning. In non-collegial groups, conflict was a serious threat that the group avoided by establishing neutral positions to maintain the status quo. By employing judgments about which no one felt strongly one way or another, conflict was dissipated with little risk of offense. The negative side of neutrality was a loss of confidence in the group's ability to respond to changing conditions. In this case, quality of task performance decreased.

Organizational potential grows as a group learns to tolerate differences and conflict. When employees are aware that their perceptions and opinions differ from others within the work group, they are able to gain understanding of organizational possibilities. This facilitates a decision-making process that is more creative and open to greater possibilities, developing through first dealing with trivial conflicts and moving on toward more difficult ones. Individuals learn to separate their interests from the decision itself. The group can work together, trusting the culture and the process to help sort out the different interests and lead the group to a very effective solution. This may require more data, a closer examination of the interests, and an openness to new insights or possibilities. In this way, the group utilizes its collective resources that are superior to any of its individual resources. The end product is of higher quality than what could have been produced from any individual member in the group.

Phillip C. Schlechty and Betty Lou Whitford (1988) write about collegial and collaborative relations, using terms such as symbiotic and organic. Symbiotic relationships are based on mutual self-interest, while organic relationships are based on a belief in the common good for all. Schlechty and Whitford favor the second—organic relations—in collaborative and collegial groups.

In symbiotic relationships, each party agrees to address the vision of the other party. The basis of the team's relationship is, "I'll help you with your concerns if you will help me with mine." In contrast, organic relationships work on visions that are mutually owned.

Thus, in addition to developing trust, mutual respect, openness, a sharing spirit, and understanding, a group must have a professional interest in being together. Members realize that the vision they have for the future can only be realized by perpetual cooperation and continuous interaction. In discussing the implications for organic relations, Schlechty and Whitford state,

> We are persuaded . . . that a common culture cannot be a by-product of collaboration; it should be its primary goal—in other words, the symbiotic must evolve into the organic. The systematic and continuous improvement of the quality of education cannot occur until education becomes a progressive profession rather than a traditional-based craft.

Collegiality in Practice

The Austin, Texas Independent School District vertical team instituted a series of dialogue sessions with groups of principals and other supervisors to discuss school effectiveness and methods of supporting one another. Dr. Nolan Estes, a professor from the University of Texas, explained that consultants were provided "to give greater insight into spiritual values and the concept of our common humanity." This was done to set the stage for the development of greater collegiality. A peer-assisted leadership program was begun in the schools represented on the vertical team and expanded to all the junior high and high schools with the exception of one. This same concept of cooperation and support was taught to students by focusing on methods of relating to and assisting others.

Dr. John Ellis, superintendent of the Austin Independent Schools, initiated dialogue meetings with principals, supervisors and officers of the Parent Teacher Association (PTA) to help improve communication and to stimulate assistance in formulating a common vision for the future. He worked with sixteen parent training specialists to focus on the concept of team building, parental involvement, and communication between home and school. Dr. Ellis's strong belief in the importance of collegiality was reflected in an emphasis on collegiality in speeches, in the district's television convocation to the entire staff, and in several television interviews and programs throughout the year.

Dr. Ellis's theme was the spirit of teamwork and cooperation needed throughout the district and community, and his message was contagious. Gary McKenzie, a board member, stated that collegiality allowed him to reduce defense mechanisms he had toward educators, and to listen to and be candid and helpful in relations with other vertical team members. He visited team members at their work sites, provided research articles, served on a team member's dissertation committee, interpreted programs and school philosophy to other board members, generally provided candid and supportive feedback to the team, and was committed to supporting team decisions.

Support groups were formed in a number of the Austin schools in order to increase collegiality. After a sense of collegiality was achieved, the groups were utilized to improve school effectiveness. Collegial support was continually stressed throughout the year. A major focus of these teams was to help unique subgroups of children be served without prejudice. Teams discussed a variety of unique students including children with Acquired Immune Deficiency (AIDS), limited English proficiency, gifted and talented, migrant, mainstream religious, new to the school, and the learning disabled, to name a few. Many highly-charged, controversial issues generated by these special childrens' needs were handled productively because the collegiality had formed a foundation of openness, tolerance, and understanding.

The effects of Austin's efforts to develop collegiality greatly improved morale among all those involved with the schools. Teachers at Blanton Elementary School said they felt very good about teaching at their school and were made to feel important from their first day. Teachers who had wanted to transfer or leave teaching no longer had those feelings. Teachers experienced a higher level of dedication, shown in the number of hours worked and in preparation for and activities within their classes. Teachers openly expressed appreciation for the sense of collegiality that existed and talked about how difficult the year would have been without such collegial support.

Teachers actively participated in making all children feel this same sense of belonging, support, and pride in their school and in fellow students. Programs were developed to help sub-groups, starting with "at-risk" students. Teacher activity at Blanton resulted in reductions in dropout rates and increases in attendance. Similar activities at Burnett Middle School resulted in dropout rate decreases of almost two percent in one year, and attendance increased one percent over the same time period. Scores on the Texas Assessment for all participating schools also improved. Team members came to understand that alone no one could obtain what together they could master.

Dr. Freda Holley, an assistant superintendent in Austin, reported,

> The rapport that developed among members of the vertical team was outstanding. Growth and trust were highly evident. Each of us expanded our sensitivity to one another. Collegial experiences were special and contagious. I have grown in my ability to work with and support others in a positive way.

Collegiality helped to close the gap in Austin that often existed between the boardroom and the classroom.

Dr. Mary Lewis Hensley (1989) concluded from the results of the Austin experience,

> Members learned to trust and to share as well as to accept others' trust and need to share. New lines of communication were opened and new perspectives were gained as a result of vertical networking. The vertical team was particularly useful as a tool to provide board members with a broader experiential base on which to make decisions when setting policy...they concurred that exposure to others' expertise and viewpoints enabled team members to function more effectively in their jobs. Each team member was able to offer personal testimony that classroom instruction had improved, student achievement was higher, communication was more open, and new levels of trust had been achieved. Aside from these expected outcomes, the team members believed the program resulted in a new sense of optimism and hope for the district.

Qualities of Collegiality

Collegiality requires opportunities to feel the warmth, caring, and support of the group while exchanging, critically evaluating, and deciding on important professional issues. Effective work relationships are characterized by helping, open, and reflective talking behaviors. Group members establish their identity by sharing their own background in a positive and personal manner. The more these behaviors are directed toward the shared purpose of the organization, and the unique contributions of the individual in achieving those purposes, the more the collegiality will be aligned to system-wide goals.

Quick, Supportive, Pro-Active Response

Participants within a group display unsuspected strengths, bravery, endurance, generosity, and loyalty when they have a strong sense of the group and feel they are important members of it. Collegiality sets the stage to allow for the discovery of professional skills. It creates the circumstances which evoke the greatest sense of wanting to contribute to the fullest. Collegiality provides a diverse set of arenas and environments in which to "talk shop." Talents that lay dormant due to earlier defeats, harsh treatment, cynicism, bitterness, self-doubt, or lack of support can be brought out within the security and caring of the collegial group. The group develops positive relationships based on an appreciation of its diversity of experiences and interests. The group builds understanding by sharing perspectives and searching for a new consensus of meaning relative to issues being discussed. The group develops a collective vision of what schooling could be.

Collegial groups come to a consensus before they move forward with any decisions. Therefore, no judgment may be incorporated into the group decision until it meets with at least the tacet approval of every member. This is not a ground rule of unanimity, wherein each person is in total agreement; rather, it represents a feeling that one can "live with" and "support" the judgment of the group. The group is at least confident and willing to give it a try.

There is a little "ready, fire, aim" in all of this. The group tries out ideas to improve the effectiveness of the school. That effort will give the group needed information to help them resolve any conflict and improve the next shot. There is no voting, trade-off, or negotiation in this form of consensus. The culture does not require voting since the climate is open to honest and frank communication about the issues. The group naturally moves toward a consensus that will allow them to work toward improvement. This is a consensus that insures that people have arrived at the same conclusion for either the same basic reasons or for complementary reasons. The class or school improvement incorporates the consensus idea.

Drs. Jay Hall and William Watson (1970) found that consensus groups reported little difficulty in adhering to the decision rules of the consensus, but the majority rule and compromise groups resulted in a bargaining approach that did not always achieve a consensus. In terms of decision quality, the consensus groups produced decisions that were significantly superior to those produced by majority rule or compromise. In terms of creativity, 75 percent of the consensus groups significantly outperformed their best individual resources while this effect was achieved by only 25 percent of the majority rule or compromise groups. These results have been replicated in a number of subsequently completed studies of leadership.

In the Danforth Foundation School Administrators Fellowship Program, consensus was defined as "the judgment arrived at by most of those concerned." It was identified as "group solidarity in sentiment and belief." Group members shared their perspectives and searched for a new consensus of meaning relative to their purpose and direction. Consensus was built upon trusting relationships. As the original Latin stem *sentiere* means *feel*, and its prefix *con* means *together*, consensus, then is an affirmation of community.

There are many possible activities that develop collegiality. The process begins with taking time for team members to "get acquainted." This is best done by sharing and discussing significant persons, high points, characteristics valued in colleagues and friends, life shaping events, early family history, and leadership styles, to name a few. The attributes of collegiality are maintained throughout the year through peer observation and feedback, team building, positive experience and value sharing, positive assistance using real life questions, and process observation.

Brainstorming is one of the most productive and least threatening first steps toward arriving at a consensus. During this process, group members may change their minds, suggest modifications, and make needed improvements until the group feels comfortable with the results. In this way, a consensus can be reached. The group works to acieve results that it can support and commit to. This is a concept of collaboration that enables local school systems to work with the multitude of reform suggestions that develop naturally .

Collegiality in Action

The Youngstown vertical team found that the spirit of collegiality created an openness and vitality that promoted school effectiveness efforts. There was substantial evidence of mutual respect and trust among team members. In describing their group work together, they stated,

> There has been a very strong willingness to share and to give others suggestions in a non-directive and harmonious fashion. Through reinforcing of the ideas of each other, there was a willingness on the part of individuals to apply suggestions made by the group. The result was an excellent working relationship as a group and fine support of one another . . . Addressing real problems, soliciting and respecting everyone's input, and arriving at mutual consensus were invaluable techniques contributing to the strength of collaboration.

Collegiality became a key "in-word" in Youngstown's schools. For example, Anthony Julian, board president and a member of the vertical team, gained support for a monthly employee recognition award presented at regular board meetings. Improved board/employee relations were evidenced by compliments from employees and in the positive publicity surrounding this awards program.

Team members were encouraged to maintain their own integrity and enhance the dignity of others, thereby encouraging honest, frank, and supportive communication and interaction. As a result, improved communication skills were practiced with greater frequency and sophistication. All administrators decided to increase their visibility to both staff and students. The collegial relations allowed teachers and students to feel more comfortable with an increased number of administrator classroom visits. Bernadine Marinelli, Principal at Woodrow Wilson High School, said the attitude changed "from not wanting me to come to their classrooms to wishing I came more often."

Julian stated,

> Working with administrators and staff through collegiality has given me more confidence in the administrative leadership of our school district. I have learned that those who decide should be among those who are most involved with the implementation of decisions.

Collegiality is a unifying thread that holds everyone together, coordinating their efforts, increasing understanding, and supporting the school spirit. The team believed that "The year was extremely refreshing, rewarding and stimulating, renewing our energy and enthusiasm to make our schools the best possible place for our children and youth."

The effects of collegiality in Youngstown have spread from the vertical teams into a number of schools. Alex Murphy, principal of Chaney High School, tried to develop greater collegiality at his school. He stated,

> The use of collegial approaches with staff has worked exceptionally well. Staff have expressed their appreciation individually and collectively. Morale and productivity are definitely on the upswing! As a result of my participation coupled with the thrust of collegiality, there has been considerable involvement of the Chaney faculty in formulating and implementing our reading and writing plans.

Richard Sheely, director of instruction, talked about the importance of increased collegiality and two-way communication in helping to resolve competing demands for instructional resources. He found that,

In asking each expert to be a true advocate for their subject area, there are bound to be tensions, especially when development is greatly restricted by limited funds.

However, Mr. Sheely also found that collaborative relations greatly reduced the tensions and helped the group to come to equitable and optimal decisions. This was especially true when members were able to give up positions and focus on the total set of interests that needed to be addressed.

This type of a synergy effect also occurred in the Cedar Rapids Public School vertical team in Iowa. Collegiality allowed each person to become a vital, contributing member of the team. This was probably best summarized by William Rainbow, executive director of high schools. He said,

> The group came together in August, made up of a group of very different professionals, each with different backgrounds and interests, and representing jobs at various levels in the organization. As time passed, we became more trusting of each other, more respectful of the knowledge and ability of others, and more capable of dealing with different points of view. Finally, the group became capable of producing work that was better than any one member might have produced.

Members of the Forth Worth Independent School District in Texas believed that the collegial experience provided a unique opportunity to communicate with one another, to develop positive relationships, and to gain greater understanding of other members of the team. This was particularly beneficial, since Dr. Don Roberts had only recently been named superintendent. Roberts and other vertical team members had an ideal opportunity to gain a deeper understanding of one another.

Although members were all from the same school district and were well aware of titles and formal job responsibilities, they quickly realized they did not know or appreciate the encompassing demands of each other's roles. Once they understood this, a sense of cohesiveness and a feeling of support for one another was created. This new understanding and approach would not have surfaced without the support and encouragement of a collegial vertical team. For example, they realized that principals in the same district and at the same grade levels do not have the same demands placed upon them. Different forces within schools made each job different. Again, this understanding allowed the district to better support and understand the unique needs of each school as a separate culture, while at the same time integrating the schools into a district-wide culture.

The development of collegiality opened up the door to true sharing and to discovering many attributes about each other's jobs that would not have occurred except as a result of the open, trusting, and non-threatening atmosphere that had been developed. This same atmosphere helped members to untangle the complex problems that existed in urban schools. Positive relations were built upon a recognition that all roles were critical to the success of the school district. Perhaps the best way to show how far the group came was the fact that two veteran high school principals on the Fort Worth team did not even know each other prior to their involvement on the team. Superintendent Roberts believed, "Such separation verifies the need for improved collegial efforts."

In her dissertation on the vertical team approach, Dr. Mary Hensley found that collegiality was an important aspect of school district effectiveness. She found,

> Team members acknowledged the development of a trusting relationship that grew among team members throughout the year. In addition, team members frequently noted an expansion of their own perspectives as a result of vertical networking. Participants became more aware of the many responsibilities of fellow team members and became more empathetic to the demands of each person's job position.

George DuPree, an assistant principal in the Waco, Texas Independent School District, found the vertical team concept to be effective because participants were made to feel comfortable, especially when expressing opinions. This encouraged participation and openness and resulted in mutual respect and support. Communication, he discovered, was real and effective. DuPree found that,

> From praise to constructive criticism, the team was sincerely involved in improving the talents of its membership. When constructive criticism is given, it should be viewed as a gift. It helps you to see yourself as others see you. We don't receive this opportunity very often.

He felt that by being a member of a collegial team, actively involved in creating a vision for the school, he was involved in not only his own development, but the school system's as well. He related, "To actually grow and develop along with your district, being a component in its growth, is fantastic." He felt that, "the chemistry was there" to take significant strides, and felt successful in the majority of his activities, stating, "By being more persistent and becoming more knowledgeable, I raised my percentage of successes."

Dr. Ron McLeod, superintendent of El Paso, Texas Independent Schools, believed that people needed to spend time together in less formal settings in order for true collegiality to develop. Dr. McLeod generalized that,

Serving on a vertical team was a valuable experience. The collegiality worked because it kept the team going. The El Paso, Texas vertical team had many collegial activities that went beyond the formality of the program. A team has to extend beyond the formality to get to collegiality.

All members of the El Paso team echoed the sentiments of Dr. McLeod, believing that "collegiality enhanced the team experience" or "collegiality was a definite asset to the success of the program." Carol Mottinger, an assistant principal, stated,

I experienced leadership growth by sharing ideas with peers as well as all levels of administrators in leadership positions. I observed members of my team bond, become cohesive in mutual regard and support, and reinforce one another's growth with regard to each member's respective goals.

H. R. Moye, vice president of the El Paso school board, concluded,

In closing, I would like to say that I feel proud of my team. The congeniality has been superb. We have all worked cohesively with one primary interest—the child. I only hope that in some way we can pass this spirit on to the entire school system.

Activities occurring at Bowie High School in El Paso provided examples of what McLeod was suggesting. The school established a goal to improve faculty and faculty/administrator rapport through increased interpersonal relationships and activities, including monthly coffees hosted by different departments, peer coaching and support, school partner employee of the month award, signed birthday cards, Christmas potluck luncheons, faculty tennis and golf tournaments, parties, thank you/congratulatory notes, and end of school celebration at the principal's home. Pete Romos, the principal, believed that the school had one of its best years as a result of increased support, encouragement, and understanding among the staff. The new dropout and at-risk program implemented at the school received overwhelming support and an across-the-board commitment that had not been seen in previous efforts.

Collegiality is the catalyst for enthusiastic participation in the improvement of schools. This is as true in union as in non-union environments. Group bonding occurs as a result of collegiality, and, no matter how time consuming, it will not take place without it. People must be involved with one another if we hope to develop a culture of excellence in American schools. This means people must be brought together in various ways so they have an opportunity to shape their vision of the ideal school and how they can work together to contribute to its achievement. People working together in collegial teams are the building blocks upon which the other characteristics of an effective work culture rest.

Team Spirit

Collegiality is the basis for group spirit and the bonds that hold a group together, allowing it to achieve extraordinary success. Once team spirit develops, the power of the team will work in almost any situation, and the results will be far superior to those achieved by the same number of individuals working under majority rule or compromise groups. This is the strength of the American military, American business, and American schools.

Dr. Lee McMurrin, superintendent of Milwaukee Schools, recognized the importance of collegiality in building team spirit. He believed that collegiality could be improved by communicating regularly and working more closely with staff, recognizing and praising their achievements, tying their activity clearly to common goals and commitments, writing notes of appreciation, asking for ideas, delivering speeches and writing articles complimenting and recognizing staff achievements, holding annual recognition events, sharing promising practices, developing a staff bulletin to recognize staff successes, and mounting public relations to gain respect for the teaching profession. He tried to implement as many of these activities as possible in order to improve collegiality and spirit within the district.

There was genuine appreciation among the Milwaukee staff for the recognition that they received. Morale and spirit improved, as did communication and work efforts. A project on Rising to Individual Scholastic Excellence (RISE) within the system received a national award. A number of staff experienced a sense of intensified commitment toward their personal development and the development of their school.

Jerome Stewart, a teacher in the Amarillo, Texas schools achieved higher levels of performance as a result of the collegial nature and spirit of the vertical team. He explained his new level of commitment and his feelings of team spirit by stating,

> Collegiality helps build bonds of benevolence and an atmosphere of goodwill. I have felt those benevolent bonds grow in our group and I have experienced a special atmosphere of goodwill. It is possible to move toward higher callings by the nurturing environment of collegiality and team spirit. The greatest growth that I have experienced has come through the friendship grown in the fertile soil of collegiality.

Our school systems must be models for this benevolence and goodwill. This same ethos must begin in the classroom and reach out and flow into the teachers' lounges, faculty meetings and principals' offices. It must reach every corner of our schools and school system. Developing collegiality can help build the foundation of benevolence and goodwill that is so desperately needed in our schools.

The Dayton, Ohio vertical team met on a regular basis for the common good of the team members and the schools. They believed that many benefits accrued from the rare opportunity for team members to share, react, suggest, complain, evaluate and dissent on a professional level with all partners equally. They continued,

> It is very unusual for educators at various levels to sit down together on a regular basis with the sole purpose of the meeting being that of improving practices and procedures in the operation of the school system. To do this on an equal partner basis is certainly unique.

In addition to policy and staff development, a number of district-wide projects were developed as a result of collaborative efforts. The team initiated ideas that developed into a leadership academy, a mentor-mentee program for first-year administrators, and a superintendent's forum for classroom teachers. Of course, the major benefit of collegiality was the opportunity to have others react to and assist in the development of both school and personal/professional improvement plans. The overriding benefit was the collective opportunity to interact with each other on a professional, rather than a positional, basis.

All team members' comments were accepted and used on the basis of their quality and not their source. Perhaps the spirit of the Dayton team was best summarized by Raymond Swann, a principal with 28 years of experience. He commented,

> I have never before experienced the quality of professional development that the vertical team provided. To me, the true collaborative experience is that "special feeling" you have because you are a part of the team . . . a team that fosters positive self-concept and encourages the honest, open, and candid thoughts of all the members.

As a result of Swann's beliefs regarding collegiality, he made it a centerpiece for his school's improvement plan. A major goal of the plan was "to build an atmosphere that fosters trust; that strengthens the commitment of the staff towards the school's mission; that encourages positive contributions; and that enhances self-esteem." Some of the actions taken were providing written articles and information; sponsoring meetings to practice skills; providing opportunities to lead, coordinate and implement; encouraging staff to express their views; publishing a school staff bulletin; recognizing staff contributions; and encouraging teachers to focus on a vision of improved academic growth for students.

As a result of these efforts, the staff shared more, was more aware of and likely to discuss educational research, and focused conversations and efforts on student achievement. Teachers became more willing to try ideas and support others to do the same. Student intervention strategies were developed and students were more actively involved in school activities. The overall culture of the school became one of participation in and support for the common or shared interests of the school.

Another example of team spirit occurred in Cedar Rapids, Iowa, where team members produced a proposal for an Outcome Based Education Model. The document was the result of intense debate, discussion, and hard intellectual work. The collegial process opened up team members and allowed them to be comfortable while actively involved in program development. Dr. Newell Lash, interim superintendent, stated, "I sensed real honesty by team members during our professional discussions. I know from experience that this professional honesty doesn't always exist." Joyce Dennis, president of the school board stated,

> Arriving at a group project that could influence the future of our district was a struggle for all of us. But once it was decided, everyone contributed in ways that made it a truly collaborative effort. Our collaborative team process evolved into a friendly, synchronized working group. As the year progressed, we came to know each other much better—our strengths and weaknesses and how each individual role fit into the total district effort. The cross-section of role responsibilities enhanced the depth and liveliness of brainstorming and discussions. Trust, credibility and respect for each other were spinoffs of the work.

The members of the team seemed to share a belief that their personal growth did not come solely from the extensive reading and research but from the team spirit that developed. John Artis, a principal at Kennedy High School stated,

> The commitment and devotion to excellence exhibited by the members of the district is simply awe-inspiring. As a team, I believe we jelled together as a cohesive, productive working unit. I have worked on similar teams before, but never with the same amount of success. Members never once reverted to their role or shied away from speaking

their minds. We argued, we listened, we helped one another expand our knowledge and thinking, and we produced an outstanding product.

Group members described the trust level as very high. Collegiality allowed group members to feel comfortable in taking risks, exposing thought, challenging ideas of others, etc. This acceptance and valuing of each other's contributions set the scene for a very successful project.

Implementing the New Vision

Change will seldom gain acceptance throughout an organization without large numbers of advocates pushing for its implementation. Those whose interests are involved should have a full understanding of and participation in a safe and open environment. The collegial group can then come to agreement or consensus, allowing the team to support and ultimately commit to the successful achievement of it's goals. Those whose future actions are affected by decisions need to feel supported while thinking through the issues.

Team members who do not verbally contribute still gain from collaboration by better understanding diverse perspectives and final decisions. They often benefit from an awareness of the rationale and method employed by more active participants in expressing their interests in the decision. They are aware of how the group came to a final conclusion and are more prepared to defend the decision, even though they did not take an active part in shaping it. These team members still serve as advocates in settings outside the initial group. Less active participants can then practice the behavior of articulating interests and defending positions—a behavior that has been modeled by more active participants.

When a members of the collegial team hear nonmembers suggesting that the central office administrators are completely out of touch, they have the experience, knowledge, evidence, and most importantly, incentive to refute such contentions. They have had direct contact with the superintendent and other administrators and have grown to understand that they each have concerns and interests that are important to the success of the school system. They know that top level administrators do have concerns about teachers and students. Collaborative participants do not stand by and watch their colleagues undermine or sabotage school efforts. All levels of the organization have advocates who speak up for one another and quell powerful and destructive rumors. In a sense, each team member not only models the culture of the team, but defends its character and the character of its colleagues. This type of collegial behavior can catch on, as the barriers between horizontal cultures within the organization begin to break down or disappear. Instead of seven or eight horizontal cultures resisting one another, a single vertical culture develops. This is equally true for the superintendent and central office administrators. When a collegial team member such as the superintendent hears other high-level administrators condemning teachers or principals, the member is prepared to defend his or her colleagues.

The superintendent realizes that this is a serious under-estimation of the ability and spirit of principals and teachers with which he or she has had direct experience as part of the collegial team. In this way, the superintendent models the needed collegial behavior for non-team members.

Collegiality also helps team members to see how others develop visions and produce results. Team members can see how others think and how their backgrounds influence that thinking, helping them learn more about the decision-making process. At the same time, they gain a greater understanding of what influences personnel at various levels within the organization. As understanding and judgment improve, the individuals' value to the organization increases, along with a capacity for exercising responsibility. Participation in a collegial team enables members to gain knowledge and develop the judgment needed for realizing the school division's vision.

In fact, the whole collegial atmosphere frees individuals from stress, tension, and fear, and the psychological factors that create anxiety and reduce their ability to use their full potential. Quality decisions are seldom reached by people who are in a stressful or burned-out state of mind. Stress causes people to become cautious and distraught over the simplest decisions. Stress can cause reduced vitality, withdrawal, detachment, rigidity, dogmatism, anxiety, and even hostility; all of which result in poor team spirit, reduced school effectiveness, and increased student anxiety. As individuals become empowered, they are able to free their minds and work on issues to help the organization. Collegiality, safety, belonging, esteem, and spirit open individuals up to share the unique abilities and skills that they have with the organization.

Kenneth Brill, a teacher in Cedar Rapids, Iowa found that participation on a vertical team was intimidating. At first, he was not able to make serious contributions or even get much out of the process other than increased anxiety. However, the collegial atmosphere that developed helped Ken to become comfortable with the group and to begin to make the type of contributions of which he was capable. He stated,

As a teacher, the thought of being a member of the vertical team was very intimidating. The sense of collegiality enabled each of us to share personal experiences with the group. The openness with which we all shared these bits of information helped foster and build a strong collegiality. From this, our team developed into a very strong working unit. As we discussed various topics and issues, all opinions were respected. Equal consideration was given to all suggestions. It was a good feeling to have everyone working toward a common goal which we knew would have a positive impact on our district.

Other members discussed this feeling of being comfortable with one another as essential to being able to actively participate. This occurred as members got to know one another, as equality began to emerge, and as members became valuable participants.

The intimidation and discomfort that team participation first creates, particularly on a vertical team, is fairly common. For example, Elva Cooper, principal at Cotswold Elementary School in Charlotte, North Carolina, stated, "to have your superintendent call you to serve on a vertical team can be a nervous and pressuring experience." However, it did not take long before the nervousness and the pressure disappeared. As a result, Cooper was able to respond more fully to the demands of participation. Before the program was over, she was expressing great satisfaction, saying that she was "privileged to rub elbows and share ideas with people who work hard, love children, and are what excellence in education is all about." She continued, "My personal experiences were enhanced by the fact that I believe even more in myself because others believe in me."

Patricia Weed, a teacher in Colorado Springs, Colorado, found that the increased sense of collegiality that she experienced helped to improve her thinking, planning, and decision-making abilities. The team served as a model to help her in her personal development and support her while she was practicing behaviors she was observing. She summarized her feelings,

> I believe that I have made more of a commitment to my own professional growth and have been able to work toward increasing my leadership abilities. My team members have been honest and supportive of each other, and I have grown through observation and discussion of problems, dreams, and realities with persons who bring diverse perspectives, diverse roles, and diverse experience to the situations we faced. I believe we developed a sense of community. We will continue to feel a sense of closeness which will enable us to continue to draw upon each other for support and advice.

There were many examples of team members in Colorado Springs cooperating on projects of mutual concern at the schools and in district-wide activities. The team concluded in their final report, "One could readily sense the respect and collegiality that exists among the team members."

Roberta Cartwright, a teacher in Clark County in Las Vegas, Nevada, found the collegial experience to be particularly beneficial in integrating parts of herself that had been interfering with her work. The collegial group provided the atmosphere in which she felt comfortable being involved in introspection, while receiving support and perspective. She stated,

> The collegiality and support I've felt from other team members, the bonds that have been created between administrators and teachers, the knowledge and opinions that have been shared, discussed, and yes, even argued, have been invaluable. I'm leaving this year's program knowing that it has enriched my life, given me new friends, and renewed a "middle-aged" teacher's belief in the joy of being an educator.

Participants on collaborative teams no longer feel mentally stressed, inhibited, uncomfortable, or jangled. Their minds work at peak efficiency because they trust and feel supported by the group. Participants realize that the other members are not "bad guys" and that they have quite a bit in common with one another. Participants do not feel threatened and are able to share their thoughts knowing that the group will accept them. They realize that each person must be heard and understood if an acceptable, quality decision is to be made.

Collegiality allows people to be natural and to call upon their full range of talents under the protection and support of the collegial team. In this way, they are better able to make sound, free, and informed decisions. They are also better prepared to implement these decisions with commitment. This leads to a pleasing sense of fulfillment as participants begin to develop and present their own characteristics to other team members, and then use those characteristics to achieve results.

Members of a group experience significant growth in resourcefulness, skillfulness, information, and effectiveness. They have a capacity to commit to and achieve results. The power to influence the group comes from skill, ideas, ability, knowledge, and interest, all of which are greatly increased by stress reduction and team spirit. The group experiences a sense of energy and feels a spirit that flows through each of its members. All members are excited about their involvement and freely enter into the work of the group. Personal information such as attitudes, values, feelings, preferences, and experiences are as important a part of the group's consideration as are information, commission reports, facts, expertise, research, statistics, mandates, memos, evaluation studies, reports, books, and successful practices.

Collegiality—Not Control—Builds Excellence

Collegiality works best when it eliminates the capricious and inconsistent use of power over less powerful members. Collegiality does not require confrontation or conforming behaviors, but allows for open discussion and consensus. Collegiality employs personal power, not positional power. Positional power is temporarily set aside, since group members communicate and cooperate in the spirit of caring for one another and the vision of the organization. Effective group behaviors are not only stated, they are understood, shared, believed in, and, most importantly, modeled.

The authoritarian and controlling styles that have been so prevalent in modern administrations run counter to collaborative cultures. Power breeds manipulation, domination, and restraint. Authoritarian and political approaches often enmesh employees in a struggle in which they do not believe.

Wielding power over others results in retarded development and vitality. Effort is based on authority and obligation as people internalize the judgments of others and deny their own. This creates the dependency which is so necessary to autocratic and political cultures. Relations are based on a debilitating legalism or materialism. This cannot promote team spirit, collaboration, or excellence. Participants have no sense of responsibility or concern for outcomes. A sense of hopelessness develops that is seldom seen in collaborative cultures.

Employee response to organizations will take one of two forms, 1.) "How can we strike back at the school division?" or, 2.) "How can we contribute more fully to the school division's success?" In collaborative cultures, the first question seldom gets asked. Collegiality runs counter to active resistance. Collegiality tends to result in satisfaction, interest, excitement, challenge, gratification, purposefulness, support, and, ultimately, increased effectiveness. With collaboration, even problems that have been disturbing or irritating seem to evaporate.

Feelings of acceptance or rejection are products of human interaction. Rejection runs counter to collaboration in that it is based on negative, hostile, or antagonistic feelings toward other, more powerful individuals within the organization. This rejection provokes distrust, tension, uneasiness, withdrawal, and, ultimately, hatred. Acceptance, on the other hand, is the basis of collegiality, resulting in trust, mutual respect and support, involvement, and a sense of personal worth.

Collegiality changes interactions from those that arouse distrust and disrespect to those that are based on mutual trust, support, and feelings of personal worth. With collaboration, people do not try to defeat one another and the organization, but work with colleagues toward success.

Drs. Raywid, Tesconi and Warren (1984) stated,

Educational excellence calls also for another fundamental change in typical school arrangements: for a great deal more team effort and collegiality. Observers have commented about the essential loneliness of the teacher, the isolation in which his or her work is typically planned and executed. As research has underscored, good schools depend upon a positive shared ethos in which colleagues are respected and student well-being and learning are central. Collaborative planning, extensive interaction, and interdependence are essential to improving educational practice. Only as a team consciousness develops can a positive ethos emerge and exert a significant claim on all staff. Collegiality can produce the coherence good schools require, and a vitality far beyond the reach of formalistic rules. In different words: In any undertaking, such as a school, where success depends on a substantial degree of autonomy, a shared ethos provides the cohesion needed to sustain individual effort.

Bibliography

Deal, Terrence E. and Kennedy, Allen A. *Corporate Cultures*. Reading, Massachusetts: Addison-Wesley Publishing Company, Inc., 1982.

Gardner, John W. *On Leadership*. New York: The Free Press, 1990. Copyright © 1990 by John W. Gardner.

Hall, Jay and Watson, William. "The Effects of a Normative Intervention on Group Decision Making Performance." *Human Relations*, 23 (1970).

Hall, Jay. *Toward Group Effectiveness*. Conroeln, Texas: Teleometrics International, 1971.

Hensley, Mary Lewis. "A Vertical Team Approach to Professional Growth, School Improvement and Collegiality in Ten Urban School Districts." Baylor University (Unpublished Dissertation), 1989.

Miller, Rina and Buttram, Joan L. "Collaborative Planning: Changing the Game Rules." In *Educational Planning: Concepts, Strategies and Practices*, edited by Robert V. Carlson and Gary Awkerman. New York: Longman Publishing Inc., 1991.

Monter, Karel, et al. *Naval Leadership*. Maryland: Naval Institute Press, 1987.

Peters, Tom. *Thriving on Chaos*. New York: Alfred A. Knopf, 1987.

Raywid, Mary Anne, Tesconi, Jr., Charles A. and Warren, Donald P. *Pride and Promise: Schools of Excellence for All the People*. American Educational Studies Association, 1984.

Reprinted by permission of the publisher from Sirotnik, Kenneth A. and Goodlad, John I. *School-University Partnerships in Action: Concepts, Cases, and Concerns*. New York: Teachers College Press, copyright © 1988 by Teachers College, Columbia University. All rights reserved. Selected quotes from sections by Sirotnik/Goodlad and Schlechty/Whitford.

Shanker, Albert. "Staff Development and the Restructured School." *Improving School Culture Through Staff Development*. Edited by Bruce Joyce, Alexandria, Virginia: Association for Supervision and Curriculum Development, 1990.

Wood, Fred and Gresso, Donn. "For Your Next Change, Think Vertically." *School Administrator*, (December, 1990). Copyright © 1990 by the American Association of School Administrators.

6

Values and Interest Lead to Trust

Trust is the foundation upon which school effectiveness is built. An effective work culture cannot develop unless trust exists within the organization. Teams, vision, collegiality, diverse perspectives, personal/professional development, long-term focus, access to information, empowerment, and school–university partnerships create a synergistic effect, however, trust serves as the catalyst. Trust allows a rich culture to develop, and allows individuals to achieve their full potential. The qualities of achievement such as self-image, identity, worth, personal development, enthusiasm, pride, wisdom, and commitment are based on a sense of organizational and individual trust. Such trust is absolutely necessary to support the action, vulnerability, and risk that is required to strive for a continuing vision of improved effectiveness for our nation's schools.

Trust develops as people expose themselves, share, and take risks together. Individuals' abilities to listen, be honest, be consistent, be trustworthy, have convictions, grow, cooperate, develop vision, support action, and be responsible for results will be exposed to the scrutiny of the toughest audience—their colleagues in the school district. This is where the personal values of respect, confidence, and self-esteem come into play as people realize that they do not have all the answers and will have to depend on one another to achieve success. Trust tends to reduce fear of dependency on others and eliminates the potentially negative effects of conflicts. The group values individuals for their strengths and encourages them to be willing to work through conflicts.

The strength of a group lies in its diversity of perspective and its ability to combine that diversity into the most effective work team. Without wide participation, trust breaks down and conflict grows, leading to wrong decisions. Even worse, the communication of such decisions must come through oral and written messages, which are often misunderstood and misinterpreted. In these cases, decisions are made on the basis of plans, reports and memoranda, formal presentations, and, ultimately, personal sources of power.

Involvement beyond the central office of the school district has been credited with bringing creativity, strength, and clarity to the content of school effectiveness. This adds to the general health of the organization where matters having to do with schooling, community, and people are being discussed. Negative conflicts are often diffused because teachers on the team are able to discuss their concerns about the deliberation taking place at the school site or in the community. This information coming to the attention of school leaders prevents matters from getting out of hand or becoming conflicts. Developing shared decision-making in a group comprised of people who come together on a regular basis and have different roles and responsibilities not only allows the best decisions to be made, but enables those decisions to be clearly communicated to members at various levels within the organization. Those participating in the decision understand it and can clearly communicate it, and can ensure that it is being interpreted and implemented correctly.

Quite often, at the conclusion of a year of shared decision making, members of the team who represented the school district administration. had comments such as: "teachers really brought good ideas to our group," "teachers had insights that we did not have," and "teachers were able to bring a different perspective to problems and potential conflicts that we did not have." Superintendents and assistant superintendents participating in vertical teams enlarged their sphere of influence through principal and teacher members of the team who went back to their places of work having heard both sides of an issue.

It takes a great deal of input in most cases to ensure that decisions are not "half-baked." However, with that input comes an increased probability of conflict as well as an increased need for trust in the process by which such conflict will be handled. The group as a whole must be able to communicate similarities and differences in views in a productive way. The talents of these individuals can be amassed, combining knowledge and skills, or it can be fragmented into power struggles, conflict, and ineffectiveness.

When a group of people is brought together there is a great opportunity for collaboration and increased productivity. These collaborative work groups are based on the premise that productive work groups can find effective ways to deal with any conflict that might develop. There is also the possibility that conflicting points of view and increased polarization might divide the group, breaking down the trust, and splintering the ability to work together.

The fear of conflict is a consistent concern regarding active participation within a work group. Educators are notorious for not actively participating in meetings and then complaining that no one listened to them. A lack of trust and empowerment makes individuals afraid to participate. Each person has his or her own view on how to proceed and which directions are most important, but they are often afraid to let anyone know.

How a group views conflict, and, more importantly, how the group deals with conflict, are very important aspects of any work culture. Even in the most collaborative group, one cannot expect each person's view to be shared or supported by all others. These different points of view inevitably lead to some form of conflict within the collaborative group. Conflict can be seen as associated with destruction, anger, disagreement, hostility, war, alienation, competition, and anxiety. In fact, many educators tend to see conflict as an activity that has few redeeming qualities. Such a view results in fear of group work and team efforts and a tendency to be a very inactive, isolated participant, or, in some cases, a participant who takes advantage of conflict as a way to wrestle control. This, however, is only one way of viewing the conflict that arises as people are brought together in work groups.

The Chinese character for conflict is made up of two equal symbols; one stands for danger and the other stands for opportunity. This is a very accurate portrayal of the potential that develops through conflict. Out of every conflict comes the chance to be beaten, embarrassed, or discredited, as well as to be reborn, reconceived, and developed more completely. Conflict can be associated with progress, strengthening, stimulating, creating, clarifying, and enhancing the organization and the individuals from which it is composed.

There is a high anxiety level associated with participation on a vertical team. This anxiety comes about because participants are not usually accustomed to such an experience, or they are concerned about what other team members will think about and talk about in such a select group. Placement on a system-wide vertical team can be interpreted as either being an opportunity to demonstrate skills and leadership or an opportunity to demonstrate weaknesses. Participants may be concerned about saying the right things to the right people, and may be afraid to be heard and to shape programs.

Because of the dual nature of such personal conflict, work groups in general and vertical teams in particular must be prepared to direct conflict in very positive ways and to diffuse negative conflict before it develops. This is an important characteristic of an effective work culture. Such work groups learn how to use different points of view to strengthen the team and ultimately the organization, not to weaken it.

Conflict can create very competitive situations where members of the group see disagreements as "win or lose" situations. Many times people in these situations become so obsessed with winning the argument that they lose sight of the team goal. This creates a very destructive, mistrusting work culture. Drs. John Bahner, Jon Paden and Jim LaPlant, from the Institute for the Development of Educational Activities, Inc., explain in their training, "As competition takes over, trust breaks down and the group effectiveness is hampered."

Collaborative groups know how to work effectively with the milieu of reforms. They learn to create the means by which they can work together to see that the instruction and learning process occurring in the schools is the best of what is known. Decisions made by collaborative work groups are congruent with the values and interests of those who make them, as well as those who are served by them.

Trust is especially necessary for vertical teams made up of members with different job levels, because these groups are particularly prone to differing viewpoints. This situation can place the participants under stress if mistrust and misunderstanding develop. Members of the team will typically have strong opinions and find it difficult to see both sides of an issue. At the same time, they will not feel comfortable speaking their minds, particularly to more powerful team members for whom they have not yet developed a sense of trust might not agree.

The work group, regardless of its horizontal or vertical nature, can become quite impotent and inert if the culture does not support trust and the free expression of interests. Without trust and openness among members of a group, hesitation, vacillation, feelings of uncertainty, and hedging of thoughts and opinions tend to occur daily. The organization feels acute stress every time a new decision or change is made. When such stress reaches a peak, the maladaptive behaviors of the various individuals and groups within the organization begin working against one another. A common maladaptive behavior is to simply continue with business as usual even though there are warning signs that changes are needed.

If a work culture does not support trust, openness, and collegiality, defensive avoidance becomes a dominant tendency. Individuals avoid exposing their interests, values, and ideas in the hope that they will not alienate others or reveal their own shortcomings to the group. As a result of this inactivity in the decision process, participants lose hope in the effectiveness of the decision even though they participated in making it. In this way, the results are no better than if the members had not participated at all—and are often worse, because considerable resentment develops over the lack of trust and openness in the process. Drs. Irving Jarvis and Leon Mann (1977) suggest that a consuming pessimism develops among those within the organization about the ability to achieve goals, resolve conflicts, or improve decision-making capabilities.

Shared Decision Making

It is important to develop not only a symbolic process of shared decision making, but one that is productive and real. The successful sharing of power in the collaborative process establishes mutual satisfaction and net gains as an ideal toward which to strive. This is not an unrealistic ideal since there are few situations that are so rigidly structured that one's gains must come from the other's losses. This is particularly true when focusing on school effectiveness and the interests and values of those concerned with the educational process. True sharing of the decision making process requires open and honest communication, sensitivity to similarities and common interests, trust, friendly and helpful attitudes, legitimacy of interests, and the time and willingness to work toward shared values and common direction.

Conflict is constructive if it emerges from a collaborative process in which values, interests, trust, and cooperation are predominant. This occurs when there is a collegial desire to discover mutual interests rather than compete to win positions. Successful athletic teams are based on helpful and supporting relationships, where one's interests and values are understood and appreciated and there is support for each member's contribution. Everyone gets satisfaction from contributing in some way to the success of others. Similarly, school success can be achieved by working in groups in cooperative settings in order to share the strengths of each individual member.

Quite simply, we are talking about school systems in which politicians, school boards, central office administrators, school administrators, union leaders, teachers, clerical staff, parents, and students spend time working in harmony to develop school effectiveness. They join together to discuss shared interests and values, to create mutually agreed upon policy and, procedure, and most importantly to create mutual trust and cooperation. In summarizing what they observed taking place in their vertical team over one year, the Duval County Public Schools in Jacksonville, Florida concluded:

> We have seen a strong bond develop among team members. A refreshing spirit of excitement and involvement was observed as team members shared new ideas and spent time gaining understanding of why team members believed as they did. A trust was developed along with

an atmosphere of respect for the ideas and opinions of others. We all observed a greater degree of sharing of what we were thinking and believing in a cooperative, supportive atmosphere. In fact, the team can be characterized by the development of trust and openness. Even when situations became difficult and conflicts emerged, the team insured that all members maintained equal status in discussing and deciding issues and that all interests were understood and addressed before any decisions were made. For example, during a lengthy discussion about the concept of school-based management and how it would be implemented in Duval Schools, it became clear that the concept meant different things to different groups of educators. The development of a shared vision of school-based management became a major undertaking of the vertical team. All points of view—of union, management, legislators, teachers, scholars, parents, other personnel, etc.—were shared. As a result of this open sharing, the team was able to lay out an approach to school-based management best suited for the Duval County Schools, which was supported by almost everyone within the school district. This theme continued as various members worked with others in the team to develop school site management plans.

The Duval team gave shared decision-making credit for improving the way that individuals at various levels within the organization worked with one another. They also believed that trust was a significant condition in making the team work, resulting in a number of quality ideas being developed that could be supported throughout the school division.

In a number of studies that have been conducted across the nation, the effects of such cooperation have been quite impressive. The concept of "shared governance" in Salt Lake City, Utah, has resulted in student performance at each grade level advancing from below national averages. The dropout rate has been slashed in half, and attendance is up 20 percent. Money spent as a result of student vandalism is down 10 percent, and teacher salaries have risen from the 19th highest in the state to the second highest. Dr. M. Donald Thomas, superintendent in Salt Lake City Schools states,

> Any friction that develops is systematically processed, negotiated, understood, and resolved. We've accomplished this by purging the idea that one side wins and one side loses and by replacing it with one objective: to make schooling a cooperative, fair and just process . . . My point is that under shared governance, teachers and administrators spend a lot of time listening to each other and letting everyone know what everyone's thinking . . . hours lost in getting everyone involved are recouped later in not having to fight over every routine decision.

The real leadership in such school systems comes from knowledge and consensus, not power and domination.

The responsibility of excellence in education lies with individuals, not organizations, and we must strengthen individuals and learn to bring them together in such ways that they can be truly effective. Collaboration, integration, and trust require that all parties in a conflict recognize and appreciate the abilities and expertise of others who are involved. In this way, the best of the group's thinking will emerge. The assumption is that the whole of the group effort exceeds the sum of the individual members' contributions. If conflict is settled through power struggles or arbitrarily resolved due to lack of time, money, or understanding, or if it is resolved by a form of power over others, the final decision will suffer.

Group Consensus

Decisions should be based on some form of group consensus, a decision arrived at by a majority of those concerned. There are some situations in which a group may simply provide information to a single decision-maker, since that person will be the only one held accountable for that decision. However, in decisions that will have an influence on the entire group, a form of consensus should be applied.

Consensus results in a form of group solidarity necessary for the members of the group to make a commitment to the implementation and the success of the decision. Consensus is built on trusting relationships and grows out of an understanding and appreciation of the values, interests, and beliefs of every member who makes up a community. Consensus cannot be forced. It develops as the understanding of one another grows along with the reasons why members of the group take the positions that they have taken.

Consensus does not grow out of conflict, but it grows out of the understanding of each individual's interests and values. The group should work together in positive ways to achieve a workable level of mutual trust and understanding. Disagreements are taken for granted but not emphasized. The group members assume that they will have differences of opinion but that they will be able to arrive at a solution with which each group member can agree. The arguments, both pro and con, are couched in terms of the organizational vision and how well the ideas to accomplish the vision meet the interests and values of those that make up the organization. Participants use the mission, purpose, and goals of the organization for guidance. The ideas are narrowed down and combined in a way that brings the group members closer to consensus. Group members can both combine and modify ideas so that they will satisfy those who did not approve of the idea in its original form. The group works within itself to agree on the two or three best and most workable solutions. The concept of "workable solutions" is quite important, since a solution will have little or no value if it is not supported by the members of the organization.

A workable solution is one that can lead toward the vision, can gain considerable support by those working within the organization, and can be implemented by the work team given the level of commitment and knowledge they are willing and able to apply. The organization works incrementally toward an ideal, making sure not to attempt more than what those working within the organization are willing to do. Solutions are selected from possible actions; solutions deal with only parts of the vision; and solutions are only loosely coupled together. Actions are based on preferences that the work teams have carefully selected. The goals of the school system become visionary; however, the achievement of visions are limited by the knowledge and attitude of the work team.

Workable solutions grow from the recognition that we have limited time, intelligence, and information, and are therefore forced to work on only small segments of a vision at one time. The work team must decide on the basis of perceptions, visions, and experience, and must choose the correct moves at the strategic time. The team is continually building upon the current situation, step-by-step and by small degrees, in order to someday achieve the vision. Supporters argue that it is the "art of the possible" as opposed to the "art of the ideal." The planning space is bound by what is already being done. Such workable solutions do not suggest that rational choices should not be made, but that the range of alternatives and ends considered are limited by the present knowledge, attitude and ability of those who work within the organization.

Workable solutions are always related to the existing organizational conditions upon which the changes will be built. Workable alternatives must be within the capability of the organization in regards to its available resources. In this way, change becomes an incremental process of continuous improvement. Planning is simplified by reducing the decision space to options that are challenging but well within the grasp of the existing organization. The planning space is reduced so that both success and vision can be integrated. Perhaps Dale Mann, in an address to the Danforth Fellows, best puts this concept in perspective:

> The remedial orientation counsels that the purpose of planning is not to Achieve Goodness, or to Eradicate Evil, but merely to keep things together and hopefully improve them—some. Freud captured the remedial orientation when he said, "Much is won if we succeed in transforming hysterical misery to common unhappiness." The remedial decision maker sets modest expectations for his decisions.

The organization trades off an immediate move to the ideal that will have limited chance of success to a much more conservative first step in the right direction, having great probability of success. In this way, the organization develops trust in leadership as it gains satisfaction through its incremental successes. A culture develops that is capable of reaching the ideal at its own pace. This is why significant change to improve the quality of education takes at least three to seven years to complete.

Trust

People's perceptions of one another are very important determinants of how well they communicate with and trust one another. For example, if one person perceives another as controlling, autocratic, insensitive, and uninterested, there is little likelihood that meaningful communication or trust will develop between these people. Such perceptions are often inaccurate, as has been disclosed by members of vertical teams after they have developed the necessary trust to communicate effectively. During the course of the Danforth Foundation School Administrator Fellowship program, individuals stated that they had a feeling of mistrust for an individual who worked at another operational level within the school system.

Trust developed, however, as individuals were able to hear people present their own ideas, beliefs, and philosophy. Often through distance, communication written by others, rumor, political tactics, and misinformation, mistrust builds between individuals who are all working toward a common vision because they have not had an opportunity to spend time together. They need time to develop their communication skills with the assistance of a facilitator who can help interpret, build trust, and provide a focus for discussion. Each person's point of view must be sought and the meaning of each must be heard and examined in order to find common beliefs and values. There is an understanding that once a person's meaning, point of view, values, and interests are truly understood, differences in beliefs will diminish or disappear. Trainees at the Institute for the Development of Educational Activities, Incorporated offer a number of helpful suggestions for building understanding and reducing misperceptions:

- seek input from all members
- define terms and their meanings
- change focus (e.g., steer discussion to a different component of the problem)
- ask questions in an effort to understand another person's point of view
- build on areas of commonality and agreement
- paraphrase a team member's side of an argument

- seek similarities and combinations
- move to higher levels of generality
- use quiet think time
- be aware of actions that contribute to consensus
- determine that consensus is an appropriate process
- know when to take a break

Trust develops as we understand people's values and interests, where they are coming from and why they take a given position. Group members need to know and understand one another; they need to know how each person became the person he or she is and understand what each member has to contribute. The more that we understand individuals' views, the more we respect, understand, and trust one another.

In sharing personal histories, group members learn of each other's different experiences. By learning about each other, group members gain an understanding of the "vastness of experiences" that exist within the group. This understanding also helps members to think about others and not just themselves. Members learn to feel a part of a group, accepted and understood. Instead of focusing on and defending particular positions, group members recognize why others have taken their positions and how interests and values are similar and different. The focus shifts from winning a position to coming up with ideas that help to recognize and address everyone's interests while achieving the shared vision.

Drs. John Bahner, Jon Paden and Jim LaPlant from the Institute for the Development of Educational Activities, Inc. suggest in their training that group facilitators need to model and foster behaviors that show respect, appreciation, and encouragement for individual identities. Each member of the group needs to respect the diverse talents and perspectives by making each person a valued contributor to the group. The facilitating process builds a positive climate for the exploration of ideas. Group members are encouraged to share their backgrounds in a positive and personal manner. The facilitation process is one of encouraging all members of the group to appreciate the diversity and commonality of experiences and interests. The group learns how to "value each person, their strengths, and at the same time encourage them to overcome shortcomings."

One of the key results of the process by which people learn about one another and ultimately learn to trust one another, is developing improved communication. Kenneth George, an assistant superintendent of the El Paso, Texas Independent School District vertical team, states,

> Communication is definitely better. I feel a more open atmosphere with everyone I work with. Essential information is more freely disbursed within and most important among different employee groups. Groups

seem to be working together rather than complaining about each other. Decision-making is more of a group decision. I am more competent about my responsibilities and I have more confidence with those at various levels within the organization.

Carol Mottinger, an assistant principal on the El Paso team, related,

> I observed members of my team bond, become cohesive in mutual regard and support, and reinforce one another's growth with regard to each member's interests values and goals. . . . The whole school division began working cohesively with one primary interest—the child.

Teams learn to work together to accomplish what they were unable to achieve separately; however, this requires a level of communication and visionary thinking among the various sub-cultures that is not often achieved.

Communication and Broad-Based Support

The purpose of a vertical team is to serve as a working model to pass on the spirit of open communication, trust, and respect to the entire school system. Jorge Descamps, the facilitator for the El Paso vertical team, described the shift that he saw occur within the team over the year. He stressed that communication had greatly improved and that team members were empowered through the open and trusting environment and their focus on a shared vision. He found that,

> Group members are beginning to incorporate a number of improved communication skills in their work. It is most obvious among several members who have particularly benefited from the interaction with team members at other levels than their own. Ron (the superintendent) continues to reinforce initiative and openness and to support a trusting, sharing environment. Ken George has become more organized with attention on communication, increased work performance, and shared planning. Carol is more relaxed, open and assertive regarding her knowledge and skills. Ben Lesley has involved teachers, parents, and central office staff as well as himself and other school administrators in better understanding effective school theory and practice in order to improve attendance, lower drop-out rate, and improve test scores. Gloria Boyer has increased her openness, visibility and assertiveness with others. Gloria has increased involvement with teachers, counselors, and parents and has provided a number of in-service activities within the district.

In describing changes at her school, Gloria Boyer stated, "A sense of collegiality was formed and a feeling of unity was created. I have learned when to lead, when to follow, and when to get out of the way."

One of the more important characteristics of an effective work culture is its ability to maintain each individual's integrity, while at the same time enhancing the dignity of each of its members. This is best achieved by encouraging honest and supportive communication and interaction among all levels within the organization. Trust results in an instinctive, unquestioning belief in and reliance upon oneself, another, and one's group. That trust allows a person to feel comfortable and safe, to express true beliefs, to unleash and thus maximize the individual's and the group's potential. Trust releases energies that were previously consumed in neurotic efforts to cover up. When trust exists, knowledge and skills are acquired most effectively and outcomes are maximized. Neil Katz and John W. Lawyer (1985) state,

> When you trust yourself, you are able to fully enter into the process of discovering who you are and can be. When you trust another, he or she can more fully enter into this process of learning, living, and being.

The trusting community helps people to be all that they can be by protecting them from political or social harm.

Personnel of Lindbergh school district near St. Louis, Missouri believed that one of the most important aspects of the functioning of their vertical team was the development of trust and understanding, which ultimately lead to very open and productive discussion of major issues facing the school district. According to Marilyn Cohn, facilitator for the Lindbergh vertical team

> . . . allocated time for personal/professional sharing was very effective in developing a sense of caring and trust with one another. The result has been a growing willingness to express feelings, beliefs, and interests in an open and honest manner. Teachers are as willing and comfortable in actively and honestly participating as our central office personnel. The progress in this area, however, was most evident during an in-basket activity on how to raise the morale of building level personnel within the district. The financial problems related to the inability of a second attempt to pass a tax levy in the district had triggered a number of budget cuts and a high degree of frustration. The exchange on how to improve morale was honest and open despite the fact that there were clearly different views of the nature of the problem and the types of action that might be helpful. The vertical team's ability to discuss this delicate, complicated and controversial subject in a forthright and honest but sensitive way revealed how far this team had come in developing an effective form of group dynamics.

The group did not debate over the positions of the various groups represented on the team, but began by gaining an understanding of where each person was coming from with a focus on how to best proceed so that the tax levy might be passed. The trust level allowed team members and representative groups to take a school district position even though it was not always best for that horizontal culture. The difference was that everyone understood the interests of all parties and trusted one another. In this way, final solutions were understood even though they might not have been exactly what a group had in mind. The group now had more vantage points from which they could view and understand the needed tax levy as it related to their shared vision.

The Lindbergh vertical team quickly recognized that one of its most important functions was to model helpful strategies for the various members to use in their horizontal culture groups. The group had to move slowly, getting to know and understand one another, but they also had to find ways to move toward the vision of achieving their goal of passing the tax levy. Dr. Gary Wright, superintendent of the Lindbergh School District, described that the group was ". . . developing a district support group which will in turn develop school teams that will make schools better for students and teachers."

The issue of improved district morale and improved schools became tied in with the need to pass the tax levy. Morale was low, teachers' salaries were frozen, there was a general sense of frustration related to lack of community support, and different perceptions existed as to what should be priorities in the district. Some of the ideas generated by the team were to:

- set appropriate time for future tax levy
- broaden involvement on Tax Levy Committee to avoid misconceptions
- determine whether passing the tax levy will solve the problem
- work harder to pass levy—teachers, PTA, mothers' club, etc.
- make an effort to express, vent, and resolve frustration, conflict and complaining and to get groups to work together on something positive
- develop fun activities around the schools—school as the community center
- gear up an effective promotion/community relations plan
- focus district finances on instruction first and other forms of activities (cut transportation and athletics) second
- come up with alternative means of raising money for the district
- stress that teachers need to experience openness and risk-taking and to be open-minded themselves
- empower everyone involved with the schools
- work more effectively with the media

Two initial activities that grew out of vertical team discussions were "World of Difference" and "Personality Fitness" programs. Employees of the school district were helped to understand the differences in people and how important each of their contributions were to the group's success. Team members believed that this program had begun to have a small impact on morale and felt a more positive spirit toward the end of the school year. The attitude had seemed to shift from frustration and complaining to a determination to make their contributions and not to let it get them down.

The elementary schools also began a program to use grandparents to serve a public relations function for the tax levy which seemed to have a very positive overall effect on school and community morale. This program began with a Grandparents' Day and the soliciting of senior citizens to participate in an elementary school tutoring program. In addition, Dawn Murray, Coordinator of Special Services, worked with the media to improve the school district's community image and to effectively communicate the School District's financial need. Efforts were initiated to provide positive reports of accomplishments of the school on a weekly basis to all forms of media. In addition, formal communication procedures were established for dealing with media during immediate, emerging, and sustained problems and crises. Murray also became involved in the Press Club and the Missouri School Public Relations Association.

Helen Ermel, a teacher at Sappington Elementary School, wanted to improve student learning and parental support by increasing contact with parents. She mailed out parental questionnaires, called at least two parents a week with positive messages, called all parents who did not come in for conferences, invited parents to visit the class, and kept parents informed of any problems their children were having. Board member Glenna Finnie increased her interactions with constituents, parents, and teachers in order to help foster an atmosphere to allow for the passage of the tax levy. She wanted to improve the climate in order to secure additional funds. She insured that the schools were seen in most positive light in local papers, at parent and community meetings, and among residents who were concerned about the schools.

These are examples of individually developed ideas that met many of the interests of those who were involved on the Vertical Team as well as the groups they represented. The process was successful and the staff of Lindbergh School District recognized these small successes and began to shift their perspective from one of gloom and frustration to hope and direction.

This is not to suggest that the process of trust and understanding on the Lindbergh Vertical Team was automatic or easy. There was a real tension among these very busy educators about the time taken to develop trusting and honest communication among all team members and pressing ahead in order to feel that something was being accomplished. Team members were concerned about what their colleagues in their horizontal culture would think when they returned talking about culture, trust, communication, and interests, and had nothing concrete to present. Team members took a considerable amount of time to feel comfortable and risk the pain of exposing their own ideas and interests to the scrutiny of other team members and of discussing controversial and delicate subjects in an open forum. They were familiar with discussions within their own horizontal cultures, but to be open and honest in a vertical culture was a new experience for them. They also found it difficult to get colleagues to accept the importance of their representation on vertical team structures as a key to their future effectiveness, as well as the effectiveness of the entire district. Some non-members felt that membership on a vertical team was another form of elitist activity and not an essential element in developing a culture of excellence. It took a while for non-team members to realize that this was an important linking activity for those struggling to make schools into better places for students, teachers, and administrators. In June, the tax levy was approved and members of the Lindbergh vertical team and their colleagues felt a sense of accomplishment and strength. After the passage of the tax levy, the staff realized that the vertical team concept had potential for being a very powerful means of bringing about change.

Interests, Not Positions

A participant on one of the vertical teams decided that large school divisions should have two superintendents. The other members of the team thought this ides was ridiculous. The more they tried to convince the participant that she was wrong, the more she resisted. The facilitator then asked the participant to explain what interests would be satisfied by having two superintendents in a school district. She stated that she believed the school division had gotten entirely too large and that everyone seemed lost in a huge, impersonal bureaucracy.

She was aware of research that suggested that "smallness in bigness" resulted in improved performance. She believed that two superintendents in the district could begin to help create a sense of smallness and provide easier access and communication. Every member of the team agreed with the participant's interest in creating more of a sense of smallness in the school district, even though they were not at all supportive of her initial position. A very important and significant discussion developed around this interest, and the team decided to focus on creating a sense of smallness as a major part of their school effectiveness efforts.

Groups that have an effective work culture distinguish between a position and an interest. The effective culture will shift to interests when the group reaches a deadlock. A person's position is a solution to a situation. Interest causes an individual to take that position. Therefore, it is important to remember that interests influence a person's position.

Values, on the other hand, have to do with what a person believes to be morally right. One's interests usually grow from one's values. The intensity of feelings toward one's interests is measured by one's emotions. A person's interests or fundamental needs in a situation are important to the person and the group.

When people "lock into" positions, the best possible outcome is a compromise. Compromise usually ends with the members of the group trying to figure out ways to incorporate a little of everyone's position in the final solution. The goals of the group tend to shift from the vision and associated tasks at hand to ways to come up with a politically sound decision in which the socio-political needs of the participants are met and everyone can "save face." The solution is not as important as the feelings and power of each of the members of the group. This seldom results in the best possible outcome. The focus becomes how the group can combine a little bit from everyone's ideas to ensure that relationships among parties involved on the vertical team are not damaged. Excellence, which needs to be addressed for school effectiveness, is given up in order to maintain an amicable solution. Drs. Roger Fisher and William Ury (1981) suggest that in positional bargaining,

> The more you clarify your position and defend it against attack, the more committed you become to it. The more you try to convince the other side of the impossibility of changing your opening position, the more difficult it becomes to do so. Your ego becomes identified with your position. You now have a new interest in "saving face"—in reconciling future action with past positions—making it less and less likely that any agreement will wisely reconcile the party's original interest.

As more attention is paid to positions, less attention is paid to the original purpose of the group and to meeting the underlying concerns of the parties. Solutions typically result in compromise rather than a solution developed to meet the needs of the organization.

To avoid these problems, effective work cultures use interests as the primary focus of negotiating the merits of various proposals. The objective of all negotiation should be to satisfy the professional interests of the team members. Effective work cultures focus on differences among representatives' needs, desires, concerns, and fears. The interests that people have are what ultimately motivate them to action in order to meet needs, satisfy desires, alleviate concerns, and achieve their vision. Interests are usually derived from passions. This is where an individual's energy resides.

The benefit of focusing on interests is that there is quite often a number of positions which will satisfy most everyone's interests. As Fisher and Ury suggest,

> When you do look behind opposed positions for the motivating interests, you can often find an alternative position which meets not only your interests but theirs as well . . . Reconciling interests rather than compromising between positions also works because behind opposed positions lie many more shared and compatible interests than conflicting ones.

Ineffective work cultures focus so intensely on positions that group members are seen as opposing turfs, cliques, enemy camps, and opponents. They think their fellow group members' positions must be opposed. Although this is very seldom the case, this attitude can destroy the team. Defending our turf results in a defensive or offensive war strategy with winners and losers. Focusing on individual interests results in an opportunity to grow in our understanding of one another.

The team process breaks down as each individual reports back to their constituents on the battles they have won or lost and what the enemy has done to them. Everyone ends up a loser in the end. Individuals cannot participate effectively if their sole concern is achieving gains and minimizing losses for their constituents. Effective employees focus on vision while shaping the various constituent interests into a quality decision. Representatives take on the role of statespeople, explaining that constituent positions are not always met because they are not in the best interest of students, teachers, or the organization. Excellent organizations develop a maturity that allows them to move from political positions to collaborative visions.

When the discussions are on interests, the constituents are usually amazed at how individuals share common interests. Team members truly have an interest in what is best for students, and they want to help improve the schools. The culture begins to share interests, common visions, decision-making and vertical structure. The group discovers that shared interests serve as building blocks for shared vertical agreement.

Trust Complements Interests

To focus on interests instead of positions is not easy, since interests are often unexpressed, intangible, and sometimes inconsistent, whereas positions are concrete and explicit. Interests are more personal and revealing than positions and they will not be discussed unless the culture is supportive, open, caring, and safe. When planning is based on interests, each individual in the group is open to fresh ideas. Members of the group remain flexible in regard to possible outcomes. They do not try to change the other person's mind, but help to develop compatible solutions. Members of the group are careful not to categorize people who take the same position as having the same interest. They ensure that there is understanding of each individual's interest.

According to Dr. Jim Hensley, superintendent from the Waco, Texas school division,

> What allowed our vertical team to work effectively together was their willingness to take time to get to know and understand one another. Out of this understanding grew a respect for one another's points of view. Everyone respected the other person, felt free to present his point of view, was interested in his colleagues within the district, and ultimately was quite willing and conscientious in bringing about school improvement. This actually spread to interest in education within the region as well, which was demonstrated by our vertical team's involvement with Black leaders in the planning of a regional observation of Dr. Martin Luther King Jr.'s birthday. The team also took part in planning a very successful program for a regional leadership conference which the group sponsored. Educators from throughout Texas participated. . . . The vertical team was especially helpful in surfacing some of the issues and interests that occurred at various levels represented on the team. Team members became more cognizant of the role fulfilled by others and gained a deeper understanding of and appreciation for the values and interests of the different groups represented on the team. I was impressed with the thoughts, insights and ideas of other team members, as well as the growth in their expertise, confidence and energy.

Linda Ethridge, the school board president in Waco, Texas, agreed wholeheartedly with Dr. Hensley and believed that she was a much better school board president because she now had a better understanding of the interests of stakeholders and the common directions that needed to be taken. She stated,

> We enjoyed being together. We did some good work together. We learned from each other. Professional respect will long endure because of the trust and understanding formed during our past year's involvement together on our vertical team . . . The vertical team reinforces an understanding that everyone has to do their part for the schools to suc-

ceed. I personally came away with a better understanding of what it takes for principals and teachers to help kids. I can make better decisions as a Board member and do more to enhance our success because of my vertical team experience.

George Dupree, Jr., an assistant principal in Waco, Texas, believed that sharing interests, being collaborative, and building team consensus had made him feel like an important contributor to the Waco School Division. He had an increased sense of dedication and energy in achieving goals that had grown out of mutually shared interests. He believed that the understanding of individual values and interests throughout the school division was essential to his growth and ultimately his ability to make a maximum contribution to the Waco Public School System. He concluded,

The opportunity to discuss shared interests and to see them shaped into district-wide plans is fantastic...The vertical team experience broadened my scope. By listening to the views of others as they focused on improving our schools, I gained a broader view of the elements which must be combined to guarantee every student a quality education. The process of working with others in such an environment uncovered the nuts and bolts of what education is all about. It places general knowledge concepts and systems in their proper prospective. By gaining a broader understanding of the issues facing the schools and the school district and the interests of colleagues related to those issues, one becomes more objective in the evaluation of his own and each other's views, more knowledgeable about desired outcomes, and possibly most important, better prepared to implement the efforts that are required to achieve the goals. The vertical team experience, in conclusion, most of all forces one to examine one's own beliefs in relation to others.

This same recognition of the importance of understanding one another and developing trust and a sense of loyalty and commitment was expressed by Lester McDowell, an elementary teacher in Waco, Texas. He said,

My colleagues on the vertical team were helpful and supportive in making me feel an important part of our school division. I came to realize that we shared many personal and professional ideologies that enabled us to better understand and trust one another. I now realize that all educators must work together to bring about the necessary changes that have been mutually derived as being important to public education in order for our children to become productive adults. As a result of my team experience, I strongly support the belief that we must all work together in a trusting environment to help the school district meet the tasks that lie ahead if we are to improve our schools. I hope to communicate this need for better understanding and to help my colleagues develop a sense of shared commitment and belonging to the school district and the very important goals we have established.

Finding the Bedrock

Team activity should be focused on the "the bedrock" issues—those issues that a group believes to be absolutely essential to its existence. This can be difficult, because there is a natural tendency to assume everyone stands on the same bedrock. This is often not the case. Neither effective decision nor support will develop when members of the group believe that their bedrock interests are being threatened. They also will not support final decisions if they do not believe they have had sufficient opportunity to express their interests or if they believe the other members of the group do not really understand those interests. This requires both a willingness to listen to and understand others as well as to explain and clarify the importance and legitimacy of their own interests. The group cannot devalue anyone's interests if an effective consensus is to be achieved. However, each person must understand that everyone's needs may not be able to be realistically met, given real world conditions. As part of the discussion process, each individual must be willing to enter into an open discussion of the legitimacy of his or her interests without arbitrarily devaluing or minimizing others.

Active listening skills must be practiced. As Fisher and Ury (1981) suggest, "if you want the other side to appreciate your interests, begin by demonstrating that you appreciate theirs." Many times the bedrock interests are quite complementary. In those cases where they are not, members quickly realize that there are a number of different interests that need to be addressed, not just their own.

The benefit of this process is that although people may not commit to a position, it is very seldom that they will not commit to their interests. This is a way in which we empower people and give them strength to achieve. The organization should focus its energies on the achievement of outcomes, not the defeating of others. The energy should not be in fighting for and winning positions, but in satisfying and accomplishing individual and mutual interests.

Organizations should not push hard against one another. This is why the time needed to focus on interests and developing mutually advantageous solutions is worth the effort. The key to all of this is to focus on vision and the group members' interests in regard to that vision. Fisher and Ury suggest, "If you want someone to listen and understand your reasoning, give your interests and reasoning first and your conclusions or proposals later."

An unknown source suggested long ago that the reasonable man adapts to the situation; the unreasonable man requires the situation to adjust to him; therefore, the whole world is controlled by the unreasonable man. This truism does not occur in productive work cultures. The emphasis of the organization is not on supporting unreasonable persons but in sharing, understanding and obtaining mutual gain. Amitai Etzioni (1988) has argued quite successfully that employees are driven by their interests, values, and emotions, which are all interrelated. Educators must spend more time getting to understand these crucial aspects of fellow colleagues.

Great achievements occur in education when we are able to work together to incorporate driving forces into our decisions. This is particularly true as we integrate groups within a vertical culture. We must stop using positional power and control to achieve educational results. We must learn to incorporate the natural drives of our colleagues into education plans. It is through shared consensus and mutual gain that the group will be able to achieve its full potential.

Effective school cultures are characterized by personnel who have learned to trust and to share as well as to accept others' needs to trust and share. Lines of communication are open within horizontal cultures and among vertical cultures. Personnel within the district continue to gain new perspectives as a result of continuous opportunities for vertical networking. The school division is constantly looking for a means to provide all those involved in education within the district with a broader base on which to perform their responsibilities and make related decisions. Administrators and others have skills in facilitating effective group process in order to assure that understanding, openness, and trust develop among all members.

The outcome of the work of the district is based on mutually agreed upon goals and plans in which the values and interests of all parties have shaped final direction and practice. The school district allows for many ways in which to integrate the knowledge, interests, and skills at all levels within the organization into a unique partnership. Exposure, at all levels, to such skill, expertise, and viewpoints enables individuals and school districts to function more effectively. Each demonstrates respect, confidence, enthusiasm, pride, commitment, and perhaps the most important, trust, so that together they will be able to achieve significant results. Trust opens up the process of communication so that shared vision and group support develop. Trust is absolutely essential to the development of excellence in American schools.

Bibliography

Cunningham, William G. *Planning for Systematic Change*. Palo Alto, CA: Mayfield Publishing Company, 1982.

Etzioni, Amitai. *The Moral Dimension Toward a New Economics*. New York: The Free Press, 1988.

Fisher, Roger and Ury, William. *Getting to Yes*. Boston: Houghton Mifflin Company, 1981. Copyright 1981 by Roger Fisher and William Ury. Reprinted by permission of Houghton Mifflin Company. All rights reserved.

Janis, Irving and Mann, Leon. *Decision Making*. New York: The Free Press, 1977.

Katz, Neil and Lawler, John W. *Communication and Conflict Resolution Skills*. Dubuque, Iowa: Kendal/Hunt, Inc., 1985.

7

Quality, Information, and Improvement

In order to participate effectively in organizational improvement, employees need to be informed. All the best organizational information is useless if it is not communicated or understood. A superintendent who wished to remain anonymous stated,

> Things I addressed in the district-wide administrators' meetings would come up in discussions in the vertical team. And as I sat and listened while the facilitator facilitated discussion, I noted that even people I had talked to directly, like the assistant superintendent, misinterpreted much of what I had said. Sometimes, what the assistant superintendents and principals were attempting to do were different from what each expected and both were 180 degrees different than what I had initially stated. I saw how other leaders used their own interpretation of information communicated without really understanding its meaning. I don't think I ever understood how differently my vision of what needed to be done was interpreted by so many different people.

This is not a unique phenomenon and was found among employees at all levels within organizations, as well as in communication with parents, community members, and policy makers.

The opportunity to freely communicate about issues of importance is absolutely essential to clear understanding. Dr. John Croghan, a Professor at the University of Miami School of Education and a facilitator for the Dade County vertical team stated,

We developed an environment in which anyone at any time could discuss items of importance to them. These items ranged from how to deal with the press after a violent incident . . . to celebrating a personal victory.

This was also a major objective of Dr. Joseph Fernandez, Superintendent of Dade County Public schools. He established the development of an effective communication and monitoring system as a priority. This was needed so that the staff would be prepared to accept more authority and responsibility for delegated assignments. Dr. Fernandez stated,

An important objective for the Dade County Public Schools is to maintain open lines of communication with school board members, business and community leaders, local colleges and universities, parents, and school and district staff. When information is shared and understood by school district personnel they will be prepared to exercise their creativity and skill in the effort of continually improving the education of the students they serve. When employees are well informed we can give individual schools, closest to the point of service impact, room to try out innovative techniques/programs and time to make them successful. The staff will need performance information to know how well they are doing and to make needed adjustments. We do not over-evaluate; yet, we do hold staff accountable for achieving a positive educational impact.

Fred Rodgers, a principal in Dade County, believed that the improved communication was the most important development resulting from the vertical team. He stated, "The first highlight was having opportunities to communicate. Oftentimes, we have such lonely feelings but in our vertical team we could share, listen, advise, and solve problems."

Without such communication, misunderstanding and misinformation become the basis of educational practice. Kenneth George, assistant superintendent in El Paso, Texas, recognized the importance of building strong systems of communication with professionals, associates, and district wide staff. He instituted weekly meetings with the office staff, and also conducted monthly meetings with all levels of employees under his supervision. This provided an excellent opportunity for two-way communication, as did minutes documenting important information from the meeting that were made available to all employees. Management by walking around (MBWA), a school vertical team, and an open door policy existed for all employees who needed information or had information to share.

Information regarding the status of various programs was reported to both subordinates and superiors. George stated that his essential theme was, "Communicate information to others which will be critical to their decision-making and job performance." In evaluating his efforts to improve communication, George stated,

> Communication is definitely better. I feel a more open atmosphere with everyone I work with. Essential information is more freely disbursed within employee groups. There is clearly less misunderstanding.

Understanding is a key element in an effective work culture. Those within an organization recognize its importance and create enough opportunities for information sharing to ensure that understanding develops. Peter Senge (1990), author of *The Fifth Discipline*, articulated the importance of greater understanding among those who work within the organization. He stated that leadership

> . . . is about helping everyone in the organization, oneself included, to gain more insightful views of current reality. This is in line with a popular emerging view of leaders as coaches, guides, or facilitators. In learning organizations this teaching role is developed further by virtue of explicit attention to people's mental models and by the influence of the system's perspective.

Visionary thinking, development, collegiality, trust, and understanding all grow from an absorption of what others have to say. Group members must understand the words as well as the meaning behind the words in order to understand the message. Senge sees this as leaders needing to have both advocacy and inquiry skills. He states,

> Specifically when advocating a view, they need to be able to:
> - explain the reasoning and data that led to their view;
> - encourage others to test their view (e.g., Do you see gaps in my reasoning? Do you disagree with the data upon which my view is based?); and
> - encourage others to provide different views (e.g., Do you have either different data, different conclusions, or both?).
>
> When inquiring into another's views, they need to:
> - actively seek to understand the other's view, rather than simply restating their own view and how it differs from the other's view, and
> - make their attributions about the other's view explicit (e.g., Based on your statement that . . . ; I am assuming that you believe . . . ; and, Am I representing your views fairly?).

In this way we are able to "think together" and to have the ability to unearth our internal pictures of the world, to scrutinize them, and to make them open to the influence of others.

Effective organizations encourage their colleagues to ask challenging questions and pose legitimate challenges when they believe that the established thinking is misdirected and off-target.

The communication that links work together so that it has purpose, direction, understanding, and achieves results is one of the more important challenges of an effective work culture. Almost all the decisions within the organization will be based on communication no matter how misunderstood or misdirected. A group's productivity is greatly influenced by this chain of communication, and their decisions can be no better than the information upon which they are based. Thus, the effectiveness of the organization is determined by how well it utilizes data transmission and verification.

Unfortunately, it only takes one bad bit of data in the chain, one communicated misunderstanding, to disturb its accuracy and the organization's effectiveness. For this reason, improving performance may not necessarily be successful if efforts are based on a lack of information, erroneous information, or a misunderstanding. Dr. Philip Crosby (1979), a total quality management expert, said,

> First, we have to recognize that the largest cause of defects and problems in any company is the paperwork and other communication system errors. The factories have their own problems, but they are working with what we give them. . . . We have to recognize that although we are hearing these words and agreeing with them, we as individuals do not really believe that they apply to us personally. This is only human.[*]

Thus, there is an implicit relationship between information, understanding, work culture, and the quality (or excellence) of the output.

The degree of free-flowing, two-way communication of information throughout an organization can be a predictor of a number of qualities of the work culture. Table 7–1 provides a chart which describes a number of these contrasting characteristics. Open, free-flowing, two-way communication means that all meaningful information is made available in the simplest and most easily understood form to each person within the organization. Closed, limited access to information means that information is tightly controlled on a very formal and stringent basis with those in power making as little information available as is possible.

[*] All references to P. B. Crosby reprinted with permission of McGraw-Hill, Inc.

TABLE 7–1   Cultural Characteristics Related to Information Flow

Free-flow of Information	*Limited flow of Information*
open communication	grapevine (rumors)
implies candidness and integrity	implies secrecy and cover-up
promotes opportunity and team work	promotes politics and power struggles
fosters convergent understanding through divergent perspectives	fosters divergent initiatives through misperception and misunderstanding
narrows or eliminates the "trust gap" between leaders and co-workers	widens the "trust gap" between leaders and co-workers
furthers confidence and assertiveness	creates and intensifies fear of impunity, defensiveness or ridicule
feeds ideas and understanding	stifles learning and development
culture with collegiality	isolation with informal factions
raises self and group esteem	reduces organizational reverence through ignorance
recognizes, ratifies, and appeases informal operatives	elicits covert operatives and clandestine activity (sabotage and subversiveness)
encourages innovation	sets up road blocks
networks people and ideas	isolates/alienates/devalues people and ideas
becomes the root of a common language	builds language barriers and rejection/low hopes
perpetuates continuous improvement	maintains equilibrium or status quo
aligns the goals and visions of many	narrows field of vision
promotes integrity, credibility, and ethical practice	promotes dishonesty, mistrust, and back-stabbing
lends itself to use for proactive planning and long term focus	shifts focus to problem-solving, nit-picking and short term focus
shares organizational information	"keeps the lid on"
promotes healthy understanding	promotes guesswork, rumors, and autocracy
means clarity, understanding, and/or acceptance	means uncertainty, ambiguity, and equivocality
multilevel brainstorming, sharing, and cooperation	messages, memos, and mandates from the great and powerful
commands accountability	accommodates successful "gun-decking," embellishment, or evasiveness
renders significance to information	devalues information

Continued

TABLE 7–1 *Continued*

Free-flow of Information	*Limited flow of Information*
solicits suggestions	imposes solutions
facilitates feedback	facilitates penalization
assesses	presumes and discounts
invites consideration	invites criticism
networks upwardly, downwardly, and laterally	flows horizontally with slight divergence
taps expertise	relies on power and force
passes information unselectively	sorts and filters
increases organizational literacy	creates organizational illiterates
motivates	debilitates
exposes multifacets of knowledge and perception	fragments facts and obscures fundamental reasoning
provides pathways for and legitimizes probing	entices the eavesdropper and spy
empowerment	impotence
teaming for synergy	one-upmanship, petty competition, and desynergism
information percolates	information stagnates
invokes spirit	creates lethargy
validates group and individual decisions	abounds with doubt and wonder
promotes vision and innovation	promotes strategy, tactics, and the status quo

In the first case, information is shared to develop and encourage greater individual participation based on knowledge and expertise. In the second, information is withheld to insure the power of those "in-the-know." One fosters candidness and integrity, the other secrecy and dependency. One brings divergent thinking and operatives out into the open while the other elicits covert and clandestine activities, including sabotage and subversiveness. One form develops networks, linkages, and bonds, the other forms, cliques, isolation, and desperation. One supports empowerment, the other supports impotence or counter-espionage. Employees are more likely to generate fertile, productive ideas when they have all the information without distortion or evasion.

Learning Organizations

If teachers do not feel that their administrators are keeping them informed, or if they see goals and directions as confused or unclear, a "trust gap" begins to develop between them. A trust gap is usually the first predictor of a crack or breakdown of the effective work culture. This trust gap becomes a self-fulfilling process as it grows, since it causes teachers not to hear what the superintendent and other policy makers say. In such a situation, confidence in the administration erodes and collapses as the culture coalesces against the administrator.

Teachers and other employees of the school system must be an integral part of creating and giving meaning to communications if they are to understand and participate in that meaning. This requires the superintendent and other key administrators to be skilled in both advocacy and inquiry. If leadership does not model good listening skills, then the employees will not listen to their leaders. Such a condition obviously inhibits innovation and the development of people and ideas that are so important in rapidly changing times. Such an organization will never achieve excellence.

Although there is no specific data on the condition of information flow in education, there was a major study of 250,000 employees in approximately 200 organizations conducted by the Opinion Research Corporation, a subsidiary of Arthur D. Little, Inc. The conclusion of this major study, reported in *Public Relations Journal* (1983), was that employees believed that they were not well informed, that management was not willing to listen to them, and that they had to rely on the grapevine for information. Moreover, the study suggested that this deteriorating quality of communication had a significant impact on productivity. The report suggested that top management was becoming increasingly remote from employees at a time when it very much needed them.

As a result, the employees responded that they got most of their information from their horizontal culture. This grapevine was not preferred by any group. Employees said that they preferred to get information from their supervisors and group meetings with the management. This separation was not only seen between workers and top management but also between middle management and top management. They concluded that both the upward and downward flows of information had suffered. Some of the recommendations from the study included:

- Regular meetings between management and employees should be held
- Management should not limit its contact with employees to formal meetings
- Managers should be held accountable for communicating

Organizations that have excellence in their work cultures insure that information and understanding flows upward, downward, and across organizational lines.

Continuous Improvement, Not Reform

The focus on quality within an organization is the focus on continuous improvement, not a focus on remediating or eliminating defects or problems or reforming and restructuring an organization. Constantly improving work means changing the ways an organization does ordinary things in order to improve quality, efficiency, or to better meet the needs of students. The development of continuous improvement is the only way to keep families satisfied and coming back. Once improvement stops an organization will start losing ground. This is what the Japanese call "kaizen." It is continuous improvement involving everyone—managers and workers alike.

This tends to run against the culture of most American organizations. Some of the mottos that have become axiomatic in American organizational life include:

> *"If it ain't broke, don't fix it."*
> *"Leave well enough alone."*
> *"Don't mess with success."*

However, many educators and American firms have learned that such thinking results in loss of ground and, ultimately, failure. In today's global world, holding one's ground is a recipe for slow death. If everyone within the organization is not constantly trying to improve, they will to be left in the dust of a fast-paced global world. With such a world view, employees cannot hold their ground; they cannot maintain the status quo; they can only stagnate.

Effective work cultures give employees the freedom and the encouragement to make improvements. No one is in a better position to improve a job than the person who does it day after day. That person is familiar with all the little things that have resulted in success, and is close to the internal and external clients and best understand their needs. The person in the job is most familiar with the work activities and process of the job, and is best able to identify opportunities for improvement. The person also will get the greatest satisfaction and benefit from practicing new ideas and knowing that those ideas are making important contributions to improving the way the job is being performed.

Effective work cultures invite and support continuous improvement from within the organization. These cultures create a long term process of systematic, cumulative improvement of educational practice. This runs counter to the reform and restructuring approach which suggests a sequence of unrelated, "one-shot" type changes. School improvement is a cultural, on going process running from milestone to milestone to achieve a shared vision. In this way, educators continuously form and reform education to meet the needs of a new generation of schools. This ultimately allows educators to get ahead of the power curve by having quicker, more supportable, and more pro-active responses to educational needs. The culture of improvement provides very stable building blocks which breed a sense of success and confidence for cumulative innovation. Continuous improvement is a sustained effort of cultural adaptation.

There are a number of personal and organizational philosophies that work against employee innovation. One is a natural fear of newness. Hindsight usually suggests, "I don't know why I didn't try that years ago." There is a natural fear of trying something new even when there is ample evidence it works. This is part of the fear of making changes or even taking small risks. One becomes enamored with security without realizing how insecure he or she is. People treasure what they can depend on even when they know the conditions are changing such that what they now depend on will not help them in the future. The work culture must develop and support individuals so they can overcome these fears and take the risks required to continuously improve the organization.

Continuous improvement is gradual, incremental, and dependent upon individual responsibility and team-work. Successful improvement requires constant work toward a shared vision of school excellence. There must be a clear vertical integration, cooperation, and a clear differentiation between causes within the worker's control and those that require management intervention. The teacher is in the best position to improve the quality of education and must be encouraged and prepared to do so. Teachers need empirical evidence to guide change. They must know how they are doing in relation to their shared vision of ideal performance.

The goal of continuous improvement should be service to the public and employee. A culture that encourages the group to deliver all it is capable of and encourages constant development is the key to success. Continuous improvement should be expected, but only as much as the system is capable of delivering. The work group has a capability and if you try to force more from them than they are capable of you will destroy the work group.

In an interview in the *Wall Street Journal*, Edward Deming used a symphony orchestra as a metaphor for a well-run organization when he said,

An example of a system well managed is an orchestra. The various players are not there as prima donnas—to play loud and attract the attention of the listener. They're there to support each other. In fact, sometimes you see a whole section doing nothing but counting and watching. Just sitting there doing nothing. They're there to support each other. That's how business should be. . . . We are all born with intrinsic motivation, self-esteem, dignity, and eagerness to learn. Our present system of management crushes that out.

Administrators cannot simply demand better results, but must provide methods by which employees can study and improve the processes to achieve better results. In fact, Deming's first 14 principles of effective management stress creation of constancy of purpose for improvement of product and service. The revised version of the famous 14 points are:

1. Create and publish for all employees a statement of the aims and purposes of the company or other organization. The management must demonstrate constantly their commitment to this statement.
2. Learn the new philosophy. Top management and everybody.
3. Understand the purpose of inspection, for improvement of process and reduction of cost.
4. End the practice of awarding business on the basis of price tag alone.
5. Improve constantly and forever the system of production and service.
6. Institute training.
7. Teach and institute leadership.
8. Drive out fear. Create trust. Create a climate for innovation.
9. Optimize toward the aims and purpose of the company, the efforts of teams, groups, staff areas.
10. Eliminate exhortations for the workforce.
11. a. Eliminate numerical quotas for production. Instead, learn and institute methods for improvement.
    b. Eliminate management-by-objective (M.B.O.) Instead, learn the capabilities of processes, and how to improve them.
12. Remove barriers that rob people of pride of workmanship.
13. Encourage education and self-improvement for everyone.
14. Take action to accomplish the transformation.

The focus on reform and restructuring decreases as we accept the idea that all educators can lead innovations and improvements. This belief must become widespread just as we now accept the tenet that all children can learn. Perhaps with site-based management as the centerpiece of the current wave of reform, that time is now upon us. Site-based, total quality, and other forms of management which empower people have much possibility for improving our schools, but they cannot be successful unless they are developed, implemented, and supported by an effective work culture. The culture of education must support systematic and ongoing efforts to achieve excellence.

Total Quality Management

School systems cannot achieve an atmosphere of excellence until they create a culture that fosters improvement for future decades. A growing number of total quality management (TQM) gurus across the globe have stressed that for this level of excellence to develop, quality improvement must be the goal of every single individual within the organization.

TQM advocates established a foothold in Japan in the 1950s and their effect has been growing and spreading ever since. Deming asks the rhetorical question,

> What's the most underdeveloped nation in the world?.... The United States of America! Because we don't use the storehouse of skills and knowledge of our unemployed. Even more appalling, however, is the misuse—the underuse—of the skills of employed workers at all levels.

Deming claims that administrators are responsible for 85 percent of all quality problems. He goes on to state,

> Improve quality and you automatically improve productivity. You capture the market with lower prices and better quality. You stay in business and you provide jobs. It's so simple.

The fundamental message of TQM advocates is that organizations should commit to quality improvement through the organization, serve the customer, satisfy customer requirements, encourage employee innovation, provide free-flow of information related to quality, attack the system (not the employees), instill pride and teamwork, and create an atmosphere of innovation and improvement.

Changes in the expectations of teachers are fundamental to the restructuring and improving of American education. Teachers will be given the opportunity to do things they have never done before. They will be actively involved in continually improving the school, and will have much greater authority and responsibility in decision making. Teachers will be asked to oversee hiring, evaluation, curriculum and instructional design, policy, practices, school structure, budgets, facilities, and resources. Linda Lentin, a teacher in Dade County, Florida, described the feeling of a supportive culture by saying,

> It widened our perspectives. We stopped looking at just our class or our grade level and began thinking about the school . . . When you . . . help shape the way a job is carried out, it makes you feel like such a professional.

These fundamentals require continuous commitment rather than a "solution-of-the-year" or a "program-of-the-day" outlook. The key to TQM is *listening to people*. Lines of communication are open, administrators hear what the employees need, decisions are made in a participative environment, employees learn group dynamics and brainstorming skills, and teamwork is encouraged and practiced. Philip Crosby (1984) found that,

> A "hassle" company is one in which management and employees are not on the same side. The "hassle-free company" is one in which all employees are together and there are no sides. It is possible to tell within fifteen minutes or so which kind of company you are visiting. "Hassle-free" offers pleasant working relationships, a smooth system, and happy employees. It also produces an environment for maximum profit and growth potential. Customers can identify this type of company and have confidence in it.

In a later book, Crosby (1988) asks,

> But why should business leaders want their employees to hate the place, or at best to be uncomfortable there? . . . Why do they accept the employee getting most of their information by rumor? . . . The kindest answer is that leaders do not know what is going on, making them insensitive to their employees. The truth is that they don't care, believing that people should make their own world and are responsible for their own happiness or discontent. The leadership becomes separated from the day-to-day reality that makes up the actual lives of regular employees.

A number of school districts in the United States have focused on hard data for school improvement in a move to create "hassle-free" schools. Blanton Elementary school in Austin, Texas, uses frequent assessment of pupil progress in order to constantly improve student and program proficiency. The results of tests results are used to make in-class as well as school-wide instructional decisions.

Freda Holley, assistant superintendent in Austin, stated,

> Low and middle achieving sixth grade students in middle schools performed on a par with sixth grade students in elementary school; high achieving middle school sixth graders, however, performed at a level .5 grade equivalents below their elementary counterparts.

Knowledge of this information has caused teachers to develop an intense interest in possible causes for these results with an emphasis on improving results for all students, placing a special focus on this one group of lower achieving students. James Wilson, principal at Burnet Middle School, said,

> Teachers committed themselves to an all out effort to help their students do better. New materials were used, resource people brought in, and extra time spent on analyzing early results. As a result of our efforts, the outcomes were very positive. In comparison to the previous year, Burnet improved its overall passing rate of 57 percent to 71 percent, an increase of 14 percentage points.

The Amarillo Independent School District used the Organizational Health Instrument (OHI), developed by Dr. Marvin Fairman, to provide information about the organization. Although this is not a measure of actual organizational performance, it does provide a picture of the overall health of the organization.

Rebecca Harrison, principal at Caprock High School, had worked with her staff to share more information and to develop a greater sense of faculty ownership for the school. She said,

> Goal focus went up 9 percent on the Organizational Health Instrument. Communication went up 8 percent and power equalization went up 12 percent. The staff has made progress in working together and working to improve the learning environment.

Using the OHI as a measure, Principal David Cargill and the Amarillo High School teachers were able to generate significant improvements in the school ethos. They improved on every single measure of organizational health in a one year period, resulting in more than a 40 percent increase in morale among those who completed the pre- and post-instrument at the school. Other areas of great increase were the adaptability and autonomy of the faculty. Much of this occurred as a result of obtaining and sharing key information.

Phillip Schmidt, a principal in the Springfield School District in Illinois, was interested in the learning climate at Lanphier High School. He discussed his interest with teachers and administrators in the school and it was decided that they needed some kind of a measurement of the general learning climate. They felt that the learning climate from the Illinois Quality of School Index (IQSI) would be quite effective and should be shared with all faculty for planning purposes. He stated,

> The IQSI learning climate segment provides paired results across 23 separate items, with one scale indicating the degree to which the school demonstrates the characteristics involved and the second scale rating

the importance of the characteristics to quality schooling. As a result of an analysis of the IQSI scale, the school focused on:

- reducing anxiety among teachers
- relationships with students
- the image of Lanphier High School
- improving the instructional practices occurring at the school

Separate groups of staff, parents, students, teachers, and administrators met to identify activities of importance in creating an improved learning climate. Many suggestions were made by these groups. Some of them include

- being a helper rather than a critic in dealing with students
- insuring proper sequencing in instructional activities
- stating specific instructional objectives
- having clear directions, expectations, and learning objectives so students know what is expected of them
- insisting that students do their assignments
- demonstrating an allowance for individual difference
- being specific in praise

Each person within the school was required to take a good deal of responsibility in accomplishing the goals of the program. In addition, data was made available to the staff so that they could measure the results of their work. The success of the Lanphier program was assessed in relation to the following criteria:

- reduction in student failures
- reduction in the number of student discipline referrals
- an increase in student attendance
- an increase in PSAT and ACT scores of students

Other Modes of Communicating Understanding

There are many means by which information is shared within organizations. Drs. Richard L. Draft and Robert H. Lengel (1986) proposed a model in which seven structural mechanisms fit along a continuum. The continuum represents the organization's capacity for reducing uncertainty and increasing the use of information in decision making. Effective work cultures support communication by as many direct contact, boundary spanning, group means as possible. Figure 7–1 presents their continuum.

The Vertical Team

One of the best flows of communication is through group meetings and face-to-face communications, since this provides both two-way communication and an opportunity to clarify misunderstanding. The vertical team is the strongest approach to effective upward and downward communication of information. Vertical teams advocate debate, clarification, and enactment instead of providing large amounts of data. If the representatives of the team are quite aware of the information on their level, they can greatly assist in achieving understanding of information at other levels within the organization. This means they must take time to share their horizontal understanding on the vertical plane and their vertical understanding on the horizontal plane. There are people at all levels who have a true understanding of information and can clarify any misunderstanding that might develop.

Members of a vertical team can get immediate feedback from each of the levels without the "filtering" that often occurs as reactions are passed through channels of communication. Was information received correctly and clearly? Was the information found to be valuable and was it received favorably? Did the messages contain inaccuracies? These and many other questions can be answered directly and quite quickly in an effectively operating vertical team.

The vertical team also provides a direct link to employee expertise. Employees at different levels have specialized knowledge and expertise

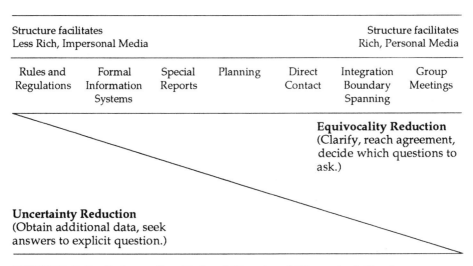

FIGURE 7–1 Information Role of Structural Characteristics for Reducing Equivocality or Uncertainty

that they can bring to the team discussions. No one knows more about a specific operation than the person who performs that operation daily. Development of a quality, service-driven culture requires a lot of communication between central administrators and school building personnel who are in direct contact with both students and parents on a day-to-day basis. Each is "in the know" to an extent that others at different levels are not.

The success of a vertical team is not automatic. The leader can stifle or squelch the candor of the vertical team by leaking his or her own ideas to subordinates before they have had a chance to state their own. Once people know what the boss thinks, the whole discussion is likely to shift in that direction.

Another possible problem is the fear of what might be discovered. Fear can make most people evasive, breaking down full and accurate disclosure. When information is not "filtered" or "distorted," it may reflect poorly on an individual or a group. That means that people must learn how to deal effectively with both the good news and the bad. Mistakes, misconceptions, and ineptitudes are bitter pills to swallow, however, when open, free-flowing forums exist, such situations are bound to occur. If they are handled gently and with courtesy and grace they can help to build trust and alleviate fear. When they are not, they will destroy the successful functioning of the team.

Organizations and clients must be able to accept responsible failures. Failures will not be tolerated for a long period, but they must be expected. Sports figures are noted for saying, "Show me a person who doesn't mind losing, and I'll show you a loser." Everyone should hate failure, but it is necessary to achieve continuous improvement. This is what toleration for risk is all about. For continuous improvement to become a reality, "permission and forgiveness" must be available.

Everyone who works together must learn to solve problems, focus on improvement, and accomplish shared visions. Employees must focus on quality in the work and not become defensive about problems they might need to correct or protecting their "territory" or "turf." Dr. Deming states, "People have to be able to tell managers when something is wrong." Dr. Crosby jokes, "Once you put on a suit no one tells you the truth anymore." Teachers must be able to share their concern with their supervisors.

The employee is, in fact, the supervisor's immediate customer. When a student has a unique problem that the teacher is unable to solve, the principal is expected to assist the teacher. For example, the principal should not consider teachers who send students to the office "poor disciplinarians," because this will result in few, if any, students being sent to the office. Customer consciousness suggests that the principal's assistance is needed by the teacher in a supportive and positive way. This type of honest and open communication is built upon mutual trust. This trust is built upon collaboration, harmony, respect, dignity, truth, support, equity, risk-sharing, and mutually shared visions of excellence for the organization.

As people are encouraged to talk about their concerns, aspirations, and hopes, opportunities for improvements, and new visions are bound to develop. Once employees see that problems are being resolved and improvements are being made, they will develop an attitude of continuous improvement. They will keep their ideal vision in mind and begin putting in the needed efforts to achieve the ideal.

Suggestion Boxes

Suggestion boxes are used to encourage employees to come up with ideas on how to improve jobs. Employees submit new ideas to their supervisors, and supervisors are expected to acknowledge receipt of the suggestion with a thank you letter within twenty-four hours of receipt. They then have a fixed period of time to communicate in writing whether the idea is acceptable for implementation.

One example of the benefit of such a suggestion system was provided by Phil Crosby (1988). An employee recognized that the unpacking of incoming deliveries resulted in an extraordinary amount of shrink wrap that was placed in costly dumpsters and hauled off at additional cost. At the other end of the plant, packing materials were being bought to be stuffed in boxes to insure safe shipment. The employee came up with a solution to these problems and suggested that the shrink wrap be shredded and used as packing material for the new shipments. The cost savings were significant and the suggestion was revolutionary for the plant, and is still having significant implications for the plant. This suggestion would never have developed prior to the change in organizational culture to stress the value of employee innovation. Management was too far from operations to be able to see this potential cost saving, and employees ideas were not valued in the culture.

Customer Research

An important source of information is customer/consumer research. A central theme of Deming's work is the focus on customer satisfaction. Customers cannot be satisfied until they are identified, their needs are determined, and an idea of good service is developed. Information must be collected regularly from consumers before any such questions can be answered .

Performance Measures and Reports

Deming (1960) and Joseph M. Juran (1992) call for statistical approaches to data analysis, reporting, and communicating. They suggest that employees need to be taught how to read and interpret statistical charts spelling out variations of the ideal vision. These charts should be produced and updated on a regular basis. Accurate and timely data regarding the performance of students, complaints, student achievement, attendance, learning problems, and extra-curricular activities must be quickly analyzed and given back to school employees for action. The actual statistical methods used include Pareto diagrams, cause and effect diagrams, histograms, control charts, scatter diagrams, graphs, and checksheets. The belief is that employees will automatically make adjustments to hit the center of the target if data is provided regarding how close they are to their goal. The absence of this feedback will naturally result in more, larger, and longer error.

Schools use various measures of performance to help achieve their own visions of excellence. In order to help El Paso teachers know how well students in their classes were performing, a special program of information feedback and planning was devised around the system of standardized testing. The program focused on raising student, teacher, and parent expectations of how well students could perform on standardized tests. This was especially important in schools that had a high percentage of low socio-economic status students and a high percentage of minorities on campus. The program was successful in that test scores over one year increased from 3 percent to 17 percent, depending on grade level and area of the tests.

Gloria Boyer, principal at Douglas Elementary School, said,

> Testing efforts at Douglas have shown gains. When results are analyzed, grade level meetings are held. In these meetings administrative and teacher expectations are expressed and discussed in view of test scores; classes are ranked by subtest scores and rankings are noted and clarified; finally, teachers and administrators rehash and brainstorm ideas that will improve students' test scores.

According to TQM experts, the timely reporting of actual performance data has been a problem in American businesses. For example, a well-run company experiencing recurring failures in its second highest volume product did not notify the plant manufacturing the failure-prone product until more than three years after they were first detected. A plant manager was shocked to find out that the waste stream leaving the plant in one year had a material value of 2.9 million dollars. A production line foreman set up a comfortable level of overfill on 50 pound packs, only to discover years later that it cost his employer $180,000 a year.

Many types of costs can be generated when people are not aware of the results of their activities. The same types of problems, although much more subtle, occur in education. Without the feedback of performance information, educators cannot be expected to work on the right aspects of quality. As Deming is fond of saying, "the control chart is no substitute for the brain." However, the interpretation of data can help the brain work more effectively for the organization.

To stimulate as much brain power as possible, output measures and charts must be highly visible. All employees must know how to interpret charts relevant to their work and know how to get data they need to determine how well they are working toward their vision. People like to be measured when the measure is fair and open and related to what they believe to be important. However, data should not become another part of the orientation process. There is no need to focus on methods of collecting perfect data. Phillip Crosby (1988) suggests that's like "someone on a tight budget keeping neat records of overspending." The reports should stimulate the brain in regards to continual improvement, not overwhelm it.

The effective organizational culture will include structures that ensure timely feedback of results to everyone within the organization. Everyone should receive some form of control chart that compares actual outcomes to the desired expectations. Measurement should reduce the variance in interpretation of success. With weekly feedback, how you're doing becomes crystal clear.

Performance Feedback

Educators agree that the intent of normed tests is to discern the level of academic growth of individual students. However, in practice, schools tend to be compared with each other. One cannot find fault with evaluation and assessment if it is used correctly—to measure student growth in key areas. Too often, however, schools, staff, and programs are compared, to the detriment of all three. Schools are individual entities, having unique school populations and uniquely different cultures, problems, and possibilities. Education should not use data to mass produce products. Schools should use data to work out their own unique needs based on accurate, appropriate information. The type of information collected should include students' scores on teacher-made tests and quizzes, as well as results from standardized tests. Such information on performance outcomes can also include students' attendance, discipline record, involvement in class sessions and extra-curricular activity, motivation for learning, and attitude toward school, the class, and themselves. The quality of learning outcomes must be continuously measured and fed back to teachers so they are aware of their success level with each student.

Teachers must know on a weekly basis if their students are attaining higher levels of achievement, becoming more involved in instruction, and expressing greater confidence in themselves and their ability to learn. Teachers believe in and practice what they find to work in their own classroom with their students. They make decisions regarding possible improvements very pragmatically, and unless the system provides measures of results for verification of new innovations and improvements, continuous improvement of their performance is highly unlikely.

In studying 61 innovative practices in schools and classrooms in 146 districts, Dr. D. P. Crandal (1983) determined that teacher commitment developed primarily after the implementation of a new idea or program. The reason for this commitment was that teachers' support for ideas grew after they had seen some positive changes in student learning within their own classrooms.

Thomas Guskey (1986) found that,

> Teachers who used the master learning procedures and gained evidence of improvement in the learning outcomes of their students expressed more positive attitudes toward teaching and greater personal responsibility for their students' learning—similar to a sense of self-efficacy. In other words, these teachers came to like teaching more and felt that they had a stronger influence on the learning of their students . . . Only teachers who used the new procedures and gained evidence of positive change in their students' learning expressed these changes in their beliefs and attitudes. In the absence of such evidence, no significant change in teachers' beliefs or attitudes was found to occur.

The important factor in changing beliefs or attitudes and improving performance seems to be feedback of performance information. Performance appraisals can be used to cover up the absence of objective data but cannot replace objective data. Teachers' beliefs and attitudes about performance are primarily a result, rather than a cause, of change in the learning outcomes of students. Without evidence of positive change in students' learning, significant change in the beliefs and attitudes of teachers is very unlikely. This requires organizations to continuously monitor and feedback outcomes. Guskey concluded,

> If the use of new practices is to be sustained and changes are to endure, teachers must receive regular feedback on the effects of these changes on student learning. . . . Therefore, plans for implementing a new program or innovation should include specific procedures by which teachers can receive evidence of the effectiveness of their efforts.

. . . Whatever the student learning outcome employed, it is critically important to plan some procedure by which teachers can receive regular feedback on that outcome to access the effects of their efforts.

The vertical team in the **Cedar Rapids School District** wanted to have a positive mechanism for getting performance feedback to individual teachers. They wanted the feedback to clarify and provide direction to the individual efforts of teachers and principals without forcing them into preconceived plans. Outcome-based (or driven) education came to be seen and accepted as a sufficiently broad and powerful concept for feedback. Outcome-based education (OBE) was seen as a method to guide the district's continuous progress for a period of years, and first surfaced in the school board statement, ". . . a school improvement focus that uses student achievement data as the basis for decision making."

The OBE initiative produced massive amounts of activity. Action plans were driven by student performance, as is recommended in the total quality management approach. Newell C. Lash, deputy superintendent, stated, "What we test is what we teach and what we teach is what derives from our objectives as suggested by Fenwick English in his curriculum auditing procedures."

Three main philosophical principles form the foundation of OBE. They are:

1. All students can learn and succeed.
2. Success breeds success.
3. School controls the conditions of success.

The emphasis is on continual growth and success as measured by student performance. The assessment component provides the data necessary to measure student progress. Assessment data is made available to teachers as quickly as possible so they can:

1. correct student deficiencies when necessary;
2. provide enrichment opportunities;
3. establish a basis for continuous monitoring of curriculum; and
4. evaluate the degree to which classroom performance has achieved district goals.

In other words, the data is used to adjust to the current situation and then, when needed, to go back and look at the real cause of less-than-satisfactory results. The data is used to help provide continuous improvement.

The emphasis is most heavily placed on helping teachers understand and implement outcome driven improvements. The results provide immediate feedback on how well the student is doing, and can be compared to how well students have done in past situations. Variances can be used to evaluate curricular and instructional approaches and measure the quality of the learning that is occurring. In this way, student performance becomes a major input in decision making.

Recognizing that a number of effective school researchers found that frequent monitoring is a key ingredient in an effective school, the Norfolk public schools established a formal system for monitoring student progress. In Norfolk, monitoring of student performance was not a single, end-of-the-year event. The monitoring system looked at student performance in every facet of the school's program. An effective monitoring system enabled administrators, teachers, and support staff to identify what had or had not been mastered, what was or was not effective, and provided timely information so that adjustments could be made.

A very important part of this student monitoring was the disaggregation of data. Student performance was measured in light of the student's socio-economic status. A teacher and school could discover whether or not the student's performance met criteria of equity and quality. Monitoring is the key in determining all forms of success, in that the teacher can examine the effectiveness of a new program on the basis of hard data and can also chart the improvement in student knowledge and performance.

In order to provide appropriate monitoring, the Norfolk Public Schools developed a computerized system called the "Monitor and Mastery Test System." The monitor tests indicated the extent to which students accomplished objectives identified by the system as being appropriate for appraising the instructional programs. The mastery test measured student performance on individual skills. Other tests included teacher-made tests, SRA achievement series, PSAT and SAT tests, and the Virginia competency tests.

Of course, there are a number of other ways to monitor progress. Homework is often used. Other measures include attendance, dropout rates, discipline, vandalism rates, participation in co-curricular and extracurricular activities, and enrollment in advanced-level classes.

Some educators argue that their work cannot be measured. When work defies measurement, it suggests that the worker is incapable of producing results. Without measurable results, there are only activities and costs. To produce results, it is necessary to know what results need to be measured. Measurement and feedback are simply collecting and reporting indicators that allow educators to conclude how close they are coming to the ideal vision they hope to achieve.

Measurements might include returning all parental telephone calls, scores on criterion referenced tests, perfect attendance at parent conferences, placing special education students properly, reducing dropouts/dropins, increased participation in extra-curricular activity, family and business support of education, successful college placements, good reports from employers, well-written essays on research assignments, improved scores on standardized tests, grades on student homework papers, and reduction of disciplinary problems.

Frances Logan-Thomas, a teacher at Meadowdale Elementary School in Dayton, Ohio, describes how she uses student performance data to help make instructional decisions and program plans. She states,

> Armed with the statistics from the California Achievement Test scores administered the previous year and my own observation, I was able to ascertain the learning level for each student. I discovered that approximately 38 percent of the youngsters were lacking the prerequisites to experience success at the second grade level. The range of abilities as evidenced by the test scores dictated that I use varied approaches, provide adequate practice time, and use different mediums to teach different students and different objectives. Using teacher-made and some commercial tests, I evaluated the students on a regular basis. If the assessment indicated that the youngster needed additional instruction, then different approaches and other correctives were put in place. The progress of each student was plotted by subject area. This was an excellent method of recording student and class performance. It provided instant feedback for both the student and the teacher and was a superb source of motivation for the students.

Input, process, and/or output can be measured. It should be up to the employees to determine what needs to be measured and to determine the quality of results. Sources of information used to determine what results are desirable and should be measured include:

- school board minutes and goals
- plans of action
- evaluations
- latest trends and research
- interviews with city council and business leaders
- media
- annual and quarterly reports
- professional associations
- PTA minutes
- personal/professional assessment
- school plans
- end-of-the-year reports
- assessment reports
- surveys

- meetings
- visits to other schools and school districts
- curriculum and instructional guides
- consultants
- vocational/career performance data
- reports on student performance
- futuristic scenarios
- publications
- suggestions from experts

Eddie West, the principal at Ottawa High School in Grand Rapids, Michigan, believes that the quality of education in his school will continue to improve as long as there is an effective feedback system on student academic progress. Multiple assessment methods are used, including teacher-made tests, samples of students' work, mastery skills checklists, criterion referenced tests, and norm referenced tests. The data is important, but the analysis of the students' progress is the essential ingredient. The results of the testing must be efficiently and effectively analyzed and used to plan ways to improve individual student performance as well as the instructional program in general.

West states,

> Administrators, teachers, and counselors will frequently review pertinent student achievement data to identify subject area and/or specific classes where overall student achievement levels are low. A specific plan of action to assist each student, teacher and department will be developed based on the results of the data reviewed. Principals, counselors, and teachers will develop a systematic method to identify students who have potential for success, but who are not progressing at an acceptable level. Overall department plans will include evidence of attainment including written departmental suggestions on how they plan to reduce student failures.

An effort is underway to computerize the assessment system so as to provide much quicker feedback regarding student progress.

Ottawa High School also incorporated the Michigan Educational Assessment of progress and other evaluation instruments into their model for evaluation. The model used outcome data and course assessment (grades/test scores) to provide feedback to teachers so that they could continuously improve the education of students and the quality of instructional programs. West continued,

The faculty and administrators will foster efforts to increase the percentile ranking of all Ottawa Hills students on the MEAP, CAT, SAT, ACT, and competency testing programs and other nationally normed tests in all areas and for achievement levels with specific emphasis on correctness of expression, the use of resource material, and problem-solving skills. All staff members will consistently stress the importance of academic achievement to all students and stress the relationship between academic success and the process of lifelong learning and success.

This is in congruence with school board goals, school plans, and curriculum and instructional guides.

The Bel-Aire Elementary school in Dade County, Florida, developed a system to measure the program/teacher effects on educational programs, student achievement, and staff effectiveness. Michael Sullivan, the principal at Bel-Aire, summarized the educational impact of a number of school proposals that were in the process of being implemented. He stated,

> Improved SAT scores, more desirable professional attitudes of staff, a larger percentage of ESOL students progressing beyond level two, increased fluency in Spanish, increased student attendance and retention, improved pre- to post-attitude assessment surveys of teachers, students and parents, increased number and frequency of parent contacts, increased attendance at PTA meetings and open houses, increased student utilization of standard English, and raising achievement averages will be used to plot the success of program implementation efforts that are now underway.

The Abraham Lincoln High School in Denver, according to principal Christine Johnson, monitors and compares grades and standardized test scores. The school completes a grade-by-grade profile comparison for each student. They also do a community needs assessment and collect various reports of progress from the individual staff and department staff during the year. They survey administrators, teachers, students, and parents on an annual basis.

At Abraham Lincoln, statistical reports are produced to determine the number of students participating in various activities and programs (such as advanced placement programs), entering student contests, receiving student recognition and awards, graduating, and making the honor roll. Reports are also produced regarding discipline problems within the school, attendance rate, suspensions, and dropouts. There is an effort to maintain records of faculty involvement in various forms of development activity and any form of staff recognition. Special displays, assemblies, programs, activities, civic group and business participation are also reported. Numbers of people involved in PTAs, booster clubs, and teacher assistance programs are also collected and reported on a periodic basis. All this information is collected and reported to help the school focus on maximizing student success and continue program improvement.

Once teachers and administrators recognize and understand the possibilities, they can create measurements to help them achieve performance improvement. Everyone must have a handle on how they are doing. Improvement begins by knowing the existing quality as well as the ideal vision of what should exist.

Performance Appraisals

Performance appraisals are typically intimidating operations in most schools. An individual, usually the principal, spends a short period of time in a teacher's class, and, on that basis, describes the quality of teaching occurring in that classroom. Sergiovanni (1992) suggests that

> evaluation systems don't matter a nickel—they're one of the biggest wastes of time in the world, because it's not important what a person does the two times that you're in the classroom observing him or her.

There are no certificates on the wall that qualify the principal to perform this highly complex act. The effect of the appraisal is very real on the teacher's professional life and ego. If there is no additional information, teachers must get their sense of success from these subjective systems such as principal, colleague, parent, and student evaluations.

The end results of performance appraisals are not as bad as they seem, since most reviews are positive and many of the forms and scales are quite innocuous. The unwritten law for principals is "be kind and gentle." Phillip Crosby (1988) sees the same situation in business, and states,

> If there is doubt about this, just examine the reviews of every single secretary in any corporate headquarters. There are none who are less than above average, and all recommended heartily. I guarantee that.
>
> The result of this is to make the reviews counter productive. They not only don't weed out the bad; they don't bring the good to the surface. And that is what drives people nuts.
>
> Dishonest evaluations show people that the company has no integrity, doesn't trust a system it forces on them, and doesn't really care about finding talent if it exists. They feel ignored and abused. . . . The

employees quickly realize that management has no way of knowing who is the fairest of them all, except through luck and instinct.

This same view is shared by a number of the other total quality management experts. In fact, Deming suggests that organizations as they now exist should eliminate yearly performance appraisals. He finds that most appraisal systems unwittingly destroy teamwork. Performance appraisal data can not and will not replace or satisfy the need for effective measures of quality performance. If the organization has time, effective appraisal systems that include an appraisal conference can serve as an effective means of communicating on performance and development. However, without time, an effective system, and an appraisal conference, they probably do more harm than good. They are not a replacement for good solid measures of outcome performance.

It is difficult, if not impossible, to achieve excellence without knowledge of performance outcomes. Student performance becomes a major part of communication regarding continuous improvement of the organization. Performance appraisals support activities, process and control; measures of performance support improved results, shared decision-making and accurate communication. The reason for existence in an organization is to achieve desired outcomes. The purpose of much of the organization's communication is to support the improvement of desired outcomes.

The Action-Oriented Culture

An effective work culture is an action-oriented culture. To support this culture, leaders must develop new mechanisms for growing, harvesting, and sharing ideas. The best way to support an action-oriented culture is with action-oriented teams of professionals from all segments of the organization. Teams should have full responsibility for generating ideas and seeing them through implementation and evaluation. Opportunities must be provided for lots of innovation, pilot tests, and prototypes. And it should not be forgotten that it is difficult, if not impossible, to achieve excellence without accurate effective communication.

Slogans like "Do it right the first time" must be eliminated. There is no "right" in continual improvement, only getting better. Experimenting with and practicing improvements is the only way to get better. Struggling with the implementation of new ideas teaches what it takes to improve.

One of the common axioms in today's education system is "more for less." However, the total quality management experts suggest that executives that use such phrases don't really understand them. They annoy employees and create hard feelings, neither of which will successfully achieve goals. Deming states,

> American management thinks the way to increase profits is to cut costs. How ridiculous! If you concentrate on building quality and eliminating mistakes, your costs will go down automatically.

Our education system will continue to play a critical role in providing young men and women with the foundation they will need to actively and fully contribute to the American pursuit of excellence. Yet, in a time when the pace of change has accelerated so rapidly, it is becoming increasingly clear that our education system, just like business and industry, must also be capable of responding to those changes. Crosby (1988) states,

> People can't last forever; the body eventually wears out. There is no way to prevent that from happening. But organizations have no need to die. . . . They can be continuously useful rather than add to the turbulence that we make of the world. They can provide something dependable rather than yet another source of disappointment.

Bibliography

Brandt, Ron. "On Rethinking Leadership: A Conversation with Tom Sergiovanni." *Educational Leadership*. February, 1992.

Crandal, D. P. "The Teacher's Role in School Improvement." *Educational Leadership*. 41, (1983).

Crosby, Philip B. *The Eternally Successful Organization*. New York: New American Library, 1988.

Crosby, Philip B. *Quality Without Tears*. New York: McGraw Hill Book Company, 1984.

Crosby, Philip B. *Quality is Free*. New York: McGraw-Hill Book Company, 1979.

Deming, W. Edward. *Sample Design in Business Research*. New York: John Wiley & Sons, Inc., 1960.

Deming, W. Edward. *Out of the Crisis*. Cambridge, Mass.: The Massachusetts Institute of Technology Center for Advanced Engineering Study, 1986.

Reprinted by permission of Draft, Richard L. and Lengel, Robert H. "Organizational Information Requirements, Media Richness and Structural Design." *Management Science*, 32 (May 1986). Copyright 1986, The Institute of Management Science.

English, Fenwick W. *Curriculum Auditing*. Lancaster, Pennsylvania: Technomic Publishing Company, Inc., 1988.

Guskey, Thomas R. "Staff Development and the Process of Teacher Change." *Educational Researcher*, 15 (May 1986). Copyright 1986 © by the American Educational Research Association. Reprinted by permission of the publisher.

Hendricks, Charles F. and Triplett, Arlene. "TQM: Strategy for '90's Management." *Personnel Administrator* (December, 1989).

Holpp, Lawrence. "Achievement, Motivation and Kaizen." *Training and Development Journal* (October, 1989).

Juran, Joseph M. *Juran's New Quality Roadmap: Planning, Setting, Reaching Quality Goals.* New York: Free Press, 1992.

Morgan, Brian S. and Schiemann, William A. "Why Internal Communications is Failing." *Public Relations Journal,* Copyright © March, 1983. Reprinted by permission of *Public Relations Journal,* published by the Public Relations Society of America, New York, NY.

Oberle, Joseph. "Quality Gurus: The Men and Their Message." *Training,* (January, 1990).

Ross, Barbara. "W. Edward Deming: Shogun of Quality Control." *Magazine for Financial Executives,* (February, 1986).

Senge, Peter M. *The Fifth Discipline.* New York: Doubleday Currency, 1990.

Senge, Peter M. "The Leader's New Work: Building Learning Organizations." *Sloan Management Review: Report Series,* 32 (Fall, 1990). Reprinted by permission of the publisher by the Sloan Management Review Association. All rights reserved.

_____. "The Gurus of Quality." *Traffic Management,* 29 (July 1990).

8

Personal and Professional Development

One of the central correlates of excellence in education is that all organizational members must focus on personal and professional development each year. The culture of excellence suggests that it is professionally immoral not to develop and grow in every single year of life. Thus, development and growth become moral imperatives within the culture of an effective work group. Development and growth and their applications to improve school effectiveness are absolutely basic to a worthy professional life. Thus, the normative environment of the organization promotes and demands personal and professional development.

The culture of development is closely related to the concepts of progress and change. Progress occurs when more people believe in and want to use new materials, new behaviors, new practices, and new beliefs or understandings. Therefore, the culture of development is linked to progress and school effectiveness, and they are one in the same in application. According to Ernest Boyer, the president of the Carnegie Foundation for the Advancement of Teaching,

> The only way we're going to get from where we are to where we want to be is through staff development . . . when you talk about school improvement, you're talking about people improvement . . . the school is the people, so when we talk about excellence or improvement or progress, we're really focusing on the people who make up the building . . . it means providing the time and the resources for people to better understand what they are trying to accomplish, to have a sense of

direction and a feeling that in the end what they will do will be recognized, rewarded, and be significant.

Effective organizations do not differentiate between people and program development. A vision for school improvement becomes reality through the life-long development process of its employees. Dr. Michael Fullan (1990) states,

> It has been well known for at least 25 years that staff development and successful innovation or improvement are intimately related. However, even in the narrow sense of successful implementation of a single innovation, people have underestimated what it takes to accomplish this close interrelationship, more fundamentally . . . we must go beyond the narrow conception of staff development to consider how it relates to instructional development of schools.

The simple premise, "nothing changes if the people within the organization do not change," becomes a foundation of all school effectiveness efforts.

All personal and professional developmental activity within the organization, although loosely defined, is designed and implemented with an eye toward increasing the effectiveness of the school and the school division. In effective organizations, concern for the transfer of employee growth and development to innovation and improved practice is minimal because the two are viewed as one in the same. The culture itself produces the mechanisms by which transfer of knowledge and skills occur by creating a climate that favors the application of development to improve organizational effectiveness. Employees will choose to apply their new knowledge because that characteristic is prized by their organization's culture.

Such beliefs develop over time and are preserved through institutional memory. Transference of growth becomes a basic value, expectation, and practice of the effective organization. Once this culture exists, there is little need to exert tight, ineffective, administrative control over what one learns. The culture keeps individual development on track.

The education challenge, then, is to generate a culture conducive to development and shared commitment to excellence. Excellence is a prominently projected value that is encouraged and supported within the work group. Extensive sharing of knowledge is modeled by all those within the organization and becomes a custom of the work culture. Excellence cannot be mandated, imposed or coerced. It grows in those who are employed within the organization. It emerges as a quality that is part of the values and norms of the organization, shared by the people who work within it.

The culture of excellence has been described as being "responsible autonomy," "collective autonomy," or "strategic independence." In this way, individuals are given freedom to have some level of control over their personal and professional development. They recognize that collaborative planning, personal and professional development, and innovation are essential to improving educational effectiveness. Mary Anne Raywid, Charles Tesconi, and Donald Warren (1984) summed up this concept quite well when they said,

> Collegiality can produce the coherence good schools require, and a vitality far beyond the reach of formalistic rules. . . . in any undertaking such as a school, where success depends on a substantial degree of autonomy, a shared ethos provides the cohesion needed to sustain individual effort.

There is significant proof that staff development and effective implementation of innovations are strongly interrelated. Successful change requires learning how to do something new. The process of change becomes complicated, in that the learner must establish his or her own developmental outcomes, and the work culture shapes the mode by which the employee transfers new behavior. This means that the culture is a primary means of establishing what an employee learns by determining what is to be implemented within the organization.

The effective work culture encourages its members to independently explore activities, while it develops a set of expectations, values, and mores that suggest that members apply what they have learned to improve the organization. Development, collegiality, shared vision, and a supportive work culture are probably the most important factors in the likelihood of any implementation success. Thus, school divisions that are characterized by these norms are much more likely to implement school effectiveness successfully.

The challenge of cultural leadership, then, is to help individuals to sustain increased development while helping them to see how it can benefit the entire organization. Effective development programs allow for this differentiation of individual and organizational needs while at the same time focusing on the goals of both. The organization must develop individually and collectively as well.

This paradox is addressed in *Changing School Culture Through Staff Development*, a book edited by Dr. Bruce Joyce (1990). The book's proposals were ambitious, yet the various contributors believed that change could occur, must occur, and would occur. In concluding, Drs. Joyce and Murphy state,

> This mission, the authors agree, requires a major restructuring of the workplace. Furthermore, this restructuring is seen as much more than

quantitative increases in instructional leadership, collegial activity, or amounts of high-quality training. Rather, it involves a transformation of the roles of all personnel and a reorientation of the norms of the workplace, including how the educator's job is constructed and how teachers, administrators, and service providers relate with and perceive one another. The challenge is to create an ethos that is almost an inversion of the one Lortie so accurately described in *School Teacher*. That is, vertical and horizontal isolation and separation of roles will be replaced by integration and collaboration. Anti-intellectualism and protectionism will be replaced by thoughtful inquiry, inclusiveness, and an overlapping of roles.

A fellow colleague in the Danforth School Administrator Fellowship Program, Dr. Daniel Duke (1987), has also written about the relationship between personal and professional development and school improvement. He believes that when development takes into account organizational culture, it serves to nurture a spirit of community and common interest. When it does not, and staff development is not effectively rooted in the local culture, divisiveness and squandered precious resources are most often the outcome.

The culture of excellence does not try to develop and improve the organization—an abstract concept destined to fail. The culture of excellence develops people and encourages them to transfer their knowledge to improve the education of youth. They share their successes with colleagues throughout the school system. Effective cultures develop the teachers and administrators so they can plan and implement the solutions that best fit their situations. The teachers and administrators figure ways that their successful solutions can be instituted.

Of course, not all members of the staff will want to exert the energy and time to transfer their development activities. Fortunately, in every organization there are groups of individuals who emerge as energized and empowered and willing to share successful activities. These are the people who become the "zealots" and the "champions" for improving organizational effectiveness. These are the people who create new approaches to educating today's youth—approaches that are based on their personal and professional development and that are shaped by the vision, mission, and goals of the entire school system. These are the ideas that grow at the grass roots level and have tremendous staying power. These are the ideas that energize and provide a positive charge to the work culture.

Results in which students, parents, community and employees take pride grow out of common efforts to achieve excellence. The personal dedication of individuals within a school make a classroom, a school, and sometimes even an entire school district display real greatness. The essence of excellence develops through the commitment, zest, energy, care, fun, friendship, enthusiasm, extraordinary individual contribution, and celebration that grows around vision and is supported by individual development and implementation efforts.

Innovation and Institutionalization

Tom Peters and Robert Waterman (1982) discovered that there were small groups within excellent organizations that created truly significant improvement efforts. These small, unofficial groups often had more significant impact than did departments up to 100 times their size who were charged with research and development. Effective organizational culture makes sure that such innovative groups have an opportunity to come forward, grow, and flourish.

In business, creativity without action-oriented follow-through is a barren form of behavior. People who have the know-how, energy, daring and staying power to implement ideas are needed. Peters and Waterman described these groups as "skunkworks." Skunkworks are groups of champions (skunks) who form a team to make innovative ideas a reality. An innovation rarely succeeds unless a skunkwork is determined to make it happen. This is how the 3M Post-It Note™ pads became a successful innovation. Not surprisingly, skunkworks often fail, but they are the creative forces that make a difference in organizations. When a practical and successful innovation occurs, it usually has a skunkwork at the heart of it.

Excellent work cultures are structured to create, support, and protect skunkworks. They develop people with the hopes that a group will form and try out some new ideas, a few of which will become the company's future direction. They provide some freedom for those individuals to test ideas, and, if successful, they encourage efforts to institute the ideas. These companies help their people to believe that they can do great things for the organization. They look to them to develop the needed ideas, products, and programs for the future.

The two "watch words" in effective work cultures are personal and professional development and innovation. These work cultures use development programs and approaches that institute innovation, and ensure that communication is integrated vertically through all echelons without barriers. Effective cultures work through informal organizational structures, the members are developed and given freedom to try new ideas, they tolerate failures, are willing to accept mistakes, and learn and grow from them. In fact, tolerance of failure is an important part of the excellent company's future.

Tom Peters and Nancy Austin (1985) expanded on the ideas of skunkworks, stating that innovating regularly is a basis for personal development and organizational improvement. The management task should be to create a culture that supports development, communication, experimentation, innovation, and the groups of people (the skunkworks) that make it all happen. In such a culture, the organization improves and new product ideas are created and able to grow. Creating this type of culture is often a sloppy, messy long term process, but it is the way that great ideas and innovations grow. Experience shows that the more an organization tries to simplify and control plans, the more innovation and success fade.

Successful innovation occurs rapidly when tested on real programs and products using real people. These tests are usually controlled, but are done before massive reports and expertise have been accumulated. Management develops its people and then lets them achieve perfection and completion by giving them the opportunity to implement what they have learned. Mistakes are tolerated, supported, and understood, however, they are corrected quickly. This only occurs in a very decentralized, site-based organizational structure.

People must champion visions or the visions die. No ordinary involvement with a new idea provides the energy required to cope with the indifference, resistance, and fear that change provokes. People must be provided an opportunity to develop their knowledge, skills, and abilities related to new ideas and directions with the hope that a small core of passionate advocates will form, experiment, and institutionalize the needed changes and new directions. A skunkwork group understands organizational vision and turns it into a mission about which it is fanatical. Typically, this mission must grow and be fed at the grass roots level if it is ever to receive cultural support and commitment. The skunkworks must be developed, fostered, and nurtured if progress and innovation are to ever become a part of the organization.

Cumulative, Incremental Implementation

In education, personal and professional development of staff members should stimulate some level of passionate skunkwork along the edges of the more traditional school district structure. Schools must have a nucleus of people who are excited and knowledgeable about a new idea that they have learned and are developing for their classroom, school, and school system.

Skunkworks can implement and test educational ideas in a very short period of time and in a very controlled situation with minimal negative impact. If the test fails, the teacher will feel quite responsible and pick up the pieces, and will make sure that everything is put back together properly. If the idea succeeds, the teacher becomes a proponent, disciple, or champion who helps to get the idea institutionalized.

Skunkwork is driven by a passionate approach to personal and professional development of every educator; it is a communication process that crosses over roles and responsibilities—like a vertical team or an educational culture that promotes understanding, ownership, trust, innovation, and commitment. It succeeds when teachers and other employees are allowed to champion their ideas in small controlled tests.

Teams of champions encourage employees to learn more about and develop their ideas and begin testing them on an incremental basis. Most advances are incremental and grow slowly as the ideas are refined. New and related ideas are attached as the innovation progresses and catches on. This is called "cumulative innovation." When educators accumulate small, incremental "wins," they are much more structurally sound than a single "big win." Overall, small, incremental changes have a stronger staying power and do not evaporate like large changes do. They become very stable building blocks for cumulative innovation. Small gains are easy to spread and preserve because they are easily duplicated by others, and there is less confusion about what needs to be done and what it takes to get it done. They are also easier to manage. Each gain requires less coordination to execute; interruptions such as those that might occur when there is a change in administration have limited effect; each small incremental change breeds a sense of success and a confidence to continue toward the goals of improved school effectiveness. Small changes allow flexibility in the combination and sequence of changes that are made.

Skunkwork and incremental change increase ownership, making everyone an owner of the success. School improvement is a "game of inches." One hundred people, each doing a little bit better, means incremental success, helping to improve schools. The types of small, incremental changes are developed and implemented with cultural support and are the lifeblood of an effective educational work culture and school improvement program.

If excellence is to be achieved in American schools, administrators must talk excellence—incrementally and incessantly. A leader must see that his or her staff is constantly being developed and is encouraged to implement what has been learned, as well as to share, share, share what has worked successfully. At the same time, failure should be tolerated and the attitude should be "let's learn and grow from that and find a better answer the next time." Leaders must encourage staff to champion the implementation of worthy ideas that could work well in other classrooms and schools. Leaders must be patient and celebrate the small, incremental improvements of their staff on a weekly and monthly basis.

It is quite important for healthy cultures to brag, display, celebrate, and promote themselves. Leadership must see that everyone believes in cumulative innovation at a pace that the organization can absorb. Personnel in leadership positions must work to see that staffs have a clear understanding of the vision and goals for the district. They must respond to the skunkworks by providing the needed structure, resources, and encouragement. Then, most importantly, they must let the site-based champions take over and develop, implement, and test ideas. They must allow this group to see that good ideas prosper throughout the organization. They must stand back and "let it happen." Then they must celebrate each incremental success.

Development in Action

In analyzing the benefits of personal and professional development for improved school culture, Dr. Fred Wood, School of Education Dean at the University of Oklahoma pointed out,

> We (Oklahoma City Public Schools) had people take new roles in the district, go back to higher education, or assume new roles within their organizations. They all ended up being in leadership spots as a result of going though the Vertical Team . . . when team members went through personal and professional growth activities, they began to discover talents within themselves. Others recognized those talents and reinforced them. There was tremendous cross-reinforcement regardless of the role. They felt trust in people. They could try out ideas they had never had a chance to try out. They could solve problems through in-basket activities. It was just phenomenal. Members of the team became catalysts for change as they took on greater leadership in improving the schools. That was typical.

Dr. Wood saw the vertical team as a learning community and personal and professional development as "discovery learning" rather than "telling learning." In addition, the combination of these two characteristics of the work culture "taught people how to collaborate and grow across role groups regardless of their role." This served as the catalyst to the implementation of new ideas.

Almost every individual who participated in the Danforth Foundation School Administrators Fellowship Program pointed to personal development, along with collegiality and the vertical team experience, as an outstanding opportunity for development and innovation. Some went as far as to say that it was one of, if not the best, growth and development experience in their professional lives. This support of the importance of personal and professional development existed among all participants regardless of roles. Almost every participant had his or her own story to tell about personal and professional growth and related innovations. Dr. Freda Holley, an assistant superintendent in Austin, Texas, concluded, "Growth and trust were highly evident. Each of us expanded our knowledge and sensitivity. . . . I know I have grown in my ability to work with and support others in a positive way."

These sentiments were shared by Yvonne Cunningham, a teacher in the El Paso, Texas, school system. Cunningham enthusiastically felt,

> I was given an opportunity to develop personally and professionally along with being able to gain greater insight into my abilities as an instructional leader. I was afforded the time and opportunity to help develop a program within my classroom that would address at-risk students (potential drop-outs). The opportunity to refresh and brush up on new techniques to implement for an effective speech program also added to my growth! A big reward is hearing about students who had thought they were "too dumb" to stay in school talk about their graduation from high school. The results of these experiences have recharged me and I plan to continue my own professional development, to continue working actively to improve the public schools, and to effectively touch the lives of the students I teach.

Cunningham was very actively involved in working with the "at-risk" student and visiting schools like Las Vegas High School to see their dropout prevention programs. In describing Cunningham, her principal said she had developed a "magic, and it was contagious." Her interest grew into a district-wide planning conference/workshop in which 95 people participated. The workshop was described by participants as a total success.

Robert Leming, a middle school principal in Springfield, Illinois, found that the greatest benefit of the Danforth Program was professional growth and development. He said,

> My own personal growth was immeasurable. I have been in education seventeen years and felt that I was well aware of current trends in education. The Vertical Team and personal and professional development experience not only helped me to discover what I did not know but also provided a forum for extensive learning. In the area of effective schools research alone, my knowledge base has grown significantly. I have been able to share with my colleagues in Springfield many new ideas and also an enthusiasm for education that derived directly from my own personal and professional development.

As a result of his development over the year, Leming was able to develop interest among teachers within his school in the study habits of the seventh and eighth graders.

A studies skills project was begun at Benjamin Franklin Middle School in Springfield. The results of a needs assessment and discussion among teachers supported efforts in this area. The program involved a pre-program inservice series for the teachers to help them and the principal in designing the program. The program was successfully designed and implemented by the teachers and principal.

Another example of a program stemming from a personal development plan occurred at Central High School in Springfield, Missouri. John Laurie, the Hillcrest High School principal, decided to focus his personal and professional development on the area of improving his knowledge of instruction. He joined a group of eight educators who brought in articles and research materials on instruction, and shared these readings related experiences on a regular basis. In addition, a major focus of all department meetings was instructional strategy and school effectiveness. People were invited to make regular state incentive grant reports to the staff on various instructional issues. Laurie also became much more knowledgeable about instructional strengths, weaknesses, and concerns at his school and closely monitored all academic programs.

As a result of this intensive year-long development, Laurie realized that there was a very small number of unmotivated, lazy students who modeled disruptive behavior. The behavior sent out a message that students didn't have to work in class. A great deal of instructional time was being used to combat the poor classroom attitude and behavior that was being modeled by those few students. Two math teachers at the high school decided to do something different with three students that were failing math because they were often sleeping, tardy, not attending, talking, or generally getting in trouble in math class. This kind of behavior had resulted in Hillcrest High School having the highest failure rate (8 percent) among all Springfield high schools. The students' excuses were, "math just don't interest me."

In an attempt to improve attendance, discipline, test scores and interest in school, the teachers designed a "contract for grades" program in the high school. The contract specified the type of behavior that was required to be successful in school—including attendance requirements, classroom behavior, study, homework, and test taking skills. If the students followed all the contracted behaviors, they were guaranteed a passing grade. On the other hand, if the students broke any of the five contracted behaviors, they were removed from class and denied academic credit for the subject. The contract was signed by the student, parent, teacher and principal. Laurie said,

The purpose of the contracts is to turn negative classroom behavior into positive classroom behavior, and the benefit of that touches more students than just the students who sign the contract. If you have three kids who put their heads down and sleep, they will have an effect on some marginal students who might take on the same type of thinking.

Teachers were reluctant to promise a passing grade without seeing results, however, preliminary results were very good and teachers were convinced that this was the hardest they had ever seen these kids work.

One of the students said, "It has me working instead of sleeping and talking with my friends and getting in trouble. I could do the work if I just sit down and do it." Average scores on a standardized math test went from 18 to 26 percent for these students to 39 to 92 percent. As a result, other teachers asked to work with Laurie to set up contracts for some students in their classrooms. Personal and professional development plans and innovations often develop out of the strong professional interest of a few individuals, as in Laurie's case.

The relationship between one's interest and one's role or profession is not always so clear. This is exactly what happened in Charles Reichert's case. As the principal of South Division High School in Milwaukee, Wisconsin, Reichert had a strong interest in urban gang life. As a major personal and professional development activity, he chose to spend a year learning as much as he could about gangs in the Milwaukee area. He contacted the Milwaukee Police Department's gang and school squads, individual officers, and the community. From this beginning he learned more about dropouts, children-at-risk, violent crime, drugs, alcohol and many other dangers flowing into the schools.

He developed a slide program and oral presentation on gang life which he presented to administrators, teachers, and community members. He raised awareness of the effects that gangs were having on the community and schools, helping to activate both to address related problems. In reviewing his development activities, Reichert said,

> I believe my staff and colleagues have developed better coping skills in dealing with gang involvement and activities due to my numerous programs. I find that my personal image as a leader has been greatly strengthened due to my continued regard and respect for my staff and student body, my more active involvement within the community, and my crusade to work effectively with the ever-growing concerns regarding gang activity. This development is naturally being positively reflected by a network of school and community programs mutually beneficial in addressing gang related problems.

Student failure in school seemed to be highly correlated with involvement in gangs. Therefore, Reichert and his teachers worked with the community to come up with a number of programs to thwart student failure, including English as a Second Language (ESL) classes, mastery learning, alternative education, bilingual programs, vocational and co-op programs, infant care, drug and substance abuse programs, as well as tutoring and adolescent health programs. Colleagues from other schools became interested in the work at South Division High and have made a number of inquiries.

The Employee as Champion

Successful development efforts usually occur when individuals become interested in a shared vision for a school system or school and begin to learn more about that vision in order to become a "champion." This is not a forced or coerced development process, but one in which the individual naturally buys into the vision, learns more about it under his or her own developmental plan, and decides to become actively involved as a champion for the cause. This, of course, is the purpose of a shared vision for the schools—to stimulate interest among employees in a shared set of goals. In this way, a number of employees will want to study these goals, their accomplishment, and determine ways in which they can develop their skills in these areas.

A classic example of individuals becoming champions for a shared vision occurred in the Charlotte-Mecklenburg school division in Charlotte, North Carolina. A task force on education and employment was formed in Charlotte in 1988. The task force was charged with evaluating local education in an effort to assist in improving local educational opportunities. The task force published a major report providing a shared vision for the public school system entitled, "Educational Imperatives: A Community at the Threshold." The task force found several deficiencies that needed to be addressed if Charlotte was to live up to its potential as a city of excellence and opportunity, such as a deplorable school dropout rate, poor teacher morale, lack of parental support, low performance by a segment of students, lack of effective assistance, and lack of basic educational skills among 20 percent of the graduates (not counting the 25 percent that dropped out). The report called for a "mosaic" of approaches that would open the door to educational excellence and make the school system's promise of equity and excellence a reality. A major emphasis was the monitoring of students' study habits, requiring appropriate classroom demeanor, discouraging mediocrity, and rewarding achievement. The report concluded that this was not only a moral imperative, it was an economic necessity.

This report became a major shared direction for the entire school system, with the dropout problem at the forefront. Dropouts often caused the
community many social and financial problems. Superintendent Peter Relic
reinforced the various findings of the report in much of his communications
with staff and community. He stated,

> What we are saying now is no more young people letting themselves be
> defeated with our passive acquiescence, their futility harming not only
> themselves, but all of society. Communication between school officials
> and parents is imperative . . . we have to teach young people that they
> must be responsible for the consequence of their actions. But to break
> the negative cycle for many students, which is resulting in failure in
> school, then dropping out, followed by years of frustration as adults,
> we must create a positive cycle of support and accountability. Adoles-
> cents need to learn that they are accountable to themselves and to their
> teachers . . . and for the health of this community and American society.
> In an increasingly competitive world, we must reach the greatest num-
> ber of students, to help them to become contributing and productive
> citizens, rather than a drain on society. We can no longer afford the
> confusion of mixed messages and the absence of standards.

The superintendent took the very important role of providing strategic
direction, but left a great deal of the operational development of the needed
programs to the staff. The superintendent and his staff did not get drawn
into becoming principals and teachers and designing programs to meet the
needs of the students. They communicated the vision and supported a culture that would allow the needed people and programs to develop from the
operational grass roots. They then provided support, resources, and encouragement as programs began to bubble up from the various skunkworks
and become part of the overall work culture.

An example of this grass roots development occurred at the middle
school level, where a heavy emphasis had been placed on the atmosphere of
learning. School effectiveness studies found that the atmosphere of learning
and student behavior in the classroom were highly correlated to student
achievement. A positive school climate was found to be vital in keeping
young adolescents in school. It was believed that the middle grades became
the breeding grounds for behavior and attitudes that caused many students
to drop out of school or become hopelessly lost by the ninth or tenth grade.
With the above in mind, Addie Moore, assistant principal at Sedgefield Junior High School in Charlotte, North Carolina, said, "My professional developmental plan grew out of a need to improve discipline." The school
system had implemented a discipline plan, however, it did not seem to be
working well at Sedgefield.

As a result, Moore read professional journals, attended professional conferences, and talked to teachers and other administrators to learn more about effective discipline programs. In describing the culture in which she worked, she stated, "My site supervisor allowed me to act without fear of criticism and even without reprimand." Moore was involved in a revision of the discipline plan so that it was more compatible with the needs of Sedgefield teachers and students and the community they served. Moore said, "The plan grew out of staff ideas and everyone committed to share responsibility for operation and implementation."

In a letter to parents, Moore and her principal described the plan as

> . . . setting limits and rules for inappropriate behavior within the school. Under this plan students accept responsibility for their behavior. Parents will be informed of inappropriate behavior and we encourage your cooperation in this effort. The Sedgefield Junior High discipline plan is based on levels of offenses and set consequences for failure to obey school rules. Consistent enforcement of the rules will occur by all teachers and administrators. . . . This plan is devised to protect your children and provide guidance and training in appropriate behavior . . . all efforts are made to keep students in school where supervision, counseling and guidance are available. Recognition will be given to students with good behavior to encourage and reinforce the positive aspects of the plan.

The actual plan spelled out responsibilities for parents and guardians, students, teachers, and administrators in handling different levels of offenses. Specific supervision, counseling, and discipline activities were related to each level. There were both in-classroom and out-of-classroom components. A committee structure was established to monitor and further refine the plan. This plan was highly effective, and was adopted by a number of other schools in the Charlotte-Mecklenburg system.

The Grand Rapids, Michigan, public school system vertical team recognized that the most pressing need within the district was a mathematics articulation program (K-12). Less than 80 percent of Grand Rapids' fourth grade students had achieved mastery in mathematics. They chose to invite Don Blanchard, a mathematics consultant with Kalamazoo, Michigan, public schools, as well as curriculum coordinators from Grand Rapids, to serve as resources in discussing a vision of what was needed in mathematics within the district. They agreed that improving the mathematics achievement of students in the four schools (represented by principals on the vertical team) would be the focal point for the year. The group came up with the following areas in which stakeholders wanted to focus attention:

1. Utilization of manipulatives
2. Linkage of mathematics programs in elementary, middle, and high school
3. Staff development in mathematics
4. Teacher and coordinator involvement in identifying math concepts and areas that need further development
5. District-level "swap shops" in which teachers share successful math approaches
6. Plans for analysis and application of expertise

The team participated in an in-depth examination of K-12 mathematics articulation and a dialogue on the best approach to use in improving mathematics education within the District. Resource personnel were asked to participate in the analysis and discussion. Team members freely shared their views and many new insights surfaced as a result of these open and frank discussions.

Teams visited model mathematics programs within the region as well as heard experts and shared their own ideas that had developed as part of their personal and professional development and school improvement plans. The focus of the mathematics improvement plan was an effort to increase the amount and openness of the mathematics articulation between elementary and secondary schools. Teachers at all levels were asked to examine content in terms of sequential delivery, continuity across grade levels, objectives, mastery, and testing.

Teams of counselors, teachers, and administrators were involved in examining evaluative data and surfacing and discussing performance early so that needs could be quickly addressed before they reached a crisis level. Administrators reported that the high schools tried to arrange opportunities to discuss and cooperate with feeder schools to develop common objectives and goals to increase student academic success in the school district. Educators' interests within the district brought about the need to develop strategies to provide specific feedback on student achievement.

Team members stated,

> Mastery learning was discussed among practitioners to guarantee students acquisition of essential skills in mathematics content areas. The faculty decided to increase the use of standardized tests, competency tests and nationally-normed tests for measures of student achievement with specific emphasis on use of resources and problem-solving skills. The theme of the district evolved into stressing the importance of academic achievement and the relationship between academic success and the process of lifelong learning and success.

Adult Growth and Development

Organizational strengths are built upon individual strengths, and individual strengths grow from personal and professional development. Therefore, staff development is the cornerstone of an effective work culture. Joseph Rogus and Elizabeth Shaw (1987) state,

> Staff development is first and foremost an attitude, a commitment to help individuals grow personally and professionally in a supportive climate. Staff development involves a broad range of activities designed to promote staff self-renewal and, indirectly, more effective learning for youngsters. Staff development activities are long-range in orientation and place the individual staff member at the heart of the growth planning process.

The development activity must be important to the individual staff member if it is to be successful.

Dr. Malcolm Knowles, the "father" of adult education, suggests that learners must establish their own development outcomes defined by their own concerns. The culture helps to provide the mechanism by which people develop a knowledge and understanding of what they will need to know and how what they want to learn can be applied to their work settings. When employees have an opportunity to be self-directed in their learning, they are likely to be highly motivated and committed to their development. Experience tells us that employees will not get much out of staff development or be very motivated to participate in activities in which they have little personal and professional interest. Motivation and commitment are the most important factors in learning and development efforts, and not recognizing their importance in such programs will result in failure.

The cornerstone of employee development must be the freedom to match what employees want to learn to their career aspirations. Almost any way in which people develop abilities and skills will improve performance; the important factor is that they continue to grow and develop. Development is best designed to coincide with significant events in the lives of learners, including stages of socialization or acculturation in the organization. Others within the organization facilitate the individuals' learning; they do not direct it.

In Dr. Knowles' book, entitled *The Modern Practices of Adult Education*, he suggests what is needed to facilitate development. These factors are based more on individual life and career planning than on organizational needs, because life and career stages provide a challenge to which the employee will be committed.

Each individual has a unique potential and a unique history presenting special opportunities, obligations, and challenges for them. No one can provide the answers for others; each must discover them for themselves. Some of the factors suggested by Dr. Knowles are:

- Encourage learner self-direction and autonomy.
- Provide groups of learners and provide them every opportunity to pool individual experiences and insights (development teams).
- Help them to analyze the challenge they are facing in their careers and work at present.
- Allow individuals to work on their own and the organization's visions, needs and personal and professional problems rather than simply trying to transmit information to them.

The major point of Dr. Knowles' work is that adults learn as a result of their own personal and professional needs. This is not to say that things external to the individuals do not create pressures that the individual will need to respond to, but no developmental activity will be successful unless the need is recognized by the individual. Dr. Knowles has pointed out that personal and professional development is a lifelong, self-directed process for all employees. Every member of the organization is actively involved in discovery of what he or she can do and become.

The lifelong learning aspect of personal and professional development is important due to the very fast pace of organizational life. Dr. Knowles suggests that the half-life of current practices is about a decade, meaning that half of all our knowledge, skill, and practice will be obsolete and outdated in ten years.

Organizations serve to help their people achieve personal and professional goals by meeting their needs for life-long learning. This is not typically well achieved by providing common staff development activities for all teachers and administrators. The problem is finding a way to individualize and personalize development in such a way that each employee's concern is addressed. This problem is solved quite well by the use of support, direction, encouragement, and freedom. Team members are responsible for their own personal and professional development plan, however, the focus of the culture on school effectiveness causes members to see how their development needs relate to the organizational needs.

Each member of the organization is encouraged and supported by others in the planning and conducting of a personal and professional development plan. The work culture supports participants in their development by serving as a resource, helping to clarify development activities and identifying possible resources and procedures that would be useful in working toward achievement. However, the individual always remains in control of the improvement plan so that he or she establishes both the direction and method of change. At the end of each year, the team verifies that the planned growth has actually taken place. In this way, the concept of personal and professional development becomes a central element of an effective, productive work culture.

The National Education Association reported that next to personal experience in the classroom, sharing experiences with fellow educators was the most significant condition and resource that affects a teacher's professional development. This grass roots strategy supports educators at various levels serving as resources to each other. The sharing of personal and professional experiences with fellow educators within the organization develops collegiality and enhances culture, while bringing a sense of importance and value to development.

Judith Warren Little (1986) suggests that school improvement, personal and professional development, school culture, and collaborative relations were all very highly correlated. She states that,

> In successful schools, teachers and administrators were more likely to talk together regularly and frequently about the business of instruction, more likely to work together to develop lessons, assignments, and materials, and more likely to teach one another about new ideas or practices. This habit of sharing . . . stands in contrast to the carefully preserved autonomy that prevailed in less successful schools.

The challenge to the administrators is to internalize and project a growth perspective, and to instill this spirit in the activities associated with personal and professional development. School effectiveness and job satisfaction are dependent on the creation of this positive support for all forms of growth in individuals, as well as in the organization itself. A development attitude must permeate the daily operation of each school.

Superintendent Support for Development

Employees must be free to take risks, be different, and make a difference if schools are to be true centers of learning. Employees must be able to see the greatness in themselves, others, and the school system. All are mutually challenged to reach their highest levels of development. All are asked to celebrate their fullest potential.

Dr. Joseph Fernandez, the superintendent of Miami-Dade County Schools, focused on a number of development issues in his personal and professional plan. Most importantly, he learned new methods by which decisions could be delegated to those closest to the problem or issue. Dr. Fernandez said, "They will know best how to develop the appropriate response or program to meet the needs of their constituency." Along with improved delegation, he wanted to focus specifically on monitoring systems which would insure that delegated assignments were appropriately completed. Dr. Fernandez wanted to,

> ... ensure that all district offices and area administrative personnel direct their professional efforts to supporting school improvement efforts at the feeder pattern, school, and classroom levels. I wanted to develop procedures and create an organizational structure that facilitates coordinating initiatives and programs, as well as monitoring their implementation. We gave individual schools closest to the point of service impact room to try out innovative techniques/programs and time to make them successful. We did not want to over-evaluate; yet, we did need to hold staff accountable for achieving a positive educational impact.

Professional growth was a major focus of Dr. Fernandez' development and refresher plan. A number of retreats and working sessions were planned as a result of his efforts, as a focus on technical support and assistance along with encouragement of staff to exercise their creativity and skill to improve school effectiveness. He shared his knowledge and leadership in the implementation of a number of ideas that came directly from his development activities.

Plans for development can be very helpful in providing insights on how one might try to do things a little differently. A major focus of personal and professional development in the Montgomery Public School System in Montgomery, Alabama was to face some very complex problems in each of the local communities requiring strong leadership skills in as many educators as possible. The focus was on serving the communities where the school children lived and went to school. Therefore, each school in each community had to have strong leadership teams in order to be effective.

The development of leadership skills became a major priority. Thomas Bobo, superintendent of the Montgomery schools, stated,

> The personal and professional development plan has had a tremendous impact upon me since I first committed to my development plan. My participation has opened new and valuable areas of communication for me. For example, I have never seen myself as a dictatorial person; however, the instruments indicated that, to some extent, I have been dictatorial. Since having that trait pointed out to me, I have attempted to

work hard on being less dictatorial. Without making changes in this area, I feel that I would not have been able to lead this system in the direction of school renewal.

This same type of outcome was noted throughout the district. Mr. Bobo continued,

An overall evaluation of our decision to focus on leadership development skills shows tremendous growth in leadership ability of all our administrative people. It has led to much professional growth. I feel that the system as a whole is bound together in looking for ways in which we can all improve professionally. There has been a kind of renewal for many of us and I feel that professional growth will continue throughout the entire system for many years to come. I feel that what we have been able to set in motion here will continue for a long, long time.

Personal Development

Personal development is now recognized as being crucial to employee performance. In a major 1986 report entitled *Staff Development*, the American Association of School Administrators reported,

In the best of today's programs, administrators address not only the professional needs of teachers, but also their personal and individual needs.

There is a strong link between self-concept, self-control, self-reliance, employee health and morale, productivity, and school effectiveness. The AASA report continues,

People need to know how to cope in every aspect of their lives. Accordingly, stress management, problem-solving skills, nutrition and exercise, financial planning, time management and interpersonal relationships should be developed as part of a total staff development program.

This was also a major finding in the Carnegie Foundation's report of the Task Force on Teaching as a Profession. The report maintained that one area that the best schools shared was a concern for the development of individuals. As the Carnegie report said,

A common corporate philosophy for inservice is to promote personal fulfillment along with professional development; it recognizes the faint, almost imperceptible line that separates personal growth from professional development.

Development begins with a positive attitude toward the importance of the employee to the school system. Unless the staff member has a positive attitude, little can be achieved in the area of personal and professional development. Neurotic organizations produce neurotic, underdeveloped individuals. The culture must clearly demonstrate, in as many ways as possible, that it values and views the person as important to the organization. This point can best be made by the organization saying that the individual is so important to them that they are concerned for the individual's physical, emotional, and spiritual health. This then is another cornerstone of an effective work culture. Development will not occur in lives that are anxious, stressful, unhealthy, and unworthy. True development is based upon a balance of physical, mental, psychological, and spiritual resources and the development of all aspects of the individual.

One of the major outcomes of a development process is to help individuals become more sensitive to their personal needs and what they need to do to meet those needs. School effectiveness requires tremendous stability and energy as well as knowledge and skill. The invocation of change requires a healthy work force, since there is sure to be great resistance, conflict, confusion, and fear. If one does not have the physical, psychological, and spiritual stamina to implement improvement, the best that can be hoped for is maintaining the status quo—an outcome that some researchers suggest is impossible.

In studying government agencies, Lance Leloup and William Moreland (1978) concluded that a strategy of moderation and maintaining the status quo was necessary for organizations that required certainty, stability, and high support of their initial efforts for organizational health. They found, however, that maintaining the status quo did not lead to agency growth and, in fact, lead to agency decline and dissatisfaction.

Some of the most important development plans are related to employees' concerns. Dan Tosado, a principal in the Miami-Dade County Schools in Florida, was concerned about his stamina and health. He would find himself out of breath, sweating profusely, and unable to keep up with heavy agendas. Tosado chose his health as a major development effort, focusing on his body and physical condition. His development plan was to lose weight and improve his health, while at the same time increasing delegation by increasing involvement in those areas of decision-making that impacted the daily operations of the school.

Tosado saw a doctor, went on a strict diet, and followed a prescribed exercise plan. In regard to increased delegation, Tosado make sure that items were reviewed by staff through group discussions, mailbox ballots, department head meetings and administrative staff meetings. He believed that the success of his development objectives were self-evident. Dr. Donn Gresso visited Tosado's middle school some months after Tosado began his development plan. Gresso walked into the principal's office area and asked to see Tosado. The secretary called in to his office, and out walked a man Donn didn't recognize. Tosado had lost a tremendous amount of weight and looked ten years younger.

Dr. Gresso shared,

> Dan took me into his office and said, "My staff, students, and others have helped me to better my performance." He showed me the grease-pencil board over his desk which had goals for personal health. In a public speech in Florida one year later, I heard Dan say his desire to initiate personal and professional lifelong growth had probably saved his life and his job by working more effectively with more energy to lead.

The importance of personal development cannot be over stressed. Most business organizations insist, and in most cases pay for, complete physicals as well as exercise and physical health programs for their middle management and above. This is not the case in education. At the very least, school systems must ask their employees to create personal development plans that focus on health. Absenteeism caused by legitimate health-related problems is a major concern in American education. This can be corrected by an increased focus on personal development.

A typical, but striking example of the benefits of health improvements occurred in the Norfolk, Virginia public school system. As a result of the focus on personal development, Dr. Edward Daughtrey, Assistant Superintendent of Instructional Support Services, sensed a need to modify his approach to life. He had been faintly aware of these messages for quite a long time, however, it was not until he began thinking about personal development that he became aware of this wise, but very quiet, inner voice. Dr. Daughtrey shared,

> Although an identified need of developing a more relaxed approach to life was not stated in the fall, I believe this need has developed during the course of my participation in the Norfolk City Schools vertical team program. This might be the most important aspect of my experience. Stopping to smell the roses has become important to me. . . . The value to me of participating in personal and professional development this year has been the realization that to be a person with contributions to

make to our organization, I must be a person who has time to enjoy and profit from a relaxed conversation with friends and fellow workers. I must stop doing everything in a hurry. I must read for relaxation and entertainment. I must be willing to listen. The vertical team experience and personal development has brought this attitude to the forefront of my personal and professional life.

His words are particularly poignant, since approximately two months after Dr. Daughtrey made this statement, he suffered a minor heart attack from which he has since recovered. The point is that personal development must become a major component of every school system's culture.

Healthy individuals are involved in a lifelong process of discovering, developing, and applying their full potential. The work culture itself has much to do with all of these unique, individual qualities, and, therefore, those who share that culture have a responsibility to the individual and the organization to create a positive and healthy climate in which to work. This culture must produce messages and feelings of employee self-direction, acceptance, self-support, reliance, esteem, understanding and confidence. Such a culture does not evaluate, categorize, label, and rate; it accepts staff for who they are and helps them to develop to the fullest potential. This culture promotes personal confidence above personal approval. The culture creates a sense of independence, self-reliance, and spontaneity that supports vitality and exhilaration. The employees are responsible for organizational outcomes and are trusted to be effective and efficient in their accomplishments.

Developmental Activities

To establish a culture of self-reliance and self-support, individuals must decide upon their own developmental activities. Ownership in planning one's own development is absolutely essential to establishing a collaborative trust. The commitment of the organization must be to assist employee growth while in the process of accomplishing organizational objectives. This is best achieved by supporting and verifying the results of staff members' achievement of personal and professional development plans. At some point, school employees will need to relate their individually developed plans to general school effectiveness or a particular curriculum innovation.

In a healthy culture, employees are constantly developing knowledge and skills, responding to the vision and goals of the organization, and taking responsibility not only for their welfare and growth but that of their students and professional colleagues. To be successful, schools need to be learning environments for teachers as well as students. In summarizing why the Los Angeles individually-oriented staff development programs were so successful, Robert DeVries and Joel Colbert (1990) suggest,

> Paradoxically, this training reflects several coherent staff development principles: needs-based, owned by participants, differentiated, experimentally/behaviorally based, cooperatively planned, individualized and involved. . . . Selected elements of the district's staff development program for teachers appear to be effective, especially those that are voluntary and reflect the principles described previously. Standard off-the-shelf programs that offer minimal interaction and little ownership are poorly attended and only moderately valued.

The actual development activities that occur within a school division can take many forms. In fact, the form they take is related to the creativity of the staff in figuring out methods that will help them and that they will be able to carry out. A partial list might include:

- readings
- attending local, state and/or national conferences
- informal conferencing with others
- group sharing session
- designing and conducting assessments/evaluations
- community involvement
- joint problem-solving
- committee and team activity (vertical teams)
- networking
- attending inservice programs (training)
- active involvement in professional associations (holding office)
- attending university classes
- mentoring, tutoring, and supervisory activity
- planning and developing new programs
- collaboration between practitioners and scholars
- therapy, counseling, and health programs
- school and school division visitations
- practicum and internship-type activity
- practice problems, in-baskets, and case studies
- writing articles, book reviews, songs, poetry, chapters, or books; delivering papers; editorials for newspapers
- designing/conducting training and courses (adjunct faculty)
- writing grants and proposals
- starting/joining interest groups
- exercise and wilderness programs

- conducting research
- volunteering at museums, health clinics, environmental agencies, youth agencies, the court systems, police department, social services
- effective parenting
- sponsoring extra-curricular activities
- school/university and school/business partnerships
- travel and field trips
- public speaking
- appearances on radio and television; participating in plays, dance, orchestras; active involvement in political or public service organizations
- running for public office
- job swapping

Creating a culture that promotes and demands continuous personal and professional development under the educators' personal control and in a spirit of collegiality across echelons will result in staff development that is far more effective and powerful than it has been in the past. To be successful, educators must have opportunities to discuss development experiences in an atmosphere of collegiality and experimentation. A chance to share perspectives and seek solutions to common problems is extremely important to the long-term growth of educators. Lucy Casarantes Fischer, a teacher from El Paso, Texas, expressed the attitude needed for personal and professional development as follows:

...may there never develop in me the notion that my education is complete but give me the strength and leisure and zeal continually to enlarge my knowledge.

Bibliography

DeVries, Robert T. and Colbert, Joel A. "The Los Angeles Experience: Individually Oriented Staff Development." *Changing School Culture Through Staff Development*. Edited by Bruce Joyce, Alexandria, Virginia: Association for Supervision and Curriculum Development, 1990.

Duke, Daniel L. *School Leadership and Instructional Improvement*. New York: Random House, 1987.

Fullan, Michael G. "Staff Development, Innovation, and Instruction Development." In *Changing School Culture Through Staff Development*. Edited by Bruce Joyce. Alexandria, Virginia: Association for Supervision and Curriculum Development, 1990.

Joyce, Bruce and Murphy, Carelen. "Epilogue: The Curious Complexities of Cultural Change." In *Changing School Culture Through Staff Development*. Edited by Bruce

Joyce. Alexandria, Virginia: Association for Supervision and Curriculum Development, 1990.

Knowles, Malcom S. *The Modern Practices of Adult Education*. New York: Association Press, 1980.

Leloup, Lance T. and Moreland, William B. "Agency Strategies and Executive Review: The Hidden Politics of Budgeting." *Public Administration Review* (May-June, 1978).

Little, Judith Warren. "The Effective Principal." *American Education* (August-September, 1986).

National Education Association, "Teachers Conference for Staff Development." ASCD Conference, San Francisco, CA: April, 1986.

Peters, Thomas J. and Austin, Nancy. *A Passion for Excellence*. New York: Random House, 1985.

Peters, Thomas J. and Waterman, Robert H. *In Search of Excellence*. New York: Harper & Row, Publishers, 1982. Reprinted by permission from Harper Collins Publishers.

Raywid, Mary Anne, Tesconi, Charles, and Waren, Donald. *Pride and Practice: Schools of Excellence for All People*. Washington, D.C.: American Education Studies Association, 1984.

Rogus, Joseph F and Shaw, Elizabeth. "Staff Development/Inservice." *Educational Leadership*, 1987.

9

Employee Empowerment

People must be able to discover the abilities that they possess in order to accomplish the greatness of which they are capable. True empowerment not only enables us to achieve our potential, but actually helps us to discover and develop it. This is not easy for most people, since their maturation process has been under the watchful and carefully controlling eye of others. We have learned to look externally for direction, first for our safety, and later on for the types of actions that get rewarded. Less effective organizations pick up on this condition with a philosophy of "what gets evaluated and rewarded gets done." This plays quite well into the disempowering maturation process of most individuals.

The strategy of effective organizations is to help individuals to continue to develop themselves and their organizations in their maturation process by using a philosophy that suggests "what is rewarding gets done." When work effort grows and is supported from within, special gifts and unique abilities are used in work. People become intrinsically motivated. They not only work for the rewards of the organization, but they work from the heart. Life and work become integrated. Work is accomplished not because the worker expects an external reward, but because the work is important. Praise does not generate greatness, encouragement does.

N. B. Garmin (1989) defined empowerment as "helping people to take charge of their lives, inspiring people to develop feelings of self-worth and a willingness to be self-critical and reflective about their actions." The concept of helping people to discover what they have to offer to the organization and then providing the support they need to develop and use their intrinsic abilities is easily intellectualized, but not often practiced. The development of unique talents takes quite a different management system and work culture than one in which the individual follows prescribed roles, goals, procedures, and structures.

Thomas Sergiovanni (1991) relates quality, control, and management to empowerment and intrinsic motivation. He states,

> Perhaps on no issue do ordinary and highly successful leaders differ more than in their beliefs about and concepts of quality control. To ordinary leaders, quality control is considered to be a management problem solvable by coming up with the right (structural) controls such as scheduling, prescribing, programming, testing and checking. Though successful leaders recognize that such managerial conceptions of quality control have their place, they are likely to view the problem of quality control as being primarily cultural rather than managerial. Quality control, they have come to learn, is in the minds and hearts of people at work. It has to do with what teachers and other school employees believe, their commitment to quality, their sense of pride, the extent to which they identify with their work, the ownership they feel for what they are doing, and the intrinsic satisfaction they derive from the work itself.

Any form of administration that is engaged in containing incompetence is involved in a fruitless and frustrating struggle. This is a struggle with a problem symptom rather than a cause, and yet, this is precisely what many educational administrators do. What is most discouraging is that such behavioral modeling by the leadership of our schools not only fails the incompetent employee, but it is likely to render the highly competent employee much less competent. Incompetence cannot be reduced by structured controls, but by helping individuals discover their competence and then providing the opportunity and support to apply that competence. This requires opportunity for individuals to discover what is important, why they are involved within the profession, and how they can contribute to it. This type of understanding cannot be shaped externally, but grows from a better understanding of oneself. This is what true empowerment is all about.

In this way, empowerment is much more than sharing governance. In fact, shared governance may not even work if the employees have not been empowered—knowledgeable of their abilities and intrinsically motivated. Once individuals have learned to look externally for direction and purpose in their lives, they find it very difficult to be involved in shared governance. They have not learned to think for themselves and their psyche does not operate that way. They are directed, coerced and controlled, but most importantly, told what to do. These directions come from leftover messages from parents, preachers, friends, bosses, colleagues, teachers, television, and many other sources, but they do not come from within. These people operate on an intense desire for belongingness, conformist behavior, approval, and law and order, and, thus, look to external guidance to give them direction.

People with such external loci of control have difficulty with shared leadership, since they have learned to live their lives based on external cues. Typically, in shared governance, they simply look to other reference groups for direction. When the cues are absent, the individuals become uncomfortable, anxious, and shaky, and look for cues elsewhere.

This is not to suggest that excellent cultures do not use shared forms of governance. In fact, excellent cultures do use shared governance, they just don't equate governance with empowerment. Effective organizations work to empower their employees so that they can actively participate in shared governance. Once the employee has become empowered, the shared model of governance is the only model that will work.

However, employees should not be empowered unless they are engaged in all aspects of an effective work culture. Empowered employees work with their own unique talents, and are intrinsically motivated and do not respond well to external directions and force. If the culture is autocratic and unchangeable, efforts to empower employees are liable to be disastrous. To achieve true school improvement, excellent school districts empower their employees so they can share governance with them. Without empowerment, participatory approaches are empty vessels.

Deming on Empowerment

One of the highest awards a businessman in Japan can receive is the "Deming Award." Deming is widely recognized in North America as a business management expert. Dr. Lewis A. Rhodes (1990) documented many of Deming's thoughts on education in a two part series that appeared in the AASA *School Administrator*. Deming focuses on the system as the catalyst and framework for change and the individual as the creator. According to Deming, "The key element for insuring improved school performance is the intrinsic motivation of the faculty and staff within the school."

In discussing Deming's ideas and influence on Japanese business, a Ford Motor Company vice president noted, "The Japanese presume you'll do your job; we U.S. managers presume you won't." Although this is a very subtle difference in practice, it has a very large effect on the culture of the workplace. Lasting change depends on the ability of the workers to bring their full level of ability and desire to create improvements in the daily operation of schools. This is very difficult in education, where educators have lost confidence in their own ability to improve instruction or modify their organizations. People will not participate if management has no confidence in them. The strengths to improve effectiveness must grow and develop within every individual.

In summarizing Deming's view of management in ineffective work cultures, Dr. Rhodes concluded,

> In short, their idea of a good manager is one who sets up a system, directs the work through subordinates, and through crisp and unambiguous assignments, develops standards of performance for his or her employees.

Dr. Rhodes states that such ineffective managers,

> . . . set goals for their staff and rate employees as objectively as possible, sometimes even calling on others to help. They identify poor performers and assist them to meet work standards or replace them. They hope, thereby, to create the most efficient system possible.

Deming contrasted this view of a less effective work culture with a more effective one. He found that effective organizations were predicated on the ideas that effective cultures provide a consistency and continuity of purpose along with the encouragement of employees to develop their natural talents.

Effective work cultures maintain a constant vision of the whole and the connections among its parts. Everyone is encouraged to achieve individual levels of excellence, however, each person understands his or her relationship to overall organization outcomes. Such a culture is predicated on the fact that staff members work in education because they want to make a difference in the lives of children, and thus make sure they have access to continuing feedback to increase their personal effectiveness.

Effective work cultures are based, according to Deming, on the acceptance that the quality of instruction depends upon the ability of staff to continually identify and meet the learning needs of students. He suggests that this will occur when people learn to take control of their own lives and develop and focus their talents on the vision of their school division and the work at hand. The staff knows where the potential for improvement of the system lies. These improvements emerge from the abilities of the staff. This means that organizational improvement depends on individual empowerment.

In summarizing Deming's beliefs about improving schools, Dr. Rhodes stated,

> The school system staff is the essential instrument in understanding what is happening at the places where the work gets done. They must

know how to determine which problems are caused by the overall system itself. Therefore, everyone in the system is involved in studying it and proposing how to improve it. Learning is part of work, driven by each person's need to be effective.

Empowering People in Practice

The vertical team in the Youngstown, Ohio, city schools described the results of empowerment when they reported,

> This experience has been especially helpful in assisting team members to maintain their own integrity and to enhance the dignity of others, thereby encouraging honest and frank, as well as supportive, communication and interaction. All educators should know that one individual does not have all the answers. He or she must encourage active participation of colleagues, at all levels within the hierarchy. Natural abilities and input are necessary to be effective in conducting the mutually supportive roles played in the education process.

E. N. Catsoules, superintendent of Youngstown schools, stressed the importance of getting to know personal strengths and weaknesses and getting to know the strengths and weaknesses of colleagues. The strengths of one team member can be used to complement weaknesses of others. In this way, the blend creates a powerful synergistic effect. The Youngstown team participants learned much about themselves and their fellow team members; discovering strengths, recognizing some of their limitations, and realizing that by working as a team they were able to overcome individual weaknesses or limits. Catsoules said,

> Support and suggestions from our team members were needed and especially useful. By encouraging individuals to develop and use their strengths, we were able to put our heads together and each one benefited from the abilities and strengths of the others.

The Youngstown team believed that the process was "extremely refreshing, rewarding, and stimulating, renewing our energy and enthusiasm." This renewed energy and enthusiasm was the catalyst for an extremely successful school improvement effort. In describing how well they were able to merge the strengths of each member of the team in order to achieve the common goals of school improvement, they said, "We have met the remedy, and it is us."

The importance of recognizing individuality and developing unique capabilities became a major theme at both Chaney and Woodrow Wilson high schools in Youngstown. A major goal was to use self-awareness and self-esteem as major tools for improving reading and writing achievement. Alex Murphy and Bernadine Marinelli, the high school principals, found that school effectiveness improved and that

> . . . morale and productivity are definitely on the upswing! There has been considerable involvement of the faculty in formulating and implementing our reading and writing plans. Staffs have expressed their appreciation individually and collectively.

Initial analysis of the Stanford Achievement Test results suggested improvement and success as a result of the program.

In describing the personal benefits of the vertical team program, Murphy shared,

> . . . overall, my vertical team participation has been very positive and has benefited me personally and professionally; I now have a greater and more finely tuned sense of "self." I am much more sensitive to my personal needs and things I should do to meet them. This has allowed me to bring more of myself to my role and to allow others to do the same. This has eliminated a strong crisis-orientation and day-to-day functioning mode that has existed at this school.

Effective work cultures like the Youngstown Public Schools recognize the essential role of the staff in both developing the effectiveness of the school system and helping to nurture and empower that staff. This occurs in a culture that encourages, supports, and channels human energy; supports innovation; recognizes and rewards ability and talent; provides resources, guidance, and encouragement; and ultimately results in the fully developed individual. Such an approach to school effectiveness avails leadership with an often untapped source of human energy and talent. Thomas Jefferson, one of our nation's founding fathers, argued often and eloquently for the notion of helping individuals to recognize and achieve their full potential in the pursuit of building stronger, more effective institutions. As he ideally expressed so long ago,

> We hope to avail the nation of those talents which nature has sown as liberally among the rich as the poor, but which perish without use if not sought and cultivated.

The Synergistic Effect of Empowerment

We have long known that individual differences and similarities within the people who make up an organization have a profound effect on performance. Dr. Peter Vail of George Washington University found that high producing organizations tend to recognize and support the individual differences of their employees. They help their employees to be comfortable with differences in themselves and those who are different from them. The mood is that individual differences play a very important complementary role, leading to much better results than when such differences are ignored or denied.

Empowerment occurs when individuals become more fully aware of their unique abilities, how those abilities can help the organization, and how they complement and interfere with the skills of others within the organization. Organizations are improved the more individuals learn about their own nature. Thus, the key to organizational effectiveness is learning how to use individual differences to the fullest. This is the exact reverse of trying to force all individuals to follow the same set of roles, rules, and regulations in order to try to make them interchangeable.

Dr. Ned Herman and the Whole-Brain Corporation (1981) conducted a study on college students and General Electric personnel and found improved productivity occurred with increased self-awareness, along with the ability to account for differences among self and others. Herman found that until people are made aware that they can think in various modes, multimodal blockages to their creativity and productivity will persist. Self-awareness and self-affirmation are two of the most important learning events for individuals asked to increase their participation in and contribution to the organization. Herman describes the free interplay of all modes of thinking within a confident individual as a "whole-brained person." He believes that "whole brains" are our best organizational assets.

Herman found that performance improved as individuals were able to bring more of their natural selves to the work, and greater cohesion was observed within the group. Communication and socialization skills, and pride increased within the group. There was an improvement in all efforts requiring team performance. The creativity of the group increased greatly as the team was better able to envision desirable outcomes. Dr. Herman found that overall, personal discovery "improves levels of trust and reduces individual differences, thus increasing the likelihood of greater group cohesion and high performance."

Dr. Susan Sayers-Kirsch, from the Northwest Regional Education Laboratory, developed a "Behavioral Matrix" model to provide a simplified paradigm for personal discovery. Because people have very different ways in which they perceive a situation, work at tasks, interact with others, and make decisions, it is important for individuals to understand their own style and the style of others. Organizations should not force individuals to assume roles or "right" ways of behaving in the organization. Effective organizations encourage employees to discover their personal operating style—the one that is most comfortable for them. The reason this is important is because the organization functions best when it capitalizes on the strengths of each individual, encouraging and celebrating such difference. This is cultural leadership.

The Challenge of Empowerment

Self-supported creative thought, feelings, or impulses are often unwelcome in education. As a result, the culture of education teaches professionals to deny or block off these individual and unique parts of themselves. They have learned to look outside to find themselves, and in so doing have denied the existence of major aspects of their identity. The self, focused on an external locus of control, builds walls within to deny the inner self its important role in providing direction. These repressed thoughts, abilities, or needs are not easy to suppress and much of the individual's energy is focused on avoiding recognition of the self so one can be controlled externally.

Employees at lower levels within the organization, the practitioner class, often have trouble recognizing their abilities and potential due to their cultural conditioning. One's natural ability, which is part of one's inheritance, is often sacrificed when one relies upon formal, authoritarian patterns of thought and action. Traditions, formalism, and legalism are used to simplify, defend, and explain behavior to others. Disempowered employees win approval by conforming to generally held norms or the views of the powerful. They bargain their ability and potential contribution for approval and safety. They repress any aspects of themselves which are not clearly accepted by those in power. They seldom have new ideas or try new experiences unless these ideas have been accepted and proven. They fear losing their sense of self-respect if they fail or are embarrassed. They learn to conform to external norms and choose not to actively participate.

The paradox of empowerment is that people are empowered by becoming aware of who they are, not by becoming something that others prefer. This is very difficult for people whose personal and professional maturation process was under the direction of external influences. Empowerment breaks the chains of external control and allows individuals to discover their true selves, or their true nature. When they get more in touch with themselves, people discover something not easily categorized as personal or

professional. However, in almost every case, personal goals are complementary and most often supportive of professional goals.

Roberta Cartwright, an English teacher at Chaparral High School in Las
Vegas, provides an excellent example of how personal empowerment and
development improves productivity and performance. She believed she
could become a better writing teacher by doing more writing herself. She
had always wanted to write a novel, but she had never taken time to allow
that feeling to develop. The vertical team program in her district encouraged such empowerment activity and supported her while she was thinking the idea through. As a result, she planned to write a novel. She soon
realized how difficult it was to write, and found this effort to be very challenging. She was not sure she would ever finish it, however, she felt much
better as a result of getting started on something that had now seemed like
a lifelong desire. This undercurrent had been a lifetime need, influencing
many of Cartwright's attitudes without her recognizing it. Growing up in
the sixties formed the subject of her novel, allowing her to wrestle with
some unfinished transactions that she now sensed were important to her.
She felt she had some important ideas to share through a novel, and it
might even serve as a small catharsis from which others could learn.
Having been a committed activist of the sixties generation, Cartwright
found herself fascinated with what had happened to,

> ... those of us in the movement who first tried to "overthrow" the
> established way of life, then, in a matter of a few short years, found
> ourselves an integral part of that establishment.

She was excited, and almost driven to get started on this venture.

The members of the vertical team supported and encouraged
Cartwright's effort. Over the next two years, they learned that this did not
take away from Cartwright's work for the school system. In fact, she did
more for the system over those two years than any she had worked in the
past. She established a very successful volunteer peer tutoring program to
develop enthusiasm and love of writing within students. The program was
geared toward students who were deficient in reading and writing skills,
and turned out to be quite a success. Some students learned about generosity, compassion and altruism while others improved their reading and
writing skills. The program received a great deal of media support and an
award for excellence from the school district. Cartwright also directed a
summer institute for teachers and served on a task force studying the district's elements of quality. She worked toward the elimination of "tracking"
by placing low-achieving students in college preparatory classes.

As in Cartwright's case, empowered, fully-developed people can use
their personal empowerment to complement and enhance their professional

lives. Empowerment helps individuals to balance their rational, logical, controlled, conservative, and material sides with their creative, conceptual, artistic, spiritual, and emotional sides Empowerment requires efforts at introspection, self-discovery and self-development. It is the struggle to be natural and authentic and takes place within a person. Empowered individuals do not look for ways to prove their worth, but look for ways in which they can creatively express their true nature.

Stages of Human Development

The basic structures of human development are like a ladder. Empowerment occurs as individuals take each step up this ladder toward the highest level of development. Perhaps Abraham Maslow (1970) was one of the first to truly understand the development process by identifying man's need as a hierarchical system with self-actualization, and later self-transformation, at the highest level. In discussing the importance of man working toward higher levels of development and ultimately actualizing oneself, Maslow states:

> We have, all of us, an impulse toward actualizing more of our potentialities, toward self-actualization, or full humanness or human fulfillment. This is a push toward the establishment of the fully evolved and authentic self . . . an increased stress on the role of integration. Resolving a dichotomy into a higher, more inclusive unity amounts to healing a split in the person and making him more unified. This is also an impulse to be the best . . . If you deliberately plan to be less than you are capable of being, then I warn you that you'll be deeply unhappy for the rest of your life.

The developmental process is described by Ken Wilber, Jack Engler and Daniel Brown (1986) in their work entitled *Transformation of Consciousness*. Their concepts are expanded by William G. Cunningham (1991) in his book, *Empowerment: Vitalizing Personal Energy*. These authors suggest that although the developmentalists use different language to discuss the developmental process, they encounter similar experiences or stages of human growth. Basic parallels emerge as they compare the stages in the various theories and constructs. They examine the rungs in the overall ladder of development by examining the interrelation of theories. Wilber et al state:

> Each basic structure, then, supports various phase-specific transitional structures or self-stages, such as different self-needs (investigated by Maslow), different self-identities (investigated by Loevinger), and

TABLE 9–1   Stages of Empowerment

Needs Development	Ego Development	Moral Development
Physiological	Presocial	Magic Wish
Safety/Security	Symbiotic	Punishment/Obedience
	Beginning Impulsive	Naive Hedonism
	Self Protective	
Social Affiliation/	Conformist	Approval Of Others
Belongingness	Conscientious	Law And Order
Self-Esteem	Conformist	
	Conscientious	
Autonomy	Individualistic	Individual Rights
Self-Actualization	Autonomous	Individual Principles/
Self-Transcendence	Integrated	Conscience
		Universal-Spiritual
Abraham Maslow	Jane Loveinger	Lawrence Kohlberg

Source: William G. Cunningham, *Empowerment.* (Atlanta, Georgia: Humanics Limited) 1991.

different sets of moral responses (investigated by Kohlberg) . . . Thus, for example, when the self is identified with the rule/role level, its self-need is for belonging, its self-sense is conformist, and its moral sense is conventional; when (and if) it subsequently identifies with the formal-reflexive level, its need is for self-esteem, its self-sense is individualistic, its moral sense is postconventional, and so on.

Table 9–1 shows various constructs of human development that make up the texture of a person. The individual passes through the stages within each of these constructs in the course of his or her growth. Although there are many stages of overall development under each of these constructs, Dr. Cunningham (1991) has synthesized and combined them both functionally and structurally into three major stages. Each stage is a higher level or order of development than the previous stage. Table 9–2 describes these stages as selfish self-indulgence, scripted self-validation, and vital self-reliance.

Selfish Self-Indulgence

In the first stage of development, humans possess various emotions, but are not distinct and separate emotional beings. Their emotions are not yet

TABLE 9–2   **Transitional Structures of Human Development**

Stages or Phases Transitional Structures	I. Selfish Self-Indulgence	II. Scripted Self-Validation	III. Vital Self-Reliance
Self-Needs	physiological security bodily desires safety, pleasure avoidance of pain	belongingness, approval conformity shared expectations praise, appreciation acceptance, support social affiliation	autonomy liberation self-actualization self-transcendence

Self-
Identities
	world & individual
	  same
	magical absorption
	  of world into
	  individual
	self-absorption
	contradiction
	impulsive,
	  symbiotic
		external, collective
		rule-role
		  expectation
		preoccupation with
		  external world
		based upon scripts
		conformist,
		  mirroring
		life-scripts, images
			natural
			personal being
			inner center
			universal
			unity
			authenticity

Self-Sense	greatness of one's
	  world
	internal motives &
	  impulses
	grandiosity
		fit-in, pleases
		  others
		belong, role,
		  position
		sameness,
		  acceptance
			individualistic
			continuity
			liberation
			balance
			boundless
			spontaneous, real

Moral
Responses
	instinctual beliefs
	individualistic
	magical wish
	punishment,
	  obedience
	hedonism
		conventional
		conform to
		  expectations
		duty, authority
		obligation
		right of society
		legality,
		  conditioning
		external validation
		approval of others
		law & order
			intuition, insight
			wisdom, judgment
			love, dignity
			freedom, justice
			humanism,
			  idealism
			individual rights
			conscience,
			  universal
			spiritual

Source: William G. Cunningham, *Empowerment.* (Atlanta, Georgia: Humanics Limited) 1991.

clearly differentiated from the emotions of others, particularly their mothers and significant others. In this stage, people believe that others feel whatever they feel, and, therefore, what is good for them will be good for everyone. There is an incapacity to have sufficient awareness of the needs of others and a strong tendency toward being self-centered.

Individuals are very self-assertive, guided mainly by selfish interests. They draw no distinction between what comes from inside and what exists in the external environment, and therefore base decisions solely on their own needs. They seldom give consideration to the consequences of their behavior on others or even themselves. They have a sense of self, but not a sense of others and the world in which they live, and therefore give total reign to self-absorption. They do not sense the joys of that world, except in relation to their own gratification. They are unable to take responsibility for their lives and blame others for every problem that develops. They cannot understand others because they cannot differentiate them from themselves.

As a result of this lack of differentiation, there tends to be an over-estimation of self and a devaluation of others. Individuals feel narcissistic and omnipotent. There is a sense of grandiosity in emotions and behaviors, as well as a sense of superiority, arrogance, perfectionism, or exhibitionism. People in this stage cannot share in the success or happiness of others, and often feel envy, humiliation, depression, emptiness, or rage. Whatever the emotion, the most recognized characteristic is that the individuals are unable to distinguish that emotion from the environment in which they find themselves.

Scripted Self-Validation

In this second stage of development, there is a preoccupation with the external world and the roles people are expected to play in that world. At this point, individuals become driven by a desire to fit in, to please others, to find a place in the group, to conform to expectations, to follow rules, regulations and policy, and, ultimately, to belong. Carried to an extreme, this can result in a disassociation with the internal, natural self and a total preoccupation with the external world.

In this stage, individuals become preoccupied with presenting themselves in regard to the external roles they fulfill. They become what they believe others would like them to be. Everything they say and do is influenced by how others will see them and respond to them. Identity and reality are based upon scripts that others have prepared. In the first stage, individuals become self-centered, but in this one they become self-imprisoned as they depend more and more on the external world for personal authenticity. This results in hidden agendas, crossed messages, confusion, distortions, and lost humanity, as the external world denies the existence of the internal one.

Due to a strong need to belong, people seek the approval of others through conformity as it relates to shared expectations. This results in a value scheme based on duty, authority, obligation, rights of the society, and the air of legality. Individuals conform to the external reference points of the group, mirroring each other in a strong external orientation. They follow literal rules and expectations, and internalize the judgments of others. This reaches an extreme point when people carefully screen and edit what they say to make sure it will be acceptable to the perceived organizational standards. Carefully prepared scripts are passed back and forth as individuals begin to lose touch with their own thoughts. At some point, they become so out of touch with their inner world that they become totally dependent on others. This is what Erick Erikson (1964) described as the "psychosocial struggle of identity vs. role confusion." It is also discussed in Eric Berne's (1964) book, *Games People Play*.

As a result of this external identity, people repress, disassociate, project, and alienate aspects of their own being. In so doing, individuals are praised, appreciated, accepted, understood, and often rewarded. They can ascertain a feeling of security, belonging, support, safety, success, and accomplishment, but at the same time feelings of meaninglessness, in-authenticity, dissatisfaction, boredom, vulnerability, unhappiness and a general lack of personal meaning in life can arise This results in organizations that lack vitality and are incapable of improving.

The recent call for site-based, total quality and participative management does not work with employees who are stuck in this scripted, self-validation stage of development. These types of employees work quite well under autocratic managers who over-manage and over-control. They wish to conform, belong, please others, receive approval, and follow law and order, which is good for autocrats and organizations that wish to maintain the status quo. However, if improvement, and constant growth is the goal, underdeveloped employees will be frustrating.

Vital Self-Reliance

The highest stage of development is reached by facilitating individual growth and development. The aim is to gain insight into human nature and how that nature is in balance with organization. A process of synthesis and adaptation between the inner personal nature and outer reality produces continuity. Only than do living and working begin to merge.

The goal is to eventually consolidate the external world and the internal self into one natural being. In this way, thoughts, feelings, and sensations are allowed into awareness without preconceived reaction to them. This stage of development leads to liberation, attainment of genuine intuition, wisdom, and judgment. A sense of identity shifts from ego-center or conformity to balance, unity, or both. All boundaries of inner and outer disappear as a boundless, universal, integrated, transcendent stage of development is achieved. This vital, self-reliant stage of development is the home of all "life juices," and provides the energy needed for fulfillment of life's responsibilities. It is the source of unique power, and the courage to be able to call upon it must be developed.

It is in this layer that self-direction, self-acceptance, self-support, reliance, esteem, understanding, and confidence are experienced. Thoughts and beliefs are reinforced internally. Individual work is based on a willingness to trust the self and let go. People develop confidence where they used to need approval. They accept resources and limits and act responsibly, without reducing self-confidence or raising self-doubts. A sense of independence, self-reliance and spontaneity is developed, supporting vitality and exhilaration. This stage of development allows employees to release their full potential in the development of vision and the work of constantly improving in order to achieve the ideal vision.

Effective work cultures encourage their employees to develop an inner sense of reality so they are not totally dependent on what others say or think about them. All persons are encouraged to define themselves, as well as be defined by others and their relation with them. They are encouraged to get in touch with aspects of themselves that are important to them and make them unique. Employees learn to develop an appropriate balance between personal and organizational expectations, trying to establish supporting and mutually beneficial relationships. There is a concerted effort to see that each employee grows to the fullest in the service of the organization. Thus, both mutually benefit.

Organizational Disempowerment

Static organizations tend to be unsupportive and inhospitable to introspection and the discovery of inner powers. Employees who function at a higher level of consciousness or development can disturb politics, bureaucracy, autocracy, and the status quo. The scripted, self-validation work culture is often poorly suited for those who are fully developed and empowered. They do not fit the comfort of "practice as usual." They are often defined by the culture as rebel-innovators who must be ostracized and neutralized so they cannot damage the status quo. The natural desire to belong and please takes over, and the individuals give up their selves in order to conform and fit in. Barring anarchy, this is the only course of action that can be taken under an authoritarian culture. It becomes the goal to go through the system visibly but quietly, unquestioningly, unobtrusively, and acceptingly.

Unfortunately, such an approach does not fit within the fast pace of modern times with the constant call for reform, restructuring, and improvement. This autocratic culture keeps the individual from innovating, thinking, being, or creating. The individual's work is molded by the continuing individual illusion of personal and organizational acceptance.

However, individuals become troubled knowing that development has not occurred. External domination requires them to be, satisfied with less than they could be resigning themselves to a barren professional life. They realize that they need something more than the direction, conformity, and acceptance they have become so dependent upon, but they are no longer quite sure what. They believe that the organization dissipates their spirit and eats up their professional lives. As they get more out of sync, they must exercise greater caution in response to their work. In this way, one-sided institutions result in one-sided individuals who are incapable of dealing with personal response, self-governance, or participatory approaches.

There is a tremendous need to change from political power to personal power. Education is a profession of great inhibitors in a society that scorns educators' inability to respond. It is not the educators, but the disempowering culture in which they are nurtured that results in the failure to respond.

As people achieve higher levels of development, they are capable of imaginative leaps, curiosity, synthesis, spontaneity, insight, wisdom, and creation. Educator John Gowan (1989) concluded that,

> If we learn to domesticate creativity—that is, to enhance it rather than deny it in our culture—we can increase the number of creative persons to the point of a critical mass. When this level is reached in a culture, as it was in Periclean Athens, the Renaissance, Elizabethan England, and our own Federalist period, civilization makes a great leap forward. We can have a golden age of this type such as the world has never seen . . .

We can achieve great leaps forward in education if educators are encouraged to develop themselves to their fullest and to fully apply their abilities.

Empowerment in Action

The Montgomery, Alabama public schools provided many opportunities for team members to discover and develop their unique interests. The vertical team took time to encourage members to focus on and develop the areas of personal interest that seemed most pressing and important to them. They showed respect for personal interests, and encouraged people to focus on and do introspective thinking about personal needs and abilities. Interests that came to the surface were treated delicately as the group helped the individuals think through unique desires and strengths in a non-threatening, understanding environment. Members were encouraged to take quiet and private time to reflect on their values, beliefs, and abilities. Members were encouraged to focus on the creative, natural side of themselves and to see how all facets could be successfully expressed within the organization.

Thomas Head, principal at Jefferson Davis High School, found that he had an opportunity to take a serious look at himself as both a person and a professional and to re-ground himself in what was really important. He discovered a sense of confidence and satisfaction in his skills that he had not thought about for a while. Thomas stated,

> The Vertical Team experience has developed an inner sense of renewed pride and a "can do" mind set that has permeated all that I do in my life. I believe that this sense of inner pride and strength has been recognized by students, faculty and parents and seems to be almost contagious. Teachers are taking a serious look at themselves and the types of attitudes and behaviors that they are bringing to the work situation. Everyone involved with the school seems to be sensing my inner desire to build spirit and pride within the school and looking into natural and comfortable ways in which they can help. Although I can't exactly put it in words, the time spent in getting more in touch with my inner nature has made me a more natural, convincing and better leader.

Head was able to renew and excite a spirit within that was infectious in his relations with faculty, staff, student body, and parents. His personal empowerment was fortified by his conviction that he had the skills and ability to make a difference in the education of children—"I am convinced I can create a better school for my community." This conviction became contagious as everyone associated with the school tried to identify the unique talents, abilities, and desires that they could apply to improve the school.

Head shared,

> I can already sense I have become a better, more real example for my faculty and school community. I feel more natural in my relationships and in the efforts I have provided to the school. I find that those around me are beginning to make an effort to identify, discover, and bring out their own natural talents and feelings and to find ways in which they can be more naturally involved in school improvement activities. This freedom to be themselves has resulted in a greater willingness and eagerness to actively participate. An opportunity to discover what is important to and natural for you creates a sense of desire, a strong spirit and a sense of reward in what you do.

This same type of experience occurred for Cindy Somerville, a teacher in Montgomery County. She stated,

> My Montgomery Vertical Team experience has been the most positive and rewarding in my teaching career. I had an opportunity to get in touch with what was important to me, to really get to know myself, and to share my beliefs with my peers. That has been a very positive thing in helping me to improve my sense of direction and to know how I wanted to spend myself professionally. This has given me a real boost in regard to my work and my active involvement in the school. I gained so much that helped me in the classroom to have my most positive year. I sensed and discovered new ways to help at-risk and marginal learners. The team gave me the wonderful positive reinforcement that helped me to become more natural and stronger.

As Somerville discovered a new sense of interest and worked to develop these interests, she became more confident and trusted herself, sharing what she had discovered about herself and her approach with her peers. She worked with her principal to set up a School Improvement Team. She began, for the first time, to do faculty inservice programs. Her attitudes toward her students were more positive, and she became actively involved in the implementation of a Power of Positive Students (POPS) program.

> I believe that my more natural approach to the classroom has improved my class atmosphere as well as my children's grades. This has probably been my best year of teaching.

Somerville also recognized how important her family was to her and spent more quality time with them. This meant that she had to say "no" more often, to readjust her schedule, and to learn to delegate more. One thing that she did not say "no" to was a very strong desire that she had been harboring to go back to school and get a master's degree. In summarizing her assessment of the experiences, she said,

> The Vertical Team experience has given me the strength and the opportunity to grow and become a stronger, more natural teacher. More teachers need to have these types of empowering experiences to expand their personal and professional growth. I learned so much that I would like to see this be more available to other teachers.

Most of the Montgomery participants involved in empowerment and self-discovery felt much more optimistic about their future and the future of the school system. The morale improved for those who were able to bring more of their natural self to their work. Dr. Talmadge Oswalt, assistant superintendent for curriculum and instruction in Montgomery, found that he had become more of a reflective thinker as a result of the empowerment process. He was better able to anchor his action in a style that was comfortable for him. He felt that his nature and experience were more complementary, resulting in an expanded sense of wisdom. He stated,

> The experience has been a professional renewal for me. I have a much deeper commitment to doing all that I can in the school system. My cynicism level has been reduced; therefore, I face the future with new hope, commitment and determination to step-up my efforts to find better ways to deliver better curriculum. My sense of inner strength has increased my ability to deal with external factors while maintaining my focus on the important needs of the district.

Dr. Oswalt's efforts resulted in the development of a more supportive, positive, psychological environment in which members of the group were free to develop and use their natural abilities. He found that empowerment was a "uniquely contagious" experience. He concluded,

> Because of my experience in the Vertical Team program, I am a more positive person. I feel better about me and my profession and this attitude seems to be contagious.

Thomas Bobo, superintendent of Montgomery public schools, was encouraged by the ways individuals and schools became more actively involved in establishing goals for themselves and their schools. He stated, "Individuals have, I feel, begun to assume ownership for themselves." He found that the empowerment aspects of the vertical team program revitalized the dedication of a number of very capable employees. He found that, "Employees of the school system have recharged energy and skills that over the years had been allowed to slip." In drawing conclusions regarding the program, Bobo states,

> An overall evaluation of our Vertical Team experience shows tremendous growth of all our administrative people ... People have brought more ownership into what is going on in their schools. It has led to much personal empowerment and professional growth. I feel the system as a whole is bound together in looking for ways in which we can all improve professionally. There has been a kind of renewal for many of us, and I feel that professional growth will continue throughout the entire system for many years to come.

Effective schools are structured by roles, sets of rules, policies, and standard operating procedures; however, there is also room for self-reliance, self-support, self-confidence, self-direction, and other energizing "life juices." Instead of depending on approval, employees learn to develop a sense of personal confidence. External support is replaced by self-support. Feelings of irresponsibility and lack of control are replaced by a sense of responsibility and inner control. Self-doubts are replaced by a self-trust that grows out of a reasoned understanding of strengths and limits and how both can be safely approached. Alex Goldman (1965) reported that John F. Kennedy told his aides that what the president of the United States needs most is support for the awesome responsibility and decisions that he faces, and not a litany of caution, concern, and danger. Professionals recognize the difficulty and danger in the tasks they face, and what they need is the courage to take the responsibility to apply their full ability and skill to do the best they possibly can do.

This does not happen in organizations in which people must turn to others for approval or where they must follow tightly prescribed plans and controls. People have no sense of responsibility for actions dictated by others, or actions supported by an external culture, so they make no dedicated efforts to act responsibly or to be concerned about consequences. Each time these individuals fail, they blame others. Each time they succeed, they attribute it to someone else. Everything is part of a cause-and-effect relationship over which nobody has control.

Energy and Excellence

Independence, self-reliance, and self-discovery support vitality, exhilaration, empowerment, and, ultimately, productivity. Empowered people do not have to do their work, they choose to. Empowered people do not use external rules, regulations, or controls as excuses not to do their best, they discover how they can best contribute toward a shared vision. Empowered people do not feel sorry for themselves and hate the organization for being so unfair; they place their efforts in improving and strengthening the organization. The effective culture demands that employees discover and apply their fullest capabilities to do their best. Empowered employees are trusted, and, thus, have the freedom to choose what they will do in a given situation, and are expected to struggle to accomplish what they decide upon. With such an outlook, self-knowledge, self-satisfaction, and self-support become important. Professional freedom does not mean that individuals give up organizational responsibilities, but that they bring their uniqueness, their strengths, their full power to these responsibilities. Energy and greatness flows from the natural self, which can only be tapped at the highest level of development.

The need to be developed, empowered, natural, and authentic is an instinct that rules personal and professional lives. The more that organizational culture denies this fact, the more the capabilities and skills of those who work within schools are lost. Empowerment is a new form of power—personal rather than collective. Edward Smith (1977) makes this point,

> . . . I cannot be other than what it is my nature to be, so to try to make myself different is destined to failure, as such a pursuit is in violation of my integrity. I am I, and the best for me is to be as fully I as I can. This means I cannot decide what I should be and shape myself in that likeness without loss of myself. What I must do is know my nature and allow that nature to flow, unfold, and be.

Organizational culture must allow employees' true nature to shape their roles and responsibilities and not allow the roles and responsibilities to shape the employees. In this way, employees gain freedom to be themselves, to reflect personal beliefs and desires, reveal true feelings, and, ultimately, improve professions and organizations.

Dr. John Ellis, superintendent of Austin, Texas, Independent School District, believes in the importance of personal empowerment to future success. His commitment to self-discovery, self-support, group-understanding and group-support was exemplified in development sessions geared toward giving greater insight into spiritual values and the concept of common humanity. As a result of the program, he believed there was an increased insight for participants. In summarizing overall impressions about the program, Ellis concluded,

> . . . the vertical team program provided the structure and support necessary to insure that each individual on the vertical team recognized his or her strengths and weaknesses. Furthermore, individuals had opportunities to improve existing strengths and to lessen and minimize weaknesses. Finally, participants came to see themselves as a part rather than a whole; to understand that alone, none could obtain what together they could master; and, to value and actively seek those parts necessary to achieve the whole.

Austin team members concurred that self-assessment and reflective thinking combined with exposure to others' introspection and viewpoints had greatly improved the effectiveness of team members to function in their jobs and to bring more of themselves to their work. Each of the participants had stories to relate about his or her self-discovery, personal growth, and personal success. The program resulted in a new sense of optimism and hope for the district.

Elena Vela, a high school principal and team member, set a major goal of sharing her empowering experiences with her teachers. She wanted her teachers to expand their knowledge and to increase their sensitivity to themselves and others. A major theme was to develop individual uniqueness while supporting one another in a positive way. She wanted the new sense of optimism and hope that developed on the Austin vertical team to spread to the faculty of her high school.

Livier Suniga, an elementary school teacher, found that the vertical team program brought out skills which were not being utilized to their fullest. She viewed her emergence as a leader at St. Elmo Elementary School as an indication of the success that can grow out of self-discovery. Examples of types of activities she was enjoying included being a member of a school district task force and PTA teacher representative for the year. Suniga believed that self-discovery and introspection was effective, "due to the support of fellow team members and to the wealth of information members shared in team meetings. The team members learned to listen to and value each others' opinions."

Suniga changed her spelling and social studies program and developed a modified brainstorming technique to use with her students to help them express and develop their ideas. She tried to bring her abilities out as much as possible and expounds on topics rather than sticking strictly to the scripts, teacher manuals, and curriculum unit guides as she had often done in the past. She also believed she was getting better at turning down activities she did not enjoy. She used her time for what she was hired to do, bringing her unique abilities to improve student learning.

When people brought their own unique abilities and perspectives to discussions, the issues and discussions came alive. This was because they could be viewed from more than one perspective, giving them a dynamic and rich quality. People were encouraged to share their thoughts and were expected to be in touch with and able to clearly articulate and support what they believed. Research, experience, teaching guides, and unit plans were all part of that articulation, but so was a wisdom and intuition for which the person cared and felt strongly about.

Self-Development and Commitment

Empowerment can be observed as liberation, spontaneity, self-understanding, poise, confidence, harmony, and freedom. Through this form of empowerment arises the higher passions of creativity and artistry, insight and intuition, dreams and fantasies, loyalty and love, dignity and drive, illusion and ecstasy, joy and peace. Empowered people are in control of their lives and know the truth and joy that come from achieving what they believe in. These are the people who stimulate hope, inspiration, and commitment for other members of the organization.

As people become more enlightened as to how to use their newly discovered energy for the universal good of mankind, they develop a sense of connection. Mind and heart become united in the soul as people become braver, more enlivened, more open, more creative, more contented, and, ultimately, more powerful. The ideals of empowerment that have been so eloquently discussed for centuries can become a reality if the culture supports them. There are many examples of this practice.

Roberta Lawrence-Walker, a teacher for the Richmond, Virginia City Schools, felt particularly good about the empowerment aspects of the vertical team program. She felt that her morale was improved and she developed the inner strength to present a workshop that she had always wanted to organize. She made a commitment to increase the sharing of information and activities among teachers at her grade level. Lawrence-Walker discovered a motivation and desire to increase her knowledge and ability in a number of areas—i.e., at-risk students, school-based management, the ministry of caring—as a result of her personal empowerment. This resulted in a renewed sense of power as she began to research expanded educational opportunities that were available to her. She concluded,

> I have been highly enlightened and charged as a result of this program. My personal growth and awareness have been raised so that I now feel a stronger commitment to truly making a positive difference in the educational arena. Overall, the vertical team experience has been probably the best revelation in my educational career. It, along with the Richmond Public Schools, has provided me with opportunities which I shall benefit from for years to come.

The general comments made by members of the Richmond City Schools' Vertical Team suggest the sense that empowerment strengthened their commitments to make needed changes. One participant stated,

> My sense of personal recognition of important educational needs increased such that I now feel a stronger commitment to making a positive difference in education. I feel empowered to take a more active role in making that difference.

Another participant suggested,

> Empowerment allowed me to discuss issues and concerns that I felt strongly about where I hadn't been able to in the past. I realize that I

had been taking out my personal frustrations of not having the strength to speak up on my administrators, colleagues and the school system.

Frances Logan-Thomas, a teacher at Meadowdale Elementary School in Dayton, Ohio, had decided to leave the teaching profession prior to her empowering experiences. As she got more in touch with herself, she began to rediscover why she had become a teacher in the first place. She increased her self-confidence and her satisfaction with her work. She concluded,

> Prior to these development activities, I had entertained thoughts of leaving the teaching profession. As a result of the past year of working with the vertical team on my professional development, my self-esteem has been bolstered. This experience has and will continue to enhance my teaching experience.

Other comments suggested that empowerment fueled interest in personal and professional development:

> Once I felt that I knew what was important to me, I was highly motivated to expand my knowledge through involvement in workshops. This total experience has been and will be invaluable to me.

There were many similar examples of people's gaining a personal sense of self in order to improve personal development and work performance. A school system superintendent found,

> ... the vertical team experience has expanded my capacity for living personally and professionally. The development of an inner strength has been very meaningful in family situations, administrative staff situations, and in working with the public and the school board. Personally, I have long had a problem of trying to be the nice guy too often. As I developed more of a personal realization and sense of inner strength, I also developed a parallel ability to eliminate positions, eliminate programs, and close schools without the undue trauma to myself.

Vital Self-Reliance in Duval County

People are different in some ways and the same in others. What they each need to do is discover what it is that is unique and powerful about themselves that they bring to their work and organizations. It will not be the same for all individuals. Each has a role to fulfill and a purpose to achieve, and together the individual contributions of many have a very significant synergistic impact. Empowerment allows each to find what is naturally within and to learn how to best bring individual skills to the benefit of the organization.

Mary Susan Huber, a teacher and member of the Duval County Vertical Team in Jacksonville, Florida, found that empowerment aspects of the vertical team program gave her an opportunity to get in touch with her educational values. She stated,

> I have used my experience on the vertical team to get in touch with my deep intrinsic personal and professional philosophy. This philosophy is directly reflected in how I assume my teaching duties, as well as how I relate to subordinates and to educational programs. The vertical team experience paved the way for my investigating and examining my own philosophies, while enlisting the ideas, input and advice of others.

The empowerment experience is often given credit for helping school personnel to share professional concerns and express personal philosophies and beliefs. Huber read a number of books and articles on empowerment of teachers, which she reported to the Duval group, and led a number of discussions in this area. The team took time to experience the concept of empowerment and, ultimately, to be more willing to be in touch with personal thoughts, beliefs, abilities, attitudes, personality styles, and to bring unique qualities forward.

This worked quite effectively to insure that group discussions were balanced, provocative, and productive. Members shared their strengths and learned how each made important contributions that were respected by the group. Team members were better prepared to use their capabilities to function more effectively as team members and teachers. Because of the success of empowerment on the vertical team, district-wide efforts were established to empower teachers.

Ron Poppel, a principal in Duval, used empowerment approaches to complete a school-wide self-assessment. He stated,

> My objective is to enable us to understand various personality types and the important and unique contributions that each make. The purpose is to help each of us to better understand ourselves as well as the people we work with in the school.

He and his staff completed a Myers-Briggs personality inventory and attended workshops to help them interpret the instrument. Members were asked to give thought to their unique strengths and how they could best participate as effective team members. They tried to find opportunities to use their strengths, and realized the importance of having members of the organization with different strengths. They learned the importance of a balanced organization.

This form of "self" and "other" understanding was successful in building appreciation, support, and effectiveness among the staff. According to Poppel, "All employees within the school felt more comfortable with themselves and the important role that they each played in the school." The improved and empowered culture of the school helped to improve student performance and standardized test scores.

The Duval team believed that empowerment allowed the team to engage in an honest and unique exchange of ideas and concerns among various levels within the organization that would not have occurred without it. The group became an important forum for critical issues as members were encouraged to bring forth their own unique thoughts. Team members concluded that,

> Individual members showed courage and initiative in offering their views, speaking out for their constituents, volunteering to prepare special reports, and, in general, freely sharing their own personal views. The attitudes of individual team members toward the notion of teacher empowerment definitely changed over the year—a change that all were most pleased to observe.

The atmosphere of the team was one of a refreshing spirit of excitement and honesty. Not only were members in touch with what they wanted to say, but they also had the courage to articulate what was important to them. This grew out of a respect for the honest ideas and opinions of others. The team members reported, "There was a noticeable growth in respect for each other."

The Call for Empowerment

Certainly, none of the correlates of an effective culture will have much of an impact if individuals are not fully developed and fully empowered. Empowered people have developed themselves fully so that they can participate and use their abilities and energies to further the mutual interests of the organization. An organization cannot be effective without the talents, abilities, skills, and passions of the individuals who make it up. The possibilities for the human is envisioned by Dr. Jean Houston (1982). She states that we must,

> . . . humbly but tenaciously educate ourselves for sacred stewardship, acquiring the inner capacities to match our outer powers. We must seek

and find those physical, mental, and spiritual resources that will enable us to partner the planet.

Empowerment is finding personal answers to our questions about human possibilities. Empowerment is an expansion of the notion of what it is to be a professional. Empowerment is drawing out one's highest aspirations and noblest actions as a professional and as a human being. Empowerment is awakening all the power that is within an individual, within an organization, so that each can fully contribute. Empowerment is discovering, feeding, and releasing the capacities within.

The visions that organization members are capable of achieving will demand a full complement of the fully developed human. This is why empowerment is so important to our modern times. Individuals within organizations must be encouraged to explore and experience all that it means to be an individual member working toward an organizational vision. Members must discover how they can bring themselves to that vision. For the visions to grow more complex and all-encompassing, choices more diverse, and schools more effective, educators must be fully in touch with themselves and capable of applying all of their unique and individual abilities to the fullest.

Bibliography

Berne, Eric. *Games People Play.* New York: Groves Press, Inc., 1964.

Cunningham, William G. *Empowerment: Vitalizing Personal Energy.* Atlanta, Georgia: Humanics Limited, 1991.

Erikson, Erik H. *Insight and Responsibility.* New York: Norton, 1964.

Garmin, N.B. "Reflection, the Heart of Clinical Supervision." *Journal of Curriculum and Supervision,* 2, (Fall, 1989).

Goldman, Alex, J. (Ed.) *The Quotable Kennedy.* New York: The Citadel Press, 1965.

Gowan, John, et. al. *Creativity: Its Educational Implication.* Dubuque, Iowa: Kendal-Hunt, 1989.

Herman, Ned. "The Creative Brain." *Training and Development Journal* (1981).

Houston, Jean. *The Possible Human.* Los Angeles, CA: Jeremy P. Tarcher, Inc., 1982.

Kirsch, Susan Sayers. *Leadership Style: A Behavioral Matrix.* Portland, Oregon: Northwest Regional Education Laboratory, 1982.

Maslow, Abraham. *Motivation and Personality.* New York: Harper and Row, 1970.

Rhodes, Lewis A. "Beyond Your Belief: Quantum Leaps Toward Quality Schools." *The School Administrator.* (December, 1990). Reprinted by permission of the American Association of School Administrators. Copyright © 1990 by AASA.

Sergiovanni, Thomas. *The Principalship: A Reflective Practice Perspective.* Boston: Allyn & Bacon, 1991.

Smith, Edward W. L., ed. *The Growing Edge of Gestalt Therapy*. New York: Bruner/Mazel, Inc., 1976 and Secaucus, New Jersey: Citadel, 1977.

Copyright Wilber, Ken, Engler, Jack and Brown, Daniel P. *Transformations of Consciousness*. Boston: New Science Library, 1986. © 1986 by Ken Wilber. Reprinted by arrangement with Shambhala Publications, Inc., 300 Massachusetts Ave., Boston, Ma. 02115

10

Sustained Innovation

One of the basic tenets of the research on effective schools is that school improvement takes time. It typically takes at least three to five years for successful innovations to become routine and fully established. Time is required for those working in the organization to adapt practices to fit the work culture. Significant improvements are translated by the culture into an operating reality within the school district. As such, the implementation of improvement is more a process of cultural adaptation than it is a structural innovation.

Cultural adaptation is the process by which individuals learn about new ideas and develop a desire to implement them. School improvement results from an on-going cultural process, not the implementation of the latest approach. Dr. Donn Gresso from East Tennessee State University states,

School improvement plans will be different in different years, but the culture and process, once developed, will be able to handle whatever the district or school chooses to pursue. Research on school improvement suggests that successful change takes three to five years, and the Danforth Foundation experience bears this out. The school system must take the time needed to establish a firm base.

Dr. Carl Ashbaugh, facilitator for the Duval County vertical team in Florida, states,

Implementing ideas like school-based management "cooperative learning" and "empowerment" takes a considerable amount of time. It requires that responsibility for the final outcome be assumed by individual members. Sufficient time must be set aside to allow for the development of ideas and responsibility so that projects can be success-fully implemented. The success of projects depends on the involvement and support of all faculty and this type of support takes time to develop. The school culture must be one of mutual support and respon-sibility and the time span must be long enough to allow these qualities to develop.

Dr. Perry Pope, principal at Spring Woods High School in Houston, Texas, discussed what he saw as ongoing goals for the school. The major theme for his school was cooperative learning. The process of fully imple-menting this project was expected to take three to four years. Materials were collected on the concept and distributed to teachers throughout the school. In addition, a campus library for cooperative learning was devel-oped. Staff development options were provided to allow the teachers to learn more about cooperative learning. Cooperative learning sessions were also provided for parents of students within the school. Dr. Pope attended several training sessions and professional meetings on cooperative learning. He held several discussions for teachers, where each shared what he or she had learned.

The teachers were encouraged to develop ways to implement coopera-tive learning within their classrooms. Their ideas were shared and dis-cussed during various staff meetings and faculty meetings, as well as through department meeting minutes and other techniques. The faculty shared ideas, research, and literature throughout the year. The focus was on continual refinement and improvement of how cooperative learning was implemented. Teachers were encouraged to continually share and discuss how their individual efforts were going. The principal also spent more time observing in the classroom and talking to teachers about any needed sup-port that would help them to better implement cooperative learning.

A committee was established to determine the best method to evaluate the results. Discussions were held to determine how to best use central administrative capacities to support the teachers in their development and implementation efforts. This was not thought of as a yearly project or as a one-time shot of the latest fad in education, but a long run commitment by the school to improve education through the use of cooperative learning. Plans were implemented as soon as teachers were ready to try out new ideas. They each had freedom to design and implement their own approaches. Teachers were supported, and there was a constant sharing, excitement, and celebration over successes that occurred.

Failures were accepted as a logical component of testing new ideas; however, they were identified and eliminated quickly. Teachers moved at their own pace, but each was part of the collective vision and was required to move forward with cooperative learning. Dr. Pope stated,

Each teacher received hands-on training, role modeling and literature on cooperative learning. The principals who visit the teachers' classrooms look for cooperative learning and comment positively when observing it. There are lots of opportunities for sharing of what works and what doesn't work. We have made a commitment to enhanced learning and social skills through cooperative learning and we will be working on that shared vision over the next two or three years.

Cultural Adaptation

The outcome of an effort to improve education depends as much on the implementation process as it does on the quality of the improvement. The process must be one that allows time for mutual participation and cultural adaptation. In a Rand study of Federal programs supporting educational change, Drs. Paul Berman and Milfrey McLaughlin (1978) found that "mutual adaptation was the only process leading to teacher change; in other words, teachers changed as they (and only as they) worked to modify the project's design to suit their particular school or classroom." The culture must be willing to invest the time and energy needed to co-adapt an innovation if it is to be successful. Short term administrative mandates and directives are not very successful in developing cultural support. Berman and McLaughlin continue, "administrative fiat was not enough to overcome so-called 'staff resistance;' it did not persuade teachers to expend the extra energy and effort to adapt to a project for which they had little responsibility." Change can only be institutionalized when it has been fully embraced by both the vertical and horizontal culture. This type of implementation process, the one resulting in stable continuation, takes a long-term focus to develop.

One superintendent, who did not want his name mentioned, lamented about the number of projects in education that seem to lack staying power and fade out of existence. He talked about a computer project that was supported by a professional association and funded by various outside groups. The announcement for submission of grant proposals had a very short lead time and involved the use of computers to help slow learners. The students would be removed from their regular class during the day to spend some intense learning time in areas of deficiency using computers in a computer lab. The entire program was overseen by a coordinator. Although the program was very strong and had great potential for helping at-risk students, the superintendent did not hold much hope for its success because of the very short time line for implementation.

The project was set up so that the proposal had to be developed in the spring term, the coordinator hired during the summer, and the project fully implemented with the beginning of school in the fall. That meant that little or no time could be used to allow all the teachers who would be influenced (releasing students from regular classes, etc.) by the plan to become familiar with it, and, more important, to support it. A planning group including a few teacher representatives wrote the project which was approved and funded in the spring. A coordinator for the project was hired during the summer (no teacher involvement) and staff development was implemented simultaneously with the project in the fall.

This project had a significant impact on the teachers' ability to schedule instructional time, particularly for students pulled for intensive instruction in the computer laboratory. As a result of this short time line that only allowed for minimal broad scale involvement, quite predictable (and appropriate) "staff resistance" developed. The culture of the organization, after all, protects it from unneeded and unhealthy changes that are not in its best interest. Healthy cultures will not allow unexpected and unsolicited changes to occur until they have embraced and understood them.

Teachers felt that this new project, however effective, had been sprung on them. They did not accept the argument that there was a short time line implemented in order to participate and obtain funding. The project affected their school day, and they believed they should have had adequate input in such planning. Even though there was great potential for the project, it started under very adverse cultural conditions and had minimal chance for long range success. The project could survive, but it will not come anywhere near the potential it might have achieved if the school district had time to allow for cultural adaptation.

The Ironies of Improvement

Many projects have been hampered by an inadequate time range, first to implement them and then to support them and work out all the bugs. The superintendent mentioned above suggested that little improvement will occur in education unless those involved in its improvement begin to see a much longer time range in which to instill needed improvements.

Dr. Carl D. Gilckman (1990) has helped us to understand the problems that schools face in mounting successful change efforts and why it takes so long. The administrators must first mobilize the forces to address needed school improvements. Improvement efforts require time and energy to build trust, confidence, community, and skill as well as to address the disturbances that improvements will cause. This must all occur at the same time that insecurity and resistance are being driven out of the culture. The culture needs time to build faith in its ability and the legitimacy of improvements.

The more different groups are brought together to focus on improving the schools, the more those involved need to know how to handle different views, tensions, and conflicts that become apparent. The collegial and shared approaches of an effective work culture tend to eliminate the enemy that holds progress back. Groups sometimes see themselves as the enemy for not having better schools, and it takes time to work through these difficulties. Failures are not seen as normal steps toward continued improvement, but as a waste of time and energy. When successes occur, people suggest that standards were lowered or the effort was doctored to make it look good. It takes time to help those involved become comfortable with both failures and successes. The more people recognize that improvements have been made, it becomes apparent that there is much to be improved. This increases dissatisfaction with what is being currently done, and increases awareness of the awesome challenge of what must be done. As a school or district improves, the more those from other schools criticize it. A long-term perspective is required to work through this natural evolution.

Schools have not been provided this long-term perspective, and have been forced to make "quick fixes" for those who are more concerned with short-term gains. Excellence requires time to stabilize and produce results. Many administrators have realized that the long term is not a frill they will be given. This is probably best exemplified by the tenure of school superintendents. The average tenure of urban superintendents is two and one-half years, which is less time than it takes to make a significant improvement. A front page article in the December 26, 1990 *New York Times* characterizes the attitude toward school improvement and a long term perspective.

> ... school superintendents around the country have been quitting in droves or have been dismissed or have retired early, often because they have failed to deliver the quick educational fixes demanded of them. More than 15 major cities are now scrambling to find school chiefs, nearly three times the usual number in a given year, experts say.

Innovation and improvement are best recognized as systematic, progressive, and cumulative improvement of educational practice. Continuous improvement is the development of an educational culture with a long term willingness to improve and a long term focus on what an ideal school looks like. It is a change from "wake me up when this one's over" to a belief that with time and effort "we can really make a difference around here."

Commitment to a long term willingness to improve the organization is difficult because that is where the really hard work begins. It takes effort and time to become competent at doing something a new way, and the time relationship is geometrically related to the number of people involved. The individual and the culture must learn and master a new way that is believed to result in a higher level of excellence. New ways whether they are improvements or not, require more effort than old ways. Without support and time everyone will revert to the old ways. When time expectations are unreasonable cultural resistance will develop.

Even very effective school improvements do not automatically take root. Continuation of projects requires a willingness to stick with them, to nurture them, and, most important, to work through all the needed effort to gain understanding and to fine tune to sustain a successful improvement. In fact, the long term focus includes both a vision of an ideal future state and a long term persistence to achieve that vision. First, it takes time to agree on improvements and for the culture to understand and adapt, and finally for teachers to implement and fine tune those improvements.

The continuing effort and commitment required to see a project that has potential through to a final acceptance, thus, takes at least three to five years. In this way, improvements are finally assimilated only after all the needed adjustments are made to make them fit the organizational culture. When this happens, corrections and improvements will take root and become institutionalized. This has not been allowed to occur in quite a number of school districts attempting to bring about a culture of excellence.

Lessons Learned

One of the critical needs in the development of educational reform is the lengthening of the nation's educational attention span. Continuous improvement requires the establishment of a mutually agreed upon vision that is worthy of professional effort and commitment. Such improvement also requires the patience that it takes for individuals and organizations to achieve greatness. One of the most often encountered enemies of successful improvement efforts is an unrealistically short time frame for implementation. Imposing a two to two and one-half year time frame on personal or organizational development is an invitation for failure. As time passes, the organization becomes clogged with incomplete initiatives. This is the condition in which we now find a number of American school districts.

Not only do the bits and pieces of abandoned plans adversely affect an organization, but so does the inability of the organization to gain "lessons learned" from the long term struggle to continuously improve a system. Instead of success, there is a series of unsuccessful, unsupported initiatives to which there has been minimal long term commitment. Because of rapid changes to new proposals, little can be gained from the last one that was tried as it begins clogging the system.

"Lessons learned" is an important concept in J. M. Juran's (1988) approach to total quality management (TQM). When long-term commitments are made to implementation and improvement efforts, a collective experience of shared knowledge about and familiarity with the whole process of innovation and continual improvement is built. Individuals gain expertise and understanding of the system and are better prepared to make needed modifications to constantly improve it.

If individuals continually throw out the latest system and begin rebuilding new ones, their collective knowledge and experience becomes much less useful and they must start over to acquire new understanding and perspective. They learn new knowledge, often incompatible with the old, and they don't get the opportunity to apply it to continuous improvement. Just when they begin to learn some essential lessons, they are off to something new, and the lessons learned no longer seem to fit.

Shifting approaches avoids the problems of fixing the system, but often leads to both a useless system and useless lessons learned. In searching for the perfect system, the organization cannot achieve an adequate system that is capable of being improved. As a result, the employees and students usually end up with neither. Many believe this is what has happened in American education, and fear that we have yet to learn our lessons.

In discussing the importance of lessons learned, Dr. Juran states,

> The value of those lessons is obvious, and it is universal for human beings to store those lessons learned in their memories as guides to action in the future. Human beings go further. They extend their memories through records and libraries; through systems of beliefs, rituals, and taboos (culture); through the design of their products and processes. Collectively, human use of the concept of lessons learned has been decisive in human dominance over all other animal species.

The purpose of lessons learned is to use them to obtain benefits later. This requires a long term perspective. If immediate success is desired, lessons learned cannot be banked for the benefit of making improvements. It is a long term, shared vision of greatness and the continuous work toward that vision that holds the greatest promise for education. The efforts associated with continuous improvement result in effective employees and excellent organizations.

Past, Future, and Present

Vision creates a precedence for all action, providing a sense of direction and consistency to all effort that follows. A three to five year perspective limits the freedom of those within the organization to make quick fixes and short term changes. At the same time, vision provides some assurance that the efforts of those within the organization will not be abandoned prior to fruition. This reduces a complex educational world to a somewhat simpler one.

The formulation of and commitment to desired, mutually supported outcomes provides a level of stability within the organization that serves as a catalyst for organizational synergy. Sequential activities can be planned and implemented while major milestones are evaluated. There is an excitement in the accomplishment of agreed upon change and a natural reward in seeing plans slowly evolve into actual practice—hopefully, improved practice. This longer range perspective allows those within the organization to adapt and continuously improve, to upgrade existing quality and resolve disagreements as the vision is being achieved. A consistent vision allows enough time for those within the organization to identify deficiencies and malalignments, as well as to make needed adjustments. Without a stable vision, it is very difficult to gain "lessons learned" and to determine what adjustments are needed.

The establishment of predetermined mileposts toward achieving a vision allows organizations to focus on and measure improvements in regard to the accomplishment of the vision. One can more quickly become aware of deviations if such milestones are established. It is much easier to make decisions about unexpected outcomes. Unexpected deviations away from the vision may demand a change in strategies or perhaps even a change in the vision.

A short term perspective typically results in organizational and individual frustration as directions constantly change, stability decreases, and crisis seems to abound. Organizations live for the moment, often persisting in ineffective activity or abandoning potentially successful activities before they reach their potential. Being able to visualize a desired future is a very wonderful gift. We are one of the few species that can see desired future outcome. We do not use the vision to create restlessness and anxiety; we use it as a beacon to provide direction and a measure of progress. We do not use a vision of an ideal future to keep us from enjoying and experiencing our present accomplishments, but it does provide us with a point of reference for the present.

The past is dead, the future is imaginary, and we have a direct influence on the present moment. Certainly, we must live in the present if we are to have any impact on the world in which we live. This does not mean that we cannot have an eye toward achieving a future vision of excellence. This is what gives present action its purpose. The vision of the future does not interrupt present living, but it provides direction and purpose. As Phillip Schlechty often suggests in his presentations,

It is not, as we commonly believe, the past plus the present that forms our vision of the future, rather the past plus our vision of the future forms the present.

We use the future to set priorities in life, to provide some stability, to think through actions, to measure progress and to gain clearer perspectives from lessons learned.

Visions are not simply or quickly achieved. They are the reason professional lives are dedicated to a particular organization. The vision is satisfying and desirable, and people are willing to commit their lives' work to the achievement of it. Visions set an organization and a work unit apart from everyone else. Visions attract both employees and clients, and they must be challenging and inspiring.

Organizational life is a one day affair followed by another day. By having a long term focus, each of those days complement one another and accumulate and add to the achievement of excellence.

The Long and Short of It

Table 10.1 highlights a number of differences between a short-term and long-term focus in sustaining innovation, improvement, and synergy. The short-term emphasis usually results in the initiators of change serving as the driving force. The long-term focus allows time for almost everyone to become part of the driving force. The short term focus is on implementation of one idea throughout the organization, and the long term emphasis is on continuous individual and organizational improvement along multiple fronts. The short term focus is based on tried and true solutions to solve problems. The long-term focus is based on continuous improvement to achieve a shared vision of an ideal school. A short-term focus depends on the structure for change to occur, and the long term focus depends on the culture for the evolution of change. The leadership style in an organization with a short-term focus leans toward selling and controlling, as opposed to a long-term focus on facilitating, supporting, and empowering.

The long-range perspective is needed to seek openness, trust, support, and consensus, to be collaborative, to be empowering, to allow for brainstorming, to encourage participation, to work through conflicts, to allow participants to develop skills, to shape vision, and to gain needed understanding for continuous improvement. Patience and long-term focus help to identify the right people in the organization, to make good decisions that they can live with, and to make them at the proper time.

TABLE 10–1   Long Term v. Short Term Focus

Short-Term Focus	Long-Term Focus
innovator(s) as driving force	shared vision as driving force
sells people	helps people
praises	encourages
autocratic	participative
problem solving, decision-making, new solutions	networks, lessons learned, feedback for future vision
centralized expertise	site-based expertise
"kick off"	planted and nurtured
a function of quick fix and control	a function of continuous improvement and effort
is deliberately implemented	is logically incremental
is imposed	evolves and adapts
underestimates effort on a single front	underestimates synergistic effect of multiple fronts
has forced momentum, few driving forces	compounds energy-growing acceptance
wears out the machinery	oils the machinery
like betting	like investing
deflates morale	fuels desire for improvement
runs over and eliminates resistance	removes barriers
aspirin	therapy
is often imported	the plan fits the place
is monitored	is facilitated
problems cause failure and abandonment	problems provide information for improvement
require new learning	requires lessons learned
new commitment	cumulative commitment
quick fix or cover-up	hard work and progress
a fad—a surge of power	a trend with staying power

Short-Term Focus	Long-Term Focus
someone else's tried and true	the progeneration of new perspective
a solution in search of a problem	a vision in search of improved direction
immediate gratification	long-term gain
weakens with assault	improves by attack and critical analysis
promotes support and marketing	encourages debate and difference
is an event	is a process
changes behavior	changes culture and internalizes new capabilities
associates change with another priority shift	associates change with the success or failure of a previous plan or program
"How will next year be different from this year?"	"What must we do differently next year to get closer to our strategic intent?"
chokes the organization	synergizes the organization
goes from beginning to end	goes from milestone to milestone

Planning requires a focus on the future consequences of present actions in regard to a vision or standard of quality. Good decisions are based on a long-term focus and are measured over the long haul, keeping the vision in mind. In this way, long-term focus is used to gain control of the future through current acts. The long-term focus allows employees to look ahead, anticipate events, prepare for contingencies, formulate directions, map out activities, and provide an orderly sequence for the achievement of visions. It also allows them to accept and correct errors made along the way.

Educational reforms should develop with a lesser sense of reactionary urgency than reforms of the past. Reforms need to be research based, locally developed from teacher expertise, and internalized and accepted by those currently employed. This will require time to develop and to dramatically change teachers' roles in improving education. Time is required for the concrete struggles that teachers will be involved in as they try new ideas, improve their classrooms, and struggle to help their colleagues to do likewise. This will require educational leaders to actively construct and share power with teachers. Time is required to structure the stories, visions, and experiences that teachers will use to organize and improve classroom experiences.

Educational improvement requires an openness to the process of development, translation, and experimentation. Leaders must understand culture, power, and ethics, and take the necessary time to influence them. These leaders will have to promote nurturing and empowering relations. Administrators and teachers must work under conditions that recognize them as professionals. Educators must be given the power to shape the conditions under which they work to produce curriculum and instruction that is suited to the needs of students.

Cultural leadership is the power to provide teachers with the culture, time, space, and power necessary to work collectively to improve American education. Henry Giroux (1992) states,

> Teaching must be linked with empowerment and not merely with technical competence. Teaching is not about carrying out other people's ideas and rules without question. Teaching requires working within conditions in which power is linked to possibility, collective struggle to democratic reforms and knowledge to the vast terrain of cultural and social differences that map out the arena of everyday life.

Today's educators must strive for the best, and as yet unrealized possibilities of American education.

Continuous Improvement in Action

The Charlotte-Mecklenburg School District in Charlotte, North Carolina, in an effort to provide a pro-active force in regard to both national and state mandates for educational reform, developed a "Comprehensive School Planning Process." The schools were provided the time and long-term perspective needed to allow teachers and principals to be involved in a school renewal process. Many within the school system believed that this could be the solution for the school system. In explaining why a long term perspective was needed in this process, superintendent Peter Relic stated,

> The implementation of the Comprehensive School Planning process in the Charlotte-Mecklenburg School System will result in a dramatic change in the way decisions are made, schools are operated, resources are allocated, and the way in which the community is involved in its schools. For this new program to be successful, it is imperative that everyone involved understands that change is a process which occurs over time. Change is not an event which results from a decision made by one or more policy makers or the superintendent. Too often good programs have struggled or failed during implementation for this reason.

The Springfield Public Schools in Illinois took two major approaches to achieve their long-term vision. They asked for a school improvement plan while providing pre-project inservice activities in relation to the school system's shared vision. The second supported the first by providing needed inservice activities prior to developing and implementing various phases of a school improvement plan.

A school improvement plan identified target groups, needs to be addressed, activities/events to address the identified needs, desired outcomes of the activities/events, starting dates, completion dates, and methods of assessing and evaluating the success of the project. The associated pre-project inservice activities included a statement of the skills and attitudes required to support the project, a list of key participants, potential inservice activities/resources, and measures of success of inservice activities. Separate groups experimented and suggested new ideas which became part of the plan if they proved to be successful.

A number of pre-project inservice activities were planned for Lanphier High School in Springfield. The overall school improvement plan for Lanphier was to increase student success. The skills and attitudes required included:

- tolerance and sensitivity to students
- being a helper rather than a critic
- proper sequencing of instructional activity
- setting specific objectives
- providing clear directions and expectations
- providing clear and related assignments and appropriate feedback
- allowing for individual differences
- being specific in feedback

Various activities were planned to develop the above skills, knowledge, and attitudes. Among the resources to be employed were the following:

- teacher conferences
- master teacher literature
- video tapes
- summer institutes
- Springfield Teacher-Staff Development

The success of the Lanphier program was to be measured in relation to the following criteria:

- reduction in student failure
- reduction in discipline referrals

- increase in student attendance
- increase in PSAT and ACT scores
- improved climate as shown on the Illinois state board climate assessment inventory

Excellence Takes Time

Many improvement plans fail because they are rushed. Teachers are asked to participate but are not given enough time to buy into the project, to adapt plans to their needs, and to shape them in a way that best meets their needs. Projects are often developed by a small group of people in the spring and summer for implementation in the fall. A brief inservice is provided, and teachers are expected to support the new, so-called school improvement. A long-term commitment to school improvement by every member of the school district based on the shared vision must be developed over time and with an extended commitment to staff development.

It is important to involve all members who will be affected by the plan in the initial planning. This will probably increase the length of time that will be required to develop a school improvement plan. Although this approach takes much longer, it results in a much more successful implementation effort.

Interview with a Superintendent

In a review during 1993, Robert C. Hill, former assistant superintendent and now superintendent of the Springfield Illinois Public School District, stated,

> Since Lanphier High School's participation in the Danforth School Administrators Fellowship program, a great deal of progress has been made with school improvement initiated in 1987. As an example, the staff focused on tolerance and sensitivity toward students. About 40 teachers volunteered beyond their regular assignments to mentor and tutor students identified as vulnerable to school failure. This strategy provided the identified students with a teacher to pupil ratio of 1:2 for special needs. The principal, Phillip Schmidt, exhibited leadership by focusing on staff development for the faculty and staff of the school and the teachers from the feeder elementary and middle schools. He was able to provide the consultants and materials through fundraising activities like candy sales. All of the planning and preparation resulted in improved attendance, reduction of student failure, reduction of discipline referrals, and achievement scores staying the same. When the

principal accepted a position in the central administration, the Lanphier school staff continued to have the same strong grassroots support for the program being implemented and for the school district.

Each decision provides direction and serves as a guide, indicating how the next improvement in the flow might be best addressed. The improvement is then implemented and evaluated as fine tuning begins. The implementation provides an opportunity to learn new lessons as the plans are continuously improved. This is not a short-term perspective. Sustained innovation is a willingness to hang in for the long term, to chart a path that leads to excellence, to adjust to changing conditions, and to prepare students who will make American schools internationally competitive. The vision is not the end of the process, but it is the beginning. It is the persistence of the culture to achieve the ideal that determines long-term success, and, ultimately excellence in our schools.

Bibliography

Berman, Paul and McLaughlin, Milbrey Wallin. *Federal Programs Supporting Educational Change, Volume VII: Implementing and Sustaining Innovation.* RAND, R-1589/8-HEW, May 1978.

Can, Clay. "Following Through on Change." *Training* (January, 1989).

Giroux, Henry A. "Educational Leadership and the Crisis of Democratic Government." *Educational Researcher* (May 1992).

Glickman, Carl D. "Pushing School Reform to a New Edge: The Seven Ironies of School Empowerment." *Phi Delta Kappan* (September 1990).

Hamel, Gary and Parahalad, C.K. "Strategic Intent." *Harvard Business Review* (May-June, 1989).

Juran, J. M. *Juran on Planning for Quality.* New York: The Free Press, Copyright © 1988 by Juran Institute, Inc.

11

School-University Partnerships in Team Facilitation

The role of the group facilitator is to provide support by serving as a catalyst during the consideration, discussion, and resolution phases of team deliberation. The facilitator must be sensitive to the culture of the group and the needs of the individual members while assisting the group to focus on its purpose. The facilitator models appropriate forms of participation and assists the individual to be as effective as possible. The major function of the facilitator is to continuously encourage and support human development, resulting in individual, team, and organizational improvement.

The success of the team requires that the group clearly understands the political, cultural, and human dynamics of improvement efforts. In excellent schools, these dynamics grow out of the expertise and commitment of team members and not the omniscience of leaders or the authority of hierarchy. The facilitator helps to broaden the understanding of power in the organization and its application for the common good. In this way, power is a form of human energy that the facilitator helps to release. The facilitator helps the group to exercise power through its membership and blocks efforts to exercise power over them. Power is shared among individuals who have the expertise, skill, and motivation to use it in the best interest of the organization. This provides potential for each member of the group to be more active in discussions or decisions related to their interests, expertise, and work.

A facilitator is someone who fosters respect by appreciating the individual identities and abilities of each group member. The *Facilitator Notebook* of the Danforth Foundation School Administrator Fellowship program states,

> Building a support group of diverse talent and perspectives requires a special sensitivity and skill to make each person a valued contributor to the group. Initial activities focus on the many strengths and experiences of individuals to build a positive climate for exploration of ideas. During this phase, facilitators establish their identities as group members by sharing their own backgrounds in a positive and personal manner. Modeling positive reinforcement of members but also sticking to a reasonable plan of action is essential for a successful group.

There are a number of skills that facilitators will be refining as they work with groups. These behaviors include such things as providing positive reinforcement of individual efforts while also finding ways to cause individuals to reach for new and uncertain goals. Facilitators need to value each person's strengths, and at the same time encourage them to overcome shortcomings. One of the key decisions facilitators make is when to keep quiet and when to intervene in the group or with an individual in the group.

The group needs to be able to share their perspectives while searching for a vision of excellence. The key is that both the group and ultimately the organization will take ownership and inspiration from the vision and related programs. This requires that the group take responsibility for the individual efforts of the members, and that the individuals take responsibility for the efforts of the group. According to the Danforth Foundation, the group becomes a team "when the group takes responsibility for the quality of success for every member of the group."

The choice of a facilitator for the vertical team is a very important decision. The person has to be able to handle the group dynamics as well as create the appropriate tone for an effective work group. The facilitator works with and through the various moods of the group. This person empathizes with the group, stays on the same wavelength, and is sensitive to the group ethos while maintaining group focus on session goals and program outcomes.

The facilitator aids the group in accomplishing its goals; enables members to satisfy needs; embodies the values, motives and aspirations of the group; represents the group's viewpoint when interacting with others; processes group conflict; and initiates group process while maintaining the group as a functioning unit. The facilitator's skills include interpersonal communication, brainstorming and consensus forming, problem solving, peer observation and feedback, agenda building, giving and receiving process feedback, and group process and leadership skills. The facilitation sets the tone for the group, thus the facilitator should be nonthreatening, supportive, and positive. In this way, the facilitator creates a climate of mutual understanding, trust, and commitment to the development and implementation of a vision of excellence within the school.

Selection of Facilitators

The Danforth Foundation Administrators believe the facilitator role provides an excellent opportunity to develop school–university partnerships. They believe that university professors have many of the qualities required of an excellent facilitator. Therefore, one of their programmatic elements is that the vertical team facilitator be a college professor. The Danforth Foundation pledge of commitment states that the school district board of education will "identify and mutually agree with the Danforth Foundation Program Director on one college/university person to serve as facilitator for the school district team."

The participating school district identifies a professor from a local university who has a desire to develop a collaborative relationship through the role of facilitator. The facilitator participates in a five–day clinical training program on facilitation skills. The facilitator is expected to coordinate the planning of an agenda, as well as facilitate and arrange locations for meetings. The facilitator is responsible for assisting the team members in the implementation of all of the major Danforth Program outcomes. The facilitator is also responsible for overseeing and coordinating the work of the team members and any reports or documentation that they produce. The facilitator fully participates in all the goals and objectives of the Danforth program. Dr. Nolan Estes, a facilitator from the University of Texas-Austin, stated, "The Fellowship program offered some of the best training for facilitators that I have ever received."

Facilitation includes the involvement with a group of strong, self-directed individuals who agreed to come together to decide collectively on a vision and the activity needed to achieve that vision. In this way, the facilitator is really a member of a "community of learners" who share the value of quality education for American youth. The roles of the members of the team are not determined by hierarchy or power but by their knowledge, information, and desire to make a contribution. The facilitator's role was to see that all the perspectives were considered during discussion.

The American Association of School Administrators chose a slightly different approach to the selection of facilitators. They came up with the concept of a pair of facilitators that could support and supplement one another in the facilitation process. The facilitating pair would operate as a team, complementing one another and working together to carry the heavy responsibilities of facilitation. This would also allow one facilitator to do some participant/process observation in order to better plan future activities.

Participant/process observation is the determination of mutually acceptable individual or team functioning criteria, the assessment of the degree to which the criteria are met, and the provision of feedback to the group to assist in making it more effective. This is not an evaluation, but an analysis and reflection upon group experience.

The facilitators work together to establish a climate of mutual understanding, trust, and commitment to program outcomes. They make each person a valued contributor to the group. The AASA staff believed that two facilitators would be better able to explore the strengths and experiences of team members, and could also build a more positive climate for the exploration of ideas. They could help group members share their perspectives and search for a consensus regarding shared vision and direction. The team becomes a support, growth, and development group in which the facilitators assist group members in being as effective as possible.

The AASA district learning leadership team documentation lists expectations for the facilitators as follows:

- build the capacities and stature of group members
- avoid creating dependence upon themselves
- nurture diverse values and perspectives among group members
- create ownership among group members
- nurture creative thoughts of others
- ask questions that help members rethink positions
- bring outside information and ideas to team process
- use effective, solid, time-tested group process to maximize efficacy of the group and its individuals
- share activities, agendas, and learnings, with other facilitators.

These are not the only models of effective group facilitation. Some believe that the highest ranking administrator within the group should serve as the facilitator. Others suggest that the individual being considered for promotion to a new administrative position should be given the responsibility of facilitator. A few have even suggested that this role might rotate so that each member of the group is a facilitator at one time or another. The important consideration is that the individual has the ability, skill, and endurance necessary for effective facilitation.

Qualities of an Effective Facilitator

A facilitator needs to be able to work well with people while helping to achieve group objectives. A facilitator needs to know when a discussion is productive and when it is time to refocus the group on the tasks at hand. The facilitator should not act as a teacher, but sharing perspectives and ideas relevant to the topics discussed can be most beneficial. The facilitator cannot be viewed as a threat to members of the group, but is solely responsible for creating group dynamics and drawing out the best potential of the group.

In discussing the qualities to look for when selecting facilitators, the AASA suggests that the facilitator

- has the confidence of the superintendent and board
- has credibility with members of the team
- is goal-directed
- has non-controlling, "others-centered" ego
- tries new ideas; models lifelong learning
- brings out the best in colleagues
- can stick with a long-term project
- can adjust to changing needs, conditions, and priorities
- is patient with and encourages colleagues' progress
- plans well, but remains flexible
- has a vision of what might be that is beyond current practice and conventional wisdom
- has strengths that may complement the co-facilitator—e.g., instructional skills, group process, extroverted, relaxed

Bonnie Wescott and Linda Seaman, principal and board member in Charlottesville public schools, commented on Dr. Dan Duke from the University of Virginia, providing a feeling for the types of relationships the facilitators develop. Their comments included,

> You have kept us moving in the right direction, encouraged us, challenged us and played with us. From a wary beginning Dan has become an outstanding mentor to us. His humor, insight, professional knowledge and task orientation have kept us working and growing together.

Another of the many positive comments about university faculty who served as facilitators was for Dr. John Croghan, from the University of Miami. Rosa Castro Feinberg, a school board member on the Dade County School's vertical team, stated,

I want to take this opportunity to thank you for the stimulating and productive Danforth Program sessions you facilitated for the Dade County school system. Those sessions provided me with focused input, directly from the field; with an overdue refresher on group process and collegial interactions; and, with the stimulus to get on with some in-depth planning in both personal and professional areas. I know the students I serve through the Board will benefit as a consequence of this experience.

Team members found that activities that gave individuals a chance to learn about each other and to learn how to function better as a work team were very important. These activities were considered absolutely essential to the development of collegiality. They provided an opportunity for team members to get to know one another better, to understand one another, and to allow the group to work together in an effective and efficient manner. Although these activities were first resisted, particularly by the more task-oriented members of the group, they proved to be the opportunities that allowed the group to actually form and bond.

An effective facilitator must be knowledgeable in these "getting-to-know-one-another" types of activities and be able to model appropriate sharing. The Danforth Foundation manual describes these as WHIP activities. The term WHIP came from the use of the "buggy whip" which is a quick and brief action that elicits a response. Each participant in the group activity is involved very briefly as the action moves from one person to another around the group. In describing these activities, the members of the Kirkwood School District Vertical Team in Missouri stated,

Evidence of this developing collegiality could be felt during the team building activity at each meeting. Initially, these exercises were viewed by the participants as something to get through. By the third meeting, the participants requested that the facilitator not place a time restraint on the activity. They felt that these activities allowed the team members the opportunity to gain a genuine understanding of each other's roles within the school district.

The most often stated concerns of the facilitators were about how rigidly they should stick to the agendas. Dr. Patricia Holland, a facilitator from the University of Houston, states,

In working with a leaderless group, the way in which an agenda is used is particularly important. If it is too rigidly adhered to it can stifle productive and creative work on the part of the group. On the other hand, if there is no agenda or if it is too vague, the group can flounder as they attempt to achieve clarity of purpose. It becomes the responsibility of the facilitator to encourage the group to assess its own process and progress, to plan and to determine the appropriate use of an agenda.

The Youngstown City Schools' vertical team stressed the importance of the knowledge and skills of their university facilitator to the success of the vertical team. They stated in their final report that Dr. Edgar Cobett from Youngstown State University,

> ... has a strong knowledge and background in administration, curriculum, and group dynamics. Equally important, Dr. Cobett has an excellent understanding and appreciation for the public schools through his close working relationship with schools over the years."

As a result of Dr. Cobett's facilitation, as well as professional development activities of the staff, it became increasingly apparent that improved communication skills were being practiced with greater frequency and sophistication among almost all members of the team.

School–University Partnerships

The facilitator is not required to be a member of a university, however the Danforth Foundation Administrators found this to be an excellent method to improve school–university cooperation and understanding. The university has a number of excellent resources for the public schools; one being a number of university professors who have many attributes of excellent facilitators. The university facilitator is not on the payroll of the organization and is a person who has demonstrated process skills in leading groups. They also have the potential to bring a wealth of resources to the precollegiate location.

Professors from local universities are most helpful in identifying resources for personal and professional development. University professors offer a new perspective on educational activities within the region and nation. They are also seen in a neutral light, since they have no roles in the school district's hierarchy. Initial research describing various forms of school–university partnerships are very favorable and suggest a bright future for these types of relationships.

Kenneth Sirotnik and John Goodlad (1988) summarized the results of a number of school–university projects nationwide. In recounting those cumulative learnings from school–university experiences spanning four decades, Dr. Goodlad found a number of successful qualities that these projects shared in common. He suggests that in order for school improvement to occur 1.) there must be a core of teachers, principals, and other stake-holders engaged continuously in inquiry about the nature, quality, and relevance of the education enterprise; 2.) there must be time away from daily demands for periods of sustained dialogue and reflection; 3.) it is highly desirable and perhaps even necessary for interpretation with other cohort groups—alternative drummers—and countervailing ideas; 4.) certain concepts, such as renewing capacity for staff (especially those closest to students), schools as the center for change, access to alternative and relevant knowledge, and the process of collaborative inquiry are more seminal and important than others; and 5.) juxtaposition of the action-oriented culture of the school and the inquiry-oriented culture of the university offers promise of shaking loose the calcified programs of both. The more these conditions exist, the less likely the school district's success will be sacrificed to "packages" or "quick-fix panaceas."

The school districts participating in the Danforth Foundation program felt that the university facilitator provided a new perspective on persistent problems. The facilitators often introduced the latest research on a given issue and a more theoretical perspective to start from. The vertical team had easy access, through the facilitator, to the expertise of not only the facilitator but the university and community as well. Faculty had the capacity to provide a theoretical context and access to research findings through the university. The district had access to the latest research, knowledge and expertise in the field. The consensus was that exposure to others' expertise and viewpoints enabled members of the school district to function more effectively in their jobs.

Phillip Schlechty and Betty Lou Whitford (1988) suggest that the model of working together will have to change from one of symbiotic relationships to one of organic relationships, if any long-term success is to be established. Symbiotic relationships emphasize mutual self interest, while organic relationships emphasize the importance of the survival of the whole as being necessary to the health of the individual. Relating this concept to school–university partnerships under symbiosis, each party addresses one or more problems that are "owned" primarily by one or another party. Then, "I'll help you with your concerns, and you'll help me with mine" is the mode of operations. This does not work in creating a culture of excellence of any long-range duration. In contrast, organic relationships focus on concerns or problems which are mutually owned.

In describing this situation, Drs. Schlechty and Whitford stated,

As long as the concerns or problems are defined in the context of any one collaborating organization, it will be exceedingly difficult, if not impossible, for all parties to the collaboration to own them jointly. This logic suggests that the problems to which collaboration is addressed must be boundary-spanning. That is, they must be problems that no party to the collaboration can solve alone or over which no party has exclusive monopoly.

One of the benefits of school–university partnerships is the possibility of assimilating another culture, the "University College of Education culture," into the vertical culture of the public schools. By having a university participant as part of the vertical team, the participant becomes the linking pin to begin connecting university and public school cultures. Thus, although each have their own unique cultures they may begin having some aspects of shared culture as well. This occurs much the same as horizontal cultures within the schools are assimilated into the vertical culture, and is the primary benefit of including a university professor as a facilitator or member of the vertical team.

Drs. Schlechty and Whitford conclude,

> The systematic and continuous improvement of the quality of education cannot occur until education becomes a progressive profession rather than a traditional-based craft. And, education cannot become a progressive profession until those who prepare educators and those who practice in the field are bound by a common culture. The building of this common culture requires that those who now function on university campuses and those who practice in the schools join together in a common organization with sufficient autonomy from the organization they now serve to work out their common destiny.

This is why the Danforth Foundation choose to use a university professor as the facilitator for the vertical team in their School Administrators Fellowship Program.

Dr. John Goodlad (1988) had some concerns about organic relationships and believed that they would not work until universities changed their views about the benefits of such relationships. He states,

> In efforts to achieve the positive potential of organic partnerships between schools (or school districts) and universities, the latter are least likely to perceive the relationship as relevant to their self-interests and, therefore, least likely to enter seriously into the marriage and to make it work.

The Professor as Learner

There were a number of areas of learning about school practice that were essential in helping university facilitators to improve their professional skills and practices, the most important being learning more about the overall school improvement process. The facilitators felt that they had gained a much better understanding of school renewal and the necessary requirements of school improvement. School improvement is an essential area of knowledge for today's professors due to the growing pressure to improve the effectiveness of American schools. The identification of supporting elements and barriers to school improvement is as important to professors of education as it is to practitioners within the schools. As a result, school improvement and effectiveness become a very strong component of mutual interest.

Dr. Marilyn Cohn, Facilitator for the Lindbergh School District in St. Louis, stated,

> I plan to systematically study the Lindbergh District's efforts at school improvement, including my own role as a facilitator, so that I can relate it to what I learned from my earlier participation in the Danforth Improvement of Instruction Project as well as my understanding of the latest research on school change. This will mean that in addition to actively working to help the district develop a process through which it can reach its school improvement goals, I will, in collaboration with members of the vertical team, carefully collect and analyze data on the facilitators and barriers to school improvement in the district. I will then present the findings, whenever possible, in local, state and national forums for others to consider.

Dr. William Grady, Dean of the School of Education at the University of Colorado in Denver also found great benefits in participating as a facilitator for the Denver vertical team. He stated,

> In my role, I have major responsibilities for addressing the needs of education in an urban setting. The vertical team experience in all its aspects greatly assisted me in fulfilling this responsibility.

The College of Education itself often benefited from the involvement of a faculty member. For example, Old Dominion University had three faculty members involved in a year-long process of facilitation. This resulted in a much more practical and real-world approach to their teaching, and, even more importantly, to the College of Education programs that were in the process of being revised. This was not a sporadic occurrence, but was observed within a number of different universities.

The University of Texas at Austin experienced similar types of benefits. Professors and students participating in the Austin program were able to apply theory and technical knowledge to practical problems. The school system provided a dynamic environment for integrating knowledge gained through formal course work. Dr. Nolan Estes, a professor at the University of Texas and the Austin facilitator, stated,

> We developed a new "spiral curriculum" which will better address needs for preparing school leaders in the future. The Danforth Vertical Team concept is being used as the cornerstone for clinical and field experiences required in this program. Faculty participation insured academic training kept pace with what was going on in the real world. Universities also began to see new research questions which needed to be addressed.

The real benefit to university faculty is to simply have an opportunity to communicate with and listen to educators at various levels within the school district. Dr. William Heller, dean of the College of Education at the University of North Carolina-Charlotte and Charlotte facilitator, stated,

> The opportunity to freely give and take, with some of the most dedicated professional educators I know, about issues of concern and consequence to Charlotte, was one of memorable proportion to me. I must say that I got so much more than I gave. This Dean has learned a lot from his colleague team members. We in higher education fail far too often to see the "big picture" of free public education and the issues that face teachers, principals, school board members, assistant superintendents, and superintendents on a daily basis. Far too often we critique from a "safe'" distance without knowing the elements of the "real" problem.

This same sentiment was echoed by Dr. Carl Ashbaugh, dean of the School of Education at the University of North Florida and Duval County facilitator. He stated,

> The fellowship program gave me a chance to establish linkages with the school system. It opened lines of communication, acquainted me with some excellent teachers and administrators, and offered a chance for me to get involved in the world of practice one again.

The idea of having an opportunity to work with practitioners was a commonly expressed benefit of the vertical team process. Dr. William Cunningham, from Old Dominion University and Norfolk facilitator stated,

> I was able to gain a much better understanding of the operation of the Norfolk Public Schools. Much can be learned through the vertical team

meetings. I was able to participate in direct communication with administrators, teachers, and board members over a protracted period of time. This is not an opportunity that has been available to me except in very structured settings. I was able to get a clear understanding of the inner-workings of the school district.

These were not the only areas of development for faculty involved in this program. Much was also learned about professional development and adult learning. The type of "community of learners" created in the vertical team program exemplified how professional education might occur within the university. Dr. Dan Duke from the University of Virginia and Charlottesville facilitator stated,

> For someone who thought he was knowledgeable about professional development, this year has been a reminder that professors have much to learn. My own professional growth must be counted among the year's achievements. I have come to appreciate the difficulties encountered by busy professionals in their efforts to grow, and I have had a chance to test a new model for promoting awareness-building and goal setting among experienced educators . . . I believe our experience this year can contribute substantially to the body of knowledge concerning adult learning and professional development.

Dr. John Croghan, from the University of Miami and Dade County facilitator, found vertical team facilitation to be an invigorating growth experience. He stated,

> This year has been a thrilling year for me personally. It gave me a unique opportunity to work with outstanding professionals from the Dade County Public Schools. We developed an environment in which anyone at any time could discuss items of importance to them. These items ranged from how to deal with the press after a violent incident, to dealing with the loss of a family member, to celebrating a personal victory. The supportive atmosphere was so powerful that it provided the impetus for individual members to work on transition plans in an attempt to recreate a similar working, yet caring, atmosphere.

Insiders and Outsiders

Many of the university facilitators felt the same concerns that other team members described regarding being enculturated into the group. The first hurdle for the university professor was establishing a level of trust and collegiality with the group. This is not dissimilar to the feelings experienced by the members of the group from within the school district. Almost all the participants felt they were in somewhat of a unique position being first time members on a vertical team.

One of the major problems with having a university-based facilitator was the fact that the professor had no direct responsibility for implementing the decision. There was a feeling that the faculty representative was an outsider who could walk away whenever the project no longer suited them. The vision and programs were for the public schools, and the university member did not feel that sense of ownership. The school system felt it had a trained facilitator who might leave the program at any time.

On the other hand, the university facilitator found it difficult to be an "insider" who was really an "outsider." Since the facilitator did not work for the district, because his world was that of the university, he did not share as deeply in the ultimate bond of collegiality that developed. Responsibility did not fall on the facilitator; it belonged to someone paid by the school district.

Both the facilitator and the vertical team gained a greater understanding of the benefits and needs of each, as they developed a shared vision of what they were all about. Drs. Goodlad and Sirotnik concluded,

> One of the most important concomitants of a school–university partnership may be the stimulation of dialogues, not only between school and university personnel as intended, but among educators within those institutions who are not ordinarily accustomed to engagement beyond the niceties of formal communication. The possibilities for sharing knowledge and expertise clearly are envisioned by Robert Sinclair and Anne Harrison in the goals of the Massachusetts Coalition for School Improvement. Indeed the concept of using people inside the coalition as resource persons in all partnership activities appears to be an operating principle. The school as the unit of change provides the setting where, potentially, the intellectual input of all actions is to be integrated into the decision-making process.

Broadening School and University Partnerships

The Coalition for School Improvement is a unique partnership joining several elementary and secondary schools in Western Massachusetts with each other and with the Curriculum Studies Program at the University of Massachusetts at Amherst. One of the objectives of this coalition is very similar to what the Danforth Foundation wanted to achieve by setting up the program to have university professors as facilitators. That objective is "To provide an opportunity for coalition members to exchange information about effective policies and practices." Professor Robert L. Sinclair, Director of the Coalition for School Improvement, stated,

> We found that the finest and most lasting reform comes through cooperation between educators from various institutions working together as equals to improve their schools. We are convinced that is the most successful way to make constructive and enduring changes.

The work of the coalition is overseen by a council made up of university faculty members, teachers, principals and superintendents. The council creates policies that assist the coalition in accomplishing its goals and encouraging schools and the university to reach their priorities for improvement. The Council is responsible for facilitating collaboration among members of the coalition.

University–school partnerships offer a number of settings in which university professors are able to develop new delivery systems for training and development. For example, as a result of his involvement in the Danforth Foundation program, Dr. William Drury, a professor at the University of Dayton, was invited to organize and conduct a series of other programs and staff development projects. These activities included a superintendent's seminar for classroom teachers, a mentor program for first-year administrators, and a leadership academy for teachers aspiring to become administrators. Dr. Jorge Decamps, from the University of Texas at El Paso and El Paso facilitator, also increased his involvement with the public schools as a result of his involvement as a facilitator. He spent every Tuesday afternoon at Capistrano Elementary School in El Paso, working with teachers on staff development. His focus was on developing ways to bridge the gap between theory and practice.

Similar types of school–university partnerships exist among five Utah school districts and the College of Education at Brigham Young University. There have been a number of patterns identified and lessons learned from the BYU-Public School Partnership. Building trust is one of the biggest hurdles this collaborative effort has faced and continues to face. No one predicted that so many pent-up fears and doubts due to previous experiences would have to be overcome before the intended collaborative work could ever begin. Another time consuming area was the shift of focus from self interests to the placement of focus on mutual interests.

In concluding over six years of research regarding Oakland University, Oakland Community College, and Oakland County Schools, Drs. Gerald Pine and William Keane (1990) determined that collaboration

- achieves the advancement of knowledge and the improvement of practice,
- reduces redundancies and overlapping of resources and finances,
- generates a cycle of knowledge-action-reflection-knowledge-action-reflection, and
- creates a new ecology for stimulating professional growth and staff development.

In a white paper prepared for a seminar sponsored by the Danforth Foundation on global education, Ronald Havelock drew some general implications from a study of three different school–university networks. These networks were at the University of Maryland, Mayville State College, and a statewide network in North Dakota. He found that school–university collaborative arrangements could be quite successful, and could be maintained over long periods of time. Such arrangements were most beneficial for participating teachers, schools, and school districts, but universities and educational faculties also gained a number of benefits. The costs of these enterprises were relatively modest in proportion to the benefits that were gained.

Dr. Havelock stated,

> Districts should look beyond inservice training needs and traditional knowledge acquisition activities and seriously consider the potential for collaboration with universities for problem-solving, curriculum and instructional reform, and other desirable changes in the process of schooling. They should also look to the involvement of personnel other than teachers and they should allow teachers and others to become involved in collaborative activities in a more prolonged and intense way. Finally, if they find that the rewards of collaboration are clear and positive, they should be prepared to back up their verbal support with long-term financial commitments.

There are some expanded benefits in regard to directly using university professors to assist public schools in that they become part of the vertical culture of American education. However, the experience of vertical team approaches are that such teams can be effective regardless of who serves as the facilitator. The important variable is that the facilitator has the skills and ability to handle the group dynamics needed to develop and sustain an effective team. An important point to consider is the process of facilitation during stages of innovation and change. During the early stages of developing a base of understanding about content, the skills of an outside facilitator are needed to clarify concerns of the parties involved. Hall and Loucks (1978) developed an instrument which represents seven stages of change experienced by people involved with innovative change. The facilitator needs to operate in isolation with regard to knowing how participants are responding to the process. The literature is very rich, with well documented and researched descriptions about the facilitation of change and the ways to measure progress and stages of behavioral change.

Bibliography

Pine, Gerald J. and Keane, William G. "School–University Partnerships: Lessons Learned." *Wright State University Record* 11 (Fall/Winter, 1990).

Sinclair, Robert L. "A Partnership in Parity: The Coalition for School Improvement." Monograph, Amherst, MASS: Coalition for School Improvement.

Reprinted by permission of the publisher from Sirotnik, Kenneth A. and Goodlad, John I., *School–University Partnerships in Action: Concepts, Cases, and Concerns.* New York: Teachers College Press, © 1988 by Teachers College, Columbia University. All rights reserved. Selected quotes from sections by Sirotnik/Goodlad, Schlecty/Whitford, and Sinclair/Harrison.

Hall, G. E. & Loucks, S. F. Teacher Concerns as a Basis for Facilitating Staff Development. *Teachers College Record,* 80 (1), 36–53, 1978.

Hall, G. E. & Hord, S. M. *Change in Schools: Facilitating the Process.* Albany: State University of New York Press, 1987.

12

Transforming School Culture

If the criteria for an effective culture described in this book sounds vaguely familiar to you, it might be because you have heard of the Total Quality Management (TQM) approach promoted by W. Edward Deming, Phil Crosby, Joseph M. Juran, Ormond Fergenbaum, and others. Their quality improvement concepts include cross-functional teams, personal/professional training, trusting employees, inspiration and vision, free-flowing information (particularly on quality measurement), long-run emphasis, lots of communication, small starts, modeling appropriate behavior, constant employee innovation, and supplier/customer emphasis and responsiveness. There are certainly many similarities between what was learned from the Danforth Foundation program with that of Total Quality Management.

The secret of good management is being able to develop and support cultures that reinforce excellence. The Danforth Foundation is involved in programs which have been doing exactly that. Effective cultures interact with structure to produce organizations of high morale, productivity and quality. The correlates are self-reinforcing and provide stability and certainty regarding individual response and behavior.

The culture tells individuals within the organization what is important and what is expected from them. The culture provides a strong sense of resistance to any activity that does not seem to fit. For example, if the culture promotes conservatism and the status quo, it will resist any efforts at change regardless of how appropriate or needed.

We have heard much about site-based management as a technique by which schools might be improved. Site-based management is an approach that changes the structure of the school system so as to share governance by pushing decision-making down into the deepest levels of the organization. This idea has much possibility for improving our schools, but it cannot be successful unless it is supported by the culture. The same is true with other reforms. Before site-based management or any other innovation can work, the culture of the school must support the innovation. The culture must set high expectations for achieving success with the innovation. These achievements are not influenced by structural changes or external pressures and mandates, but are influenced by the cultural and behavioral characteristics of the organization. Planned improvements, regardless of whether they are national, state, or local initiatives, will neither be successful nor long lasting if they are in conflict with the local culture. The best way to insure that this does not happen is for improvements to be developed, implemented, and supported within the culture.

The culture must emphasize the values that make a classroom, a school, and a school district display greatness. The culture of excellence emphasizes the personal qualities of achievement such as self-image, skill, knowledge, respect, confidence, identity, worth, personal development, enthusiasm, pride, wisdom, and commitment. These attitudes develop around certain correlates of effective culture that have emerged in a number of different arenas. The individual efforts of employees supported by an effective culture tend to lift educational efforts to greatness. The central themes of these are vertical teams, individual efforts, vision and optimism, collegiality, values and interests, diverse perspectives, personal and professional development, long-term focus, continuous improvement, performance information and understanding, quality expectations, cooperation, communication, trust, empowerment, bold action, vulnerability, commitment, and risk.

This type of culture cannot be managed from an office exerting paper control over people; operating and deciding on the basis of formalized long-range plans, reports and memorandums; implementing structural changes; or, evaluating and taking pride in process, reports, or documents. This is where personal values of respect, confidence, self-esteem, high expectations, and commitment must come to play. Great schools are developed by organizations that develop the essence of excellence through enthusiasm, extraordinary individual efforts and celebration. They do not occur by applying the bureaucratic authoritarian centralism from the industrial era to our post-industrial society.

Organizational excellence emerges, or fails to emerge, based on the culture the organization is able to create. Excellence can not be mandated, bought, imposed, or coerced. Excellence develops from the understanding, trust, and expectations that are created and shared by all those who work within the organization. It is cultivated by the commitment that grows within people. More precisely, excellence does not develop from a single effort by a very capable individual, but it grows in the culture of the work group. Schools must expand the number of people who achieve what in the past only those at the top of the hierarchy achieved. Excellence grows from the efforts of every single person working in the school division and the crucially important culture, climate, ambiance, ethos, or order in which they work and relate.

John Saphier (1985) suggests,

> Essentially, the culture of the school is the foundation for school improvement... if certain norms of school culture are strong, improvements in instruction will be significant, continuous and widespread; if these norms are weak, improvement will be at best infrequent, random and slow ... giving shape and direction to a school's culture should be a clear, articulated vision of what the school stands for.... The development of "school excellence," the development of a bright educational future for American youth depends on the creation of a rich and supportive culture .

The view people take of their jobs, organizations and clients is a matter of their association with their work culture. Effective and ineffective work performance is most often created by a combination of culture and management. Knowledge, views, and behavior have a subjective element, however it is equally as obvious that people are significantly influenced by the culture to which they belong. To understand why teachers are successful or unsuccessful, we must look into the work culture from which they have acquired their beliefs and attitudes. How were they socialized into the school division? What is socially transmitted within the work culture that directs the behavior of its members? What is their sense of identity with purpose?

Michael Fullan (1991), Marvin Fairman (1982), and others have placed these cultural questions in relation to organizational health and effectiveness. Leadership must recognize the importance of organizational health and its relation to organizational culture, and, ultimately, organizational performance. Leaders in the year 2000 must be able to reflect on and understand their organizations as living, working cultures. As they begin seeing the school as a living organism, they will become interested in the health of that organism. This mode of thought has the potential to greatly improve American education.

The Culture for Excellent Schools

The first wave of educational reform in the 1980s emphasized a theme of "back to the basics"—of emphasizing order and discipline, core curriculum, equal opportunity, accountability, testing, and national evaluation. The 1990s ushered in the second wave of school reform, based on the premise that the mandate-driven, externally imposed, and peripherally developed modifications of the 80s, leaving basic school practices unaffected, are likely to prove futile. The educators of the second wave of reform are advocating fundamental change and restructuring of educational practices.

A third wave of culturally led reform is necessary if public education is to succeed, or even survive, in the twenty-first century. This reform cannot be directed by omnipotent leaders who want to improve educational practice using a hierarchal perspective. Nor will it occur by practicing leadership as usual. It is for educational leaders with the foresight and strength to be able to work through the culture to achieve a vision of excellence in American education. A new kind of American education requires a new kind of education.

Rather than the quick solutions tried in the 80s, or the reform and restructuring of the early 90s, the new wave requires insights on how to begin and maintain a remaking of the American school. These type of changes require a period of years. School systems, and even individual schools, will need years to explicate their vision, build collegiality, develop a professional renewal ethos, and accomplish school improvement. The development of a culture that supports the creation of excellence in schools is not a quick approach. The creation of excellence does not provide quick solutions to restructuring and renewal, nor does it provide the semantic changes that political policy makers and public administrators have been employing in campaign rhetoric.

The cultural approach lays the necessary groundwork by which educators will be able to begin and maintain a remaking of the American school. The correlates of excellence support an effective school culture that can remain on the cutting edge of today's reform efforts. The response to educational reform can no longer be a series of bureaucratic "how-to-do-its." We must have the courage to support our American teachers in their efforts to improve American education.

Education must move from "A Nation at Risk" to "A Nation on the Move." In his 1988 report to the president entitled, *American Education: Making it Work*, William J. Bennett, the U.S. Secretary of Education concluded,

> Education reform is a two-step process. The first step is to identify where we stand and what needs to be done. That step has largely been

finished. We know what needs to be done. But there is a second step: We must exert the will and demonstrate the resolve to overcome the obstacles that block reform. We must make education reform a reality. If we now act forthrightly and decisively, American education tomorrow will work much better than it does today. And we will provide our children with the schools they deserve.

Although all may not agree with the contents of this report, most who read the report have come to agree with its conclusion. This is well documented in Carl Glickiman's (1991) work.

This call for a new model of educational reform was supported by almost all of the past secretaries and commissioners of education. For example, Harold Howe II, (1986) a former commissioner of education, believed that past school reforms had been woefully lacking. However, he was encouraged by more recent thinking. Dr. Howe II stated,

> . . . there is a refreshing aspect of the school reform movement that sees schools as places in which teachers, parents, and principals can work together to fashion an education that serves the needs of students. In this view, each school has some freedom to draw on creativity of those concerned with it, particularly teachers. Some latitude exists for schools to be different from each other, to invent their own futures, and to take pride in their uniqueness.

This call for renewal and reform was the basis for the Governor's Conference on Education at the University of Virginia in 1990. The president and the Governor's Task Force on Education jointly developed national goals about restructuring and revitalizing the educational system of the United States. They were designed to encourage a "renaissance" in American education. They expressed a national challenge, stating,

> These national education goals are not the president's goals or the governor's goals, they are the nation's goals. Achieving them will require a strong commitment and concerted effort on the part of every section and every citizen to improve dramatically our nation's education system and the performance of each and every student.

Dr. Christopher Cross, Assistant Secretary for Education, in reflecting upon the national goals stated,

> Education reform had been sweeping the United States for the better part of a decade when, in 1990, it received a boost—the release by President Bush and the 50 governors of national goals for American

education. By the year 2000, they agreed, American children should begin school ready to learn; graduate from school at a rate of 90 percent; demonstrate competence in challenging subject matter and be prepared for citizenship; rise to first in the world in mathematics and science; attend safe, disciplined, and drug-free schools; and join the workforce as literate adults and responsible citizens . . . The degree to which a school is able to achieve excellence, according to recent research, is highly correlated with the degree to which that school operates autonomously—that is, independent of externally imposed rules and regulations. In other words, according to this study and other research, a school's autonomy or lack there of is a key determinant of its success.

Dr. Arthur G. Wirth (1993) has taken this point even further, and stated that most of education's factory-era administrative styles are dysfunctional. He argues persuasively that we have barely begun to create the education system required for the century. In providing direction for the needed efforts, he states:

> I have argued that we can find the beginnings of appropriate postindustrial education in the futures of the school restructuring movement that have gained force in the 1990s. The most promising restructuring efforts seek to invigorate the education system by adopting participative styles of management that support local creativity, autonomy and problem solving.

Many have recognized the possibility of autonomy, involvement, and commitment at the school level. Schools cannot be renewed or made excellent except by those who work within them on a daily basis. Yet, the reform efforts of the past ten years tend to suggest that the educators have not yet been invited into the process, and this has been the cause of failure. Dr. Theodore Sizer, in *Horace's Compromise*, (1984) found that

> Teaching often lacks a sense of ownership, a sense among the teachers working together that the school is theirs and that its future and their reputation are indistinguishable. Hired hands own nothing, and are told what to do, and have little stake in their enterprises . . . Not surprisingly . . . teachers . . . often act like hired hands.

Basically, there is a school culture underlying all efforts for renewal and reform, and if this culture is healthy or not in a position to be able to handle change—even if it is significant improvement—little can be done regardless of the efforts of outsiders.

In an April 18, 1991 speech at the White House, President George Bush stated,

> Across this country people have started to transform the American school. They know that the time for talk is over. Their slogan is: Don't dither, just do it. Let's push the reform effort forward. Use each experiment, each advance to build the next American century. New schools for a new world.
>
> So, to sum it up . . . the revolution in American education has already begun. Now I ask all Americans to be points of light in the crusade that counts: the crusade to prepare our children and ourselves for the exciting future that looms ahead. At any moment in every mind, the miracle of learning beckons us all.

The culture of excellence places the responsibility of reform and restructuring firmly on the shoulders of those who work with students on a daily basis, and this is where the responsibility belongs. That does not suggest that non-educators do not have an important and necessary role in achieving success but we must be very clear on what the various roles are before we move forward to achieve the national dream of using "each experiment, each advance to build the next American Century."

President Bill Clinton has established a record of willingness to immerse himself in the culture of education in order to change it. Perhaps his greatest educational legacy in the state of Arkansas was not the laws that were passed, but his active involvement at the grassroots level to nourish local involvement in and an attitude toward education. Clinton barnstormed the state as governor to change the culture in Arkansas to create an excellent school system while providing the autonomy to do so. His educational message was to get involved and make the system better. Since 1985, Arkansas has had a fourteen percent rise in the number of students who attend college. They moved from the 40th to the 60th percentile in mathematics and reading on the national assessment. The *Arkansas Gazette* summarized Clinton's impact as "He just changed people's values. Arkansas now believes in education."

It is time to let the educators set the vision for American schools and for the communities, politicians, and businesspeople to support and contribute to the achievement of the vision. This is the hope for American educational reform.

Local Autonomy in Educational Reform

Local capacity and will are most important to any policy outcome. The energy and effort required to sustain a successful reform activity grows out of the culture which supports it. This culture or local capacity is beyond the reach of federal, state, and, often, even school board policy makers. Changing policy, programs, funding plans, mandates, or players seldom seems to work, particularly in a well-imbedded culture. The inspiration, motivation, and related attitudes for successful renewal and restructuring of American education must grow from its culture and not from its reactions to policies, mandates, and outside directives.

Each school and school district has its own unique personality—each is different in fundamental and consequential ways. Those working within it understand those variabilities. However, as we move up the local, state, and federal hierarchies, those essential differences are lost and schooling is incorrectly viewed as having a sense of uniformity for which policy and often even practice is prescribed. In addition to being unavoidable, this variability is a good thing since it is built upon local clientele, values, traditions, histories, resources, and, most important, by local "grassroot" efforts. Grassroot control is the basis on which our forefathers designed American government and our history reaffirms it. In fact, these superior local efforts have made America great. John Chubb (1991), senior fellow at the Brookings Institute, found that local autonomy was the prime factor affecting successful school performance because it led to the development of effective school characteristics. Dr. Chubb said,

> It seems to me that educators ought to be cutting back on regulations governing personnel, curriculum, and instruction. They should be doing everything they can to treat teachers as professionals, to encourage principals to be leaders, and to give schools more freedom and incentive to chart their own courses. These are now somewhat familiar lessons, but our research shows more clearly than ever that if they are practiced, they make a real difference.

In this way, policy, and, more specifically, projects, developed outside the locale often decrease the quality of output by paradoxically diverting energies from the more basic goals of improvement seen by the local educators. This domination and control of education by those who spend their professional lives outside the culture often generates hostility, frustration, helplessness, and professional depression among practicing educators.

The restructuring, reform, and renewal efforts envisioned for American education are steady work for those involved in education. The problems that need to be addressed in education are not acute, they are chronic. They are not bound and short-term, they are multiple, simultaneous, interrelated and dynamic. Local educators are the experts in the job and we all must learn to depend upon them. This cannot occur unless there is a strong educational culture that supports respect and trust. The culture of American education must support systematic and ongoing efforts to achieve excellence.

The Third Wave of Reform

Dr. Milbrey McLaughlin (1990) completed a very interesting reconsideration of the results of an earlier Rand Change Agent study in light of today's change practices and reform efforts. He described factors that seemed especially promising which are becoming quite familiar but which are not directly influenced by policy. He believed that the new wave of reform must be directed toward cultural change. Dr. McLaughlin concluded,

> The factors that enable practice—productive collegial relations, organizational structures that promote open communication and feedback, and leadership that "manages" opportunities for professional growth and nurtures norms of individual development, for example—are not amenable to direct policy fixes because they do not operate singly or consistently across settings . . . in order for shared mission and supportive leadership to enhance classroom practices, institutional structures need to be in place that provide regular feedback about teachers' performance, permit teachers to be heard in the area of curriculum decision making, and promote collegial integration. All of these enablers, in turn, are enhanced by the presence of multiple opportunities for teachers' professional growth. By itself, any one of these factors can promote better practice, but only in the short term. Sustained support for effective classroom practice assumes the co-occurrence of these and other enabling factors at the school site.

A shift in school district culture from district control to school control requires everyone to change roles, routines, and relationships. Culture that defines and sustains educational excellence needs to successfully practice the following characteristics:

- schools that focus on improvements to positively influence what happens to students
- collegiality, trust, integrity, and sufficient time for open, free-flowing communication
- an explicit mutually shared vision of the ideal school
- a climate of mutual support, growth, and inovation
- a three- to seven-year perspective for improvement
- face-to-face involvement of appropriate stakeholders
- work with values, interests, and expertise

- continuous improvement that is incremental and systematic
- staff development, character, and skill as the essential components to school improvement
- cooperation among home, school, and community
- empowerment and encouragement of staff to experiment, innovate, and share success
- constant monitoring and feedback of results
- central administrative support of individual school efforts

A vertical culture provides the cohesion needed to sustain the efforts of both individuals and groups. These cultural characteristics produce the coherence that quality improvements within the school require.

Variability in innovation is a positive result in that it builds upon the values, traditions, myths, histories, resources, and, most important, the culture in which they develop. The ideas that promote, foster, and sustain excellence in our schools come from teachers, principals, central office staff, or parents and members of the community. The key factor is that they can be developed and nurtured within the culture of the school.

Cultural Leadership and Participation

Dr. Perry Pope, principal at Spring Woods High School in the Spring Branch Independent School District outside of Houston, Texas, in an effort to improve the school culture, worked with school staff on an effort "to attain higher levels of cooperation, respect and involvement between and among parents, teachers, and students." This goal was based on feedback received on the Secondary School Attitude Inventory and the Effective Schools Survey. Dr. Pope, along with representative staff, attended sessions offered on cooperative learning. A campus library on cooperative learning was established and all teachers were encouraged to check out and read relevant publications. Faculty were encouraged to attend sessions related to cooperative learning at professional meetings, universities, and/or with discussion groups. Teachers were encouraged to discuss cooperative learning techniques informally, and time was set aside in staff meetings and faculty meetings to share information. Faculty were then encouraged to use cooperative learning in their classrooms and to evaluate and present results.

The shared vision that developed at Spring Woods High School was the implementation of instructional strategy to enhance student learning and social skills. Dr. Pope and the teachers who received training in cooperative learning provided a cadre of trainers within the school who provided training to all other teachers and staff. Each teacher received "hands on" training, role modeling, and literature on cooperative learning. Teachers worked together to develop a plan to implement cooperative learning as part of their regular classroom instructional process. The school administrators visited classrooms in an effort to help in the development and sharing of successful cooperative learning techniques. Administrators looked for cooperative learning, commented positively when observing it, and encouraged teachers to share effective ideas. The teachers within the school planned and staffed a cooperative learning session for parents.

The teachers and students both found cooperative learning techniques to be quite effective. Jim Stones, a teacher, had a great deal of success in implementing the techniques. He asked for unofficial follow-up from department members on the cooperative learning being practiced. He thought it would be very helpful if teachers shared techniques that were working for them. Chris Lee, a student member of the Campus Improvement Committee, said, "Students have noticed the implementation of cooperative learning in several of their classes and the general consensus is that it works great!"

Parent attendance at activities within the school grew, and the senior parents worked with the assistant principals to coordinate graduation activities. Alex Vana, associate principal in the Spring Branch District held a meeting with freshman parents to create a rapport and support system to help insure the students' success throughout their high school experience.

Another example of a culturally driven program occurred at Southridge High School, the Cultural Center for the Humanities in the Dade County Public Schools in Florida. The faculty, under the leadership of Fred Rogers, the principal, developed a shared vision of global and cultural awareness as their plan for "Building for the twenty-first Century." The theme of their efforts was to promote cultural and global awareness in the school for the 90s. They planned to continue to develop their global education, cultural literacy, geography, world religions, foreign language, world literature, European history, and world history programs. They also planned to expand their international exchange program with France and Italy to include Russia, Costa Rica, and Germany. They expanded their Black History, Mayfest, International Food Fest, and Global Awareness programs. They added Global Awareness courses in Portuguese, Hebrew, Classical Greek, Western Civilization, and Japanese. Student choices of curriculum would be based on interests, expectations, performance, and career goals. School staff worked on a grant proposal in order to secure monies to develop teachers and curriculums, prepare courses, articulate concepts, select subjects, and become Great Books Foundation program trainers.

In another culturally based reform that included educators, parents, and community working together, the Charlotte, North Carolina Chamber of Commerce produced a report entitled "Educational Imperatives: a community on the threshold." As a result of this report, the Charlotte-

Mecklenburg School District recognized, along with many other school systems nationwide, the importance of forging school and business partnerships. This began with the Education Council of the Charlotte Chamber of Commerce developing a mission statement that paralleled and complemented the school system's mission statement. The school district education mission statement was,

> The Charlotte-Mecklenburg school system is an important determinant in the future quality of life as our community commits and dedicates itself to become the top integrated, urban, public school system in the Southeastern United States and one of the premier school systems in the nation by the year 2000."

The complementary mission statement for the Education Council of the Chamber of Commerce is,

> "The greater Charlotte Chamber of Commerce commits its unique expertise, resources, and abilities in support of the Charlotte-Mecklenburg School's board, administrations, and teachers—to forge our public schools into the top integrated system in the southeast and one of the premier school systems in the United States by the year 2000.

This symbolic coordination and support was formed in everything the chamber did for the schools. For example, businesses in Charlotte built educational understanding and support; encouraged parent, civic group and volunteer involvement; supported and recognized classroom teachers and school principals; shared know-how and skills; and, helped educators to influence policy-makers. Some of the specific policies recommended for adoption included:

- Employees will be allowed reasonable work time to meet with their children's teachers to confer and support their children's education.
- Employees are encouraged to seek leadership and participate in PTAs and other support groups.
- Employees should be their children's role models in the home, positive about the benefits of education, assist with homework when appropriate, and structure home time for school work.
- Employees may volunteer to make classroom presentations, serve as a curriculum resource, tutor or counsel and represent our company using their unique education and experience.
- Parents should develop regular communication with their children's teacher through open houses, telephone contact or letter.

Other suggestions included awarding fellowships and sabbaticals for teachers, establishing incentive and recognition grants, offering paid summer internships in business, lobbying for higher teacher and principal salaries, establishing occupational exchange days, offering scholarships for local students majoring in teaching, establishing courtesy recognition programs, providing state-of-the-art equipment, sponsoring joint-use facilities, insuring affordable, high quality preschool child care, supporting increased funding, providing feedback on graduates, and providing input on program planning.

James Jynes, chairperson of the Educational Council of the Chamber, stated,

> As a parent and business person, and what I hear from teachers and administrators, increasing parental involvement in schools is one of the most important things we in business can do. That is, encourage and find ways to get our employees, who are parents of school children, and other volunteers to get reinvolved in the schools and in their young person's education. The teacher can't do it alone and we need to support them. Everyone needs to be interested in their children's education.

He went on to say,

> We not only want to encourage our employees to be involved in education, but show them how at school and at home. We need to think about allowing employee-parent time, either paid or unpaid, to visit their student's teacher when needed.

The Chamber sponsored "Parent Leadership" workshops which they hoped to expand to include all parents. Dr. Peter Relic, superintendent of the Charlotte-Mecklenburg Schools, said of the chamber's efforts,

> The commitment of the Chamber to work with schools and our community for quality education is one of the most positive signs I've seen from business. We have set the course to be the very best, and the Chamber is central to this commitment.

In adding his support to this effort, John Georgius, chairperson of the chamber, stated,

> I'm extremely pleased we have a meeting of the minds, a vision of where we want to go with our school system. The chamber wants to lead the business community in helping make our schools some of the best in the nation.

Culture as the Capacity for Excellence

The focus on educational improvement as a cultural change is not a entirely new concept; however, it is receiving more attention now than in the past. Dr. John Goodlad, in an interview appearing in *Educational Leadership,* stated,

> For nearly two decades I have been espousing the idea that the individual school is the key unit of change. I have also noted, though, that individual schools can be very lonely, fragile places . . . For a school to become the key unit for educational change requires a substantially different stance at the district level than now exists. Improvement programs tend to be district-wide; they are usually an effort by all schools in a district to attack the same problem at once. In elementary schools, for example, it is typically the improvement of reading or the improvement of math. These efforts have gone on repeatedly over the years, and we would have to conclude they haven't been very successful—so we need to be looking for something else. . . .The something else is for the district to encourage the individual school to come up with its plans based on its own analysis of that school. The principal, teachers, students and parents need to think their problems through and determine their priorities, using as much data as possible . . . Then the resources of the district should be brought to bear on helping the individual school do what it has defined and received approval to do.

The American Federation of Teachers, in a study funded by a grant from the Bureau of Labor-Management Relations and Cooperative Programs, concluded,

> With respect to public schools, the need for change is not only paramount but urgent. There is often little to be gained from striving to perfect existing strategies or to perform the same tasks better. In many cases, systematic change is necessary which must involve school employees at every level and be supported by a broad constituency of stakeholders in the community.

The major themes reported by the American Federation of Teachers for improving and renewing American education were:

- Some of the most acclaimed restructuring programs resulted from a beachhead in a single school or organizational subsystem by a small group of committed teachers and administrators.
- Relationships must be redefined, power must be redefined, power must be viewed differently and more professionally, authority and decision-

making must be more widely dispersed, and all members of the organization must take responsibility.

- We need to develop a common vision of what we want students to be accountable for and how to utilize performance-based assessment as a means of evaluating results.
- We must encourage risk-taking and leadership through enhanced autonomy at the school site.
- Teachers, administrators and school board members should take the most active role in renewing schools, however, educators should encourage the attention and support of parents, business and community and local state and federal governments that are necessary in innovation.
- Mid-level management should serve as a resource for, rather than policeman of, school operation, and all employees of the system should be included in framing and executing the school mission.
- Investment in human resource development is essential to restructuring schools.
- Teachers and administrators need to develop experience in group process skills and facilitation techniques.
- Educators must utilize communication vehicles that allow both inter- and intradistrict sharing of information.

The America 2000: An Educational Strategy (1991) source book reported,

Yet few elements of this strategy are unprecedented. Today's best ideas, dedicated education reforms, impressive innovation and ambitious experiments already point the way . . . real educational reform happens community by community, school by school, and only when people come to understand what they must do for themselves and their children and set about to do it.

Awakening to Our Future

When taken together, the characteristics of the culture of excellence help schools to develop the cultural foundations that are needed in order to build preeminence in American schools. The concepts help schools to achieve the educational renewal and reform that is being called for in almost every segment of American society. In fact, this restructuring is well underway. There is considerable testimony that change can and will grow out of the efforts of the individuals who are responsible for American education. They are the experts, because they educate American children on a daily basis. They are the point where all changes are made and sustained. They are those upon which American education stands or falls.

The recent research, whether on vertical team approaches, site-based management, total quality management, or participative team management, stresses the importance of involvement, shared governance, and cultural leadership to organizational effectiveness. On a global scale, its effectiveness can be seen in the economic output and social conditions of the democratic nations. The culture of excellence is a testimonial to the characteristics and benefits of the application of democratic principals.

The culture of excellence encourages the development of all educators to their fullest potential. It must give them an opportunity to come together frequently to develop their vision along with programs, practices, and tasks needed to achieve that vision. They must trust, support, and empower one another as they face the challenges required to foster continuous improvement in American schools.

As our society grows more complex, science more all-encompassing, and choices more diverse, we need organizations that can match the complexities of the society in which they are embedded. We all must be able to work together to revise, reform, and renew our organizations to adapt to the fast-paced times in which they are now set. Multiple levels of reality, new notions about purpose and practice, expanded states of awareness, staggering technological advances, diverseness of people, and a global world (perhaps even a planetary one) will require an equally expanded view of our organizations.

Culture can prolong our discomfort with the world we serve, or it can allow us to build a better world. The culture of preservation and tradition can protect the status quo from which it grows, but it is incapable of keeping up with modern society. The practice of external mandate can intrigue politicians and soothe business people, but it cannot improve our schools. Our culture can block or foster the constant improvements that are required. A culture of excellence results in an organization that is imaginative and active enough to rescue itself from the perils that the future might bring. Alvin Toffler, in *Future Shock*, accurately foretold that we need "a multiplicity of visions, dreams, and prophecies—images of potential tomorrows. . . . " That time is upon us as we prepare our organizations to handle this complex realism.

Tomorrow will bring thrilling opportunities if our cultures are prepared, or scary, cataclysmic disappointments if they are not. We are entering a new world of autonomous dependency. We are asking fewer questions for which we already have answers. We are facing the greatest number of uncertainties ever confronted by man. We have reached the edge where we must make the transition from one era to the next, and we must be prepared to create what we want this society to be—that which will nourish the next generation.

We must have organizations that are prepared to deal with the multiplicities of our new frontiers of democracy and freedom. Dr. Jean Houston, a professional in human development, calls this the "Rhythm of Awakening." Some welcome it with joy and hopefulness, while others see it with gut-gripping terror. Our organizations must be designed to help both to continue to be productive professionals in this ever changing world.

Our present problems are not rooted in political or economic solutions. They are rooted in the full use of our humanity, and the full complement of human resources. Organizations must be designed in such ways that they bring forth and orchestrate the culture to support a new order. Our organizations can no longer block and diminish the capacities of those ordinary professionals of which they are composed. In describing this new human revolution, Dr. Jean Houston states,

> A sleeping giant, it wakes in the hearts and minds of millions. Four hundred thousand years of being humans-in-search of subsistence, seven thousand years of being humans-in-search-of-meaning, and two centuries of modern economic and social revolution have prepared the way for the deepest quickening in human and cultural evolution. The events of recent centuries were the social and political churnings of the change. They were the manifestations of the deep seismic seizures happening and rehappening in the depths of ourselves. And what is happening constellates around the ideas of human freedom and human possibilities. The idea of freedom is expanding because the idea of what is to be a human being is expanding . . .

Organizational leadership will fail or succeed on the basis of how well the culture supports this new organizational order. The type of renewal needed in this third wave of reform is the type that grows from the individual efforts of not only thousands, but millions of educators across this great nation. It is not the type of improvement that is externally mandated or centrally coordinated, but the type that grows out of the hearts and minds of millions of people putting in joint efforts to improve the education of their students. What becomes important in this grass roots process is the development of an ongoing culture that enables educators and schools to deal with whatever renewal efforts they want to pursue.

School improvement plans might be different among different schools, or even for the same school among different years, but the culture once developed will be able to support whatever the teachers, school or district chooses to pursue. Good seeds will grow if we can develop a nourishing culture. America is a shining tribute to this truism. Cultural leadership creates the foundation upon which we can work together for world class schools.

Bibliography

_____. *America 2000: An Educational Strategy.* Washington, D.C.: U.S. Department of Education, 1991.

American Federation of Teachers. *A Call for Professionalism.* Washington, D.C.: American Federation of Teachers, 1985.

Bennett, William J. *American Education: Making It Work.* Washington, D.C.: U.S. Government Printing Office, 1988.

Brandt, Ron. "On Local Autonomy and School Effectiveness: A Conversation with John Chubb." *Educational Leadership* (January 1991).

Deal, Terrence E. and Peterson, Kent D. *The Principal's Role in Shaping School Culture.* Washington, D.C.: U.S. Government Printing Office, 1991.

Fairman, Marvin and Clark, Elizabeth. *Organizational Problem Solving: An Organizational Improvement Strategy.* Fayetteville, Arkansas: Organizational Health Diagnostic and Development Corporation. 1982.

Fullan, Michael. *The New Meaning of Educational Change.* New York: Teachers College Press, 1991.

Glickman, Carl D. "Pretending not to know what we know." *Educational Leadership* (May, 1991).

Houston, Jean. *The Possible Human.* Los Angeles, CA: J.P. Tarcher, Inc., 1982.

Howe II, Harold. "The Prospect for Children in the United States." *Phi Delta Kappan* (November, 1986).

McLaughlin, Milbrey W. "The Rand Change-Agent Study Revisited: Macro-Perspectives and Micro-Realities." *Educational Researcher* (December, 1990). Copyright 1990 by the American Educational Research Association, Reprinted by permission of the publisher.

National Commission on Excellence in Education. *A Nation at Risk: The Imperative for School Reform.* Washington, D.C.: U.S., Office of Education, 1983.

Quinby, Nelson. "Improving the Place Called School: A conversation with John Goodlad. *Educational Leadership* (March, 1985).

Saphier, John. "Good Seeds Grow in Strong Cultures." *Educational Leadership* (March, 1985) Reprinted with permission of the Association for Supervision and Curriculum Development. Copyright 1985 by ASCD. All rights reserved.

Sizer, Theodore. *Horace's Compromise.* Boston: Houghton Mifflin, 1984.

Task Force on Education and Employment. *Educational Imperatives: A Community at the Threshold.* Charlotte Chamber of Commerce, July 19, 1988.

Toffler, Alvin. *Future Shock.* New York: Random House, 1970.

Wirth, Arthur G. "Education and Work: The Choices We Face." *Phi Delta Kappan* (January, 1993).

Name Index

Subject Index